Freedom, Only Freedom

Freedom, Only Freedom

The Prison Writings of Behrouz Boochani

Behrouz Boochani

Translated and Edited by Omid Tofighian
and Moones Mansoubi

Foreword by Tara June Winch

BLOOMSBURY ACADEMIC
LONDON • NEW YORK • OXFORD • NEW DELHI • SYDNEY

BLOOMSBURY ACADEMIC
Bloomsbury Publishing Plc
50 Bedford Square, London, WC1B 3DP, UK
1385 Broadway, New York, NY 10018, USA
29 Earlsfort Terrace, Dublin 2, Ireland

BLOOMSBURY, BLOOMSBURY ACADEMIC and the Diana logo are trademarks of Bloomsbury Publishing Plc

First published in Great Britain 2023

For legal purposes the Acknowledgements on p. xviii constitute an extension of this copyright page.

Cover design by Adriana Brioso
Cover image © Kai Schwoerer/Getty Images

A catalogue record for this book is available from the British Library.

A catalog record for this book is available from the Library of Congress.

ISBN: PB: 978-0-7556-4935-8
ePDF: 978-0-7556-4266-3
eBook: 978-0-7556-4267-0

Typeset by RefineCatch Limited, Bungay, Suffolk
Printed and bound in Australia by Griffin Press

To find out more about our authors and books visit www.bloomsbury.com and sign up for our newsletters.

Contents

Foreword

I first exchanged correspondence with Behrouz Boochani in the weeks leading up to the 16th Ubud Writers and Readers Festival in Indonesia, where I was to interview him, his tireless translator and collaborator Omid Tofighian and two other refugee writers on the topic of seeking asylum. In October 2019, I remember that despite the instability of internet connection between Port Moresby and Ubud, the conversation between us was effortless. We've been writing colleagues since that time. We are both Indigenous writers – Wiradjuri and Kurdish – ours is an oral tradition, our histories are not monumental but connected to the land and our ancestor's survival in living history. Behrouz is not only a colleague though, today I consider him one of my closest friends.

Within this incredibly important collection, are the voices also of both colleagues and friends. Here, remembered, are those men imprisoned alongside Behrouz and the people incarcerated in Nauru and other Australian detention centres, those brothers and sisters who made it, and those who did not. Journalists who worked to earth his voice from the rubble and write alongside him, academics and creatives who have responded to his works and brought them into academic study, and definingly, Omid Tofighian and Moones Mansoubi, whose extraordinary roles helped expose Australia's detention industry.

In this collection, we see Behrouz's transition from MEG45 to a reclamation as a journalist and a man with a name, to a witness, a soothsayer, an award-winning literary writer, who changed the way Australians and the world viewed those seeking safe passage in a system built on lies, built to suspend lives and built to destroy. Instead of torture performed in secrecy, through Behrouz's emphatic words, under his critical eye, it was seen in the light. In the process of this transition, Behrouz became a defender of human rights, but moreover, a defender of human dignity.

This text, alongside *No Friend but the Mountains: Writing from Manus Prison*, is part of a movement of resistance knowledge – it is a scream in response to the settler-colonial canon. In the reverberation and echo of this anti-colonial truth-telling, a new language beyond journalism has been writ large in our literary history and in our consciousness.

Operation Sovereign Borders – and the ruthless border regimes directly preceding it – were not only brutal border-control operations aimed at racializing outsiders who powerful people claimed threatened 'Australia's sovereignty', but a mythology created during the frontier wars of Australia's colonial assimilation and annihilation of Indigenous peoples. Here lies the structure of invasion, which has perpetuated these events today.

Refugees and First Nations Australians share an affinity – we've taken control of our narrative and contributed to the retelling of time and space and linguistics, of the past and present and future. Behrouz speaks the language of testifying on our continent. Reading these words in their entirety, written at the edge of the jungle and in the aftermath, and from that uncomfortable position of being free, is not easy, but we must read them. James Baldwin wrote that 'Nothing can be changed until it is faced', about another inhumanity, and yet the truth remains just so. Here in these pages is everything we must face if we are to save ourselves from the horror of repetition.

Tara June Winch, 2022

Acknowledgements

We wish to express our sincere gratitude to friends and allies for their important role in this book: Victoria Grieve-Williams, Warraimaay intellectual who was the first to publish Behrouz in an academic publication and who has also been publishing with us – her connections to Bloomsbury helped make this book happen; Anne Surma for her support of our work in academic contexts and assistance during the editing process; all media organisations and literary and academic publications that gave us permission to republish the articles and poems; Rory Gormley from Bloomsbury for his support and editing work during the process; and all collaborators and contributors for being part of this project.

Moones, Omid, Behrouz

Behrouz would also like to thank Ngāi Tahu Research Centre (NTRC) at the University of Canterbury for their support and the opportunity to work with them. He is also grateful to the University of Canterbury College of Arts and Creative New Zealand for granting him the 2021 Ursula Bethell Residency in Creative Writing.

Writing in Languages of Freedom

Introduction

Omid Tofighian

The journalism and poetry in this book were written between 2013 and 2020. From 2013 to late 2019, Kurdish Iranian writer and cultural advocate Behrouz Boochani was indefinitely detained in Australia's 'invisible' offshore immigration detention system. Boochani – along with tens of thousands of others in recent decades – travelled to Australia by boat to ask for refuge. Since the early 1990s, instead of providing protection and safety, the Australian Government has passed laws that allow, in contravention of international law, the mandatory and indefinite detention of people fleeing danger and discrimination, including (since 2001) offshore detention. The Australian Government exiled Boochani to Manus Island in Papua New Guinea, even though he had committed no crime, without a hearing or clear explanation for why or for how long he would be detained, and with no access to practical legal representation or the judicial system.

The writing in this book was produced during Boochani's time in detention, with the last two chapters consisting of articles written soon after he was free. These writings are accompanied by reflections from twenty-one invited researchers, writers and confidants (including pieces by the two editors/translators of this book).

Boochani fled Iran because his activist journalism and cultural advocacy on behalf of the Kurdish people there put him in danger. It is fitting that this book is dedicated to the journalism he wrote under extreme duress, a practice he has been committed to for a significant part of his life and which he was willing to risk his life doing, a practice for which his colleagues in Iran are regularly punished. After first fleeing to Indonesia, he engaged a people smuggler to help him escape persecution and discrimination.[1] The first boat he boarded for Australia sank in Indonesian waters, almost leading to his death.[2] The second boat was rescued by the Australian Navy on 23 July – Boochani's thirtieth birthday[3] – and he was detained initially on Christmas Island (an Australian territory) for a month,[4] before being banished to Manus Island.[5] For the first four years of his time in detention, he was held in the Lombrum Naval Base (officially called the Manus Regional Processing Centre, MRPC) which had first been converted into an immigration prison in 2001.[6] Originally built during the Second World War, the conditions were squalid. After their arrival in 2013/2014, over 1,300 detainees were forced to sleep mostly in tents, converted containers or hangars, and had to endure extreme tropical heat, inhumane treatment from authorities and substandard basic services.

It is one of the extraordinary features of Boochani's work and the person he is that, on arrival at Manus, he was able to establish and maintain a wide range of networks beyond the prison using the very few resources available to him and limited English-language skills. Initially, he made use of the slow and unreliable computers in the prison, which he was permitted to use for a short time once a week. When he managed to smuggle in a mobile phone, he was able to work more effectively; however, he had to operate clandestinely with vacillating internet reception, and was always at risk of having his phone confiscated. Sometimes, his phone would be found by the prison officers and Boochani suffered the consequences. In the early years, the journalists he connected with incorporated his reporting into their own articles but they did not endeavour to publish his own writings. He was often referred to as a 'source' from inside; the fact that he was not acknowledged as a journalist infuriated him and increased his cynicism regarding journalism and its practices. This changed later as a result of his persistence: first he began publishing regularly with *The Guardian* and *The Saturday Paper* and then with many other outlets in Australia and internationally. In the beginning, Boochani was worried about the repercussions he might suffer if he wrote under his real name, but this fear subsided after he realized that his situation would not change whether he was known for his journalism and activism or not. Also, once he was confident that his network was strong enough and would never abandon him, he was convinced that he had to become more prolific and visible.

The journalism and poetry in this book – and the intricate and collaborative translation process involved in producing them – were written while the author was living under horrific circumstances. Boochani typed all his work on mobile phones he smuggled into the prison in exchange for cigarettes and other available items. Moones Mansoubi and I translated the work, receiving each article via WhatsApp. In some cases, the events he was writing about on his phone were occurring in real-time. While he reported on and analysed his experiences in the prison, he also began to write literature, storing the pieces of each chapter in various dormant contacts in his WhatsApp contacts list. This writing would become his multi-award-winning autobiographical novel *No Friend but the Mountains*.[7] Once he was satisfied with what he had produced, Boochani would send the pieces, whether a single sentence, full paragraph or whole page, to Mansoubi to store in chapter files for me to translate (in consultation with Mansoubi and Sajad Kabgani, whose work also features in this book).[8] We approached all our translations, especially Boochani's novel and the writing in this volume, with a collaborative sensibility and a collective aesthetic.[9]

From the beginning, Boochani's writing examined the history of Australia's colonialism, migration policies and the racism, all underpinning the border regime that incarcerated him in an abject offshore prison. The prison's structure and procedures, the impact of the Manus detention centre on the Indigenous Manusians,[10] and the logic, implementation and impact of systematic torture are explored in detail in the articles in this book. So, too, are the experiences and identities of those detained with Boochani, together with the political and economic machinations that have determined the fate of the tens of thousands of people seeking protection from the Australian Government in recent years.

After over six years in detention, in November 2019, Boochani managed to escape to New Zealand after winning a slew of prestigious awards for *No Friend but the Mountains* and having been invited to attend a literary festival in Christchurch, Aotearoa New Zealand.[11] Soon after his arrival, on the day of his thirty-seventh birthday, he was granted permanent protection.

This book is a kind of chronicle of the years dedicated to resisting, critiquing, exposing and attempting to abolish Australia's brutally strategic and racialized programme of border control. The book's structure reflects this unique and complex, yet horrific, timeline of events. The chapters are designated by key moments: beginning in 2013, after Boochani was banished to Manus Island and ending in 2020, after he arrived in Aotearoa New Zealand, and was granted refugee status. Each chapter marks a significant phase in his imprisonment; each chapter documents a particular period, with articles representing many noteworthy events, people and experiences. The articles also introduce or develop key ideas and theories in Boochani's critical analysis of a neocolonial experiment involving exile, incarceration and torture. The invited respondents to the journalism are academics, writers and activists who have collaborated with Boochani over several years. Their work is intertwined in the narratives of resistance that have emerged from Australian offshore and onshore immigration detention, and they have all been vital researchers and supporters in this space.

Political context, geography and critical place-based reporting

While Boochani's writing centres on his experience in the Australian-run immigration facilities on Manus Island, the history of Australia's inhumane policy of mandatory and indefinite offshore detention for people arriving in Australia by boat without a visa provides the disturbing context of the writing in this book.

In 2012, approximately a year before Boochani was detained, and in an attempt to 'stop the boats', Julia Gillard's Labor government reopened the offshore immigration detention centres on Manus Island and Nauru. This move activated phase two of the Pacific Solution – the policy of offshore 'processing' for people seeking asylum who attempted to arrive in Australia by boat, first implemented by John Howard's Liberal–National Coalition government between 2001 and 2008.

In 2013, Kevin Rudd (who had shut down phase one of the Pacific Solution in 2008, in his first term as prime minister) replaced Gillard as prime minister of the Labor government. On 19 July 2013, Rudd introduced what Boochani calls the 'exile policy': the mandate that anyone travelling to Australia by boat seeking protection would never be permitted to settle in the country. An example of how the Labor Party continued to bend to political pressure from the conservatives, this intensified the same offshore regime Labor had disbanded years before.[12] When the Liberal–National Coalition government led by Tony Abbott won the 2013 federal election, it further militarized the border, with the then Minister for Immigration, Scott Morrison, helping to establish Operation Sovereign Borders. This particularly punitive and discriminatory version of border control has continued until the time of writing, under Prime Minister Anthony Albanese.

From 2013 to 2017 – the initial phase of his detention – Boochani and up to approximately 1,350 people were locked up by the Australian Government in the Lombrum Naval Base (on Manus Island). Boochani refers to this carceral site as Manus Prison;[13] he also used the phrase to describe how the entire island had become a prison for the refugees (after the doors were first open in 2016), and after its official closure in 2017 he used the same phrase to refer to other carceral sites on Manus Island, and later in Port Moresby. As Boochani wrote, researched and reflected on his experiences in Manus Prison together with Mansoubi and me, the term became an important concept we used to refer to and analyse a broad and complex ideologically driven structure of refugee imprisonment and control in Papua New Guinea (PNG), Australia and beyond. We call this structure Manus Prison Theory.

Manus Prison Theory

The foundations of Manus Prison Theory pervade all of Boochani's journalism and features prominently in a number of articles in this collection.[14] This combined theoretical and activist framework brings together political, scholarly, cultural and aesthetic approaches and fuses genres in unprecedented ways to produce a unique literary and analytical tapestry: philosophical reflections, psychoanalytical examination, anti-colonial political commentary, as well as new forms of storytelling, poetry, myth, epic and folklore. In addition to Persian literature and cultural-political history and elements of Indigenous Manusian knowledge and heritage, Boochani's Indigenous Kurdish heritage plays a crucial role. The history of Kurdish resistance, creativity and intellectual life informs the collaborative works in this book and earlier projects.[15]

Manus Prison Theory also draws on different experiences of displacement and exile and is particularly attentive to the ways settler-colonialism and border politics manifest in Australia and around the world. Thus, the writing in this book investigates the symmetrical relationships between the violence inflicted on the border and within the nation.[16] In Part Seven of this book, Boochani's writing and that of Mahnaz Alimardanian and Helen Davidson explore Manus Island and Australia together, tied up in a vicious exchange in which they randomly and interchangeably impact on each other. This occurs through the role of multinational companies, such as Paladin, within the border-industrial complex; the fostering of suspicion, enmity and competition; the silencing of displaced and exiled peoples and their demonizing through the use of reductive, damaging and dehumanizing tropes;[17] and the function of indefinite detention as a neocolonial experiment.

Key to Manus Prison Theory is the role of hope, joy, celebration, pride and love as political acts.[18] One of the most important aspects of Manus Prison Theory is that it is a collective endeavour that grows and expands with every new contribution and collaboration. The articles in this book both highlight the need for creative and collaborative approaches and strategies for dismantling malignant border regimes, as well as for showcasing this collective approach in action.

Another key theoretical underpinning of this book is what Boochani refers to in Farsi as *system-e hākem*, which I translated as the 'kyriarchal system', drawing on the neologism 'kyriarchy' introduced by radical feminist theologian Elisabeth Schüssler Fiorenza.[19] In the context of Australia's border regime – similar to Schüssler Fiorenza's use of kyriarchy in her feminist biblical hermeneutics – the kyriarchal system is best described as interlocking and mutually reinforcing structures of violence obsessed with oppression, domination and submission, structures also characterized by their replication and multiplication. Boochani uses the kyriarchal system as both a literary and political technique for identifying and naming the colonial logic and ruthless structures that pervade the detention centre, Australia's border regime as a whole, and, by extension, the foundations, social systems and conditions of the Australian settler-colonial state. His writing in this book critically analyses this kyriarchal system and the way it morphs, invigorates and conceals itself within the historical timeline of Manus Prison.

The horrific and surreal dimensions of Australia's border regime are unpacked with visceral quality and analytical verve in this book. Boochani's articles illuminate the intricacies of the kyriarchal system. They consider the fact that the detention of people seeking asylum is indefinite; the inadequacy of any judicial system or review to determine the legitimacy of their detention; the externalization of state borders; and the extraterritorial and extrajudicial practices of border control and confinement. Other prominent themes that attest to the horrific and surreal aspects of immigration detention include the weaponization of time and the use of bad faith as a tool of torture. In order to expose the nature of the kyriarchal system, Boochani's articles address indefinite detention as a policy of deterrence and punishment; the extrajudicial nature of that punishment; the censorship surrounding media coverage and investigation into what occurs in detention centres; the ways in which the detention industry encourages hate, malice and competition between everyone either held or working within; and the ambiguous and ever-changing laws surrounding Australia's border regime. In order to help critically analyse a horrific, surreal and extremely complex system, both Boochani's articles and many contributions in this book detail the corruption and secrecy around the political economy of the detention industry and wider border-industrial complex, the damaging physical, psychological, emotional and spiritual tactics and strategies that comprise systematic torture in immigration detention, and so much more.

The role of time and identity: The structure of this collection

The structure and themes of this book are determined by some of the most significant periods and events of Boochani's imprisonment and eventual escape. Like much of his work, the journalism in *Freedom, Only Freedom* can be described as anti-genre: a mix of historical document, political critique, on-the-ground reportage, philosophical reflection, psychoanalytical examination, poetic expression and epic. Boochani draws on multiple styles and frameworks in order to capture the complexity of the refugee experience in offshore indefinite detention; the lived reality of systematic torture; and the horrifically surreal nature of the island prison.[20]

Weaponizing time through indefinite detention and malevolent bureaucracy, and stripping human beings of their identity by cutting them off from family and denying them even the use of their own names are tactics integral to maintaining Australia's border regime.[21] Boochani was forced to grapple with the damaging physical, emotional and psychological impact and deep loss associated with these two aspects of indefinite detention. In order to survive and resist these oppressive conditions, he and fellow detainees reimagined the meaning and role of philosophical notions such as temporality and autonomy.

Certain events, experiences and political decisions would become psychological and emotional markers for Boochani and the other detained refugees. Therefore, chapters in this book present key incidents and events within each year, including the deaths inside the prison, the 23-day siege, various federal elections and policy shifts, the making and distribution of *Chauka, Please Tell Us the Time*, the release of *No Friend but the Mountains* and subsequent accolades, and Boochani's escape to Aotearoa New Zealand. They remind us that within the context of indefinite detention, and in an environment just south of the Equator, time and confrontations with power function in radically political ways and take on heightened significance. The chapters are arranged in chronological order, and each chapter highlights temporal markers, personal stories and lived experience. These key temporal reference points reflect the way Boochani and the other detained refugees battled against the use of time as torture, reclaimed their identities and restored a sense of their agency. Each chapter begins with a narrative that includes a number of key dates and events relevant to the period under consideration in order to help orient the reader. This information also helps account for our selection by providing a historical and political backdrop to the articles within individual chapters.

What kind of journalism is this?

Writing in 2017, after enduring 23 days under siege in the Manus Island detention centre (featured in Part Five of this book),[22] Behrouz describes his work as a 'duty to history'.[23] During his TEDxSydney 2019 talk, he states: 'For me, writing has always been an act of resistance . . . writing and creating is a way of fighting to get my identity, humanity and dignity back.'[24] He was fighting against a system that only recognized him as MEG45. Also, Boochani often states that we need a new language and new narratives;[25] he often claims that literature draws from life, coupling this with the well-known Kurdish saying – especially important for Kurds in Rojava – *Barxodan Jiana* or 'resistance is life'.[26] The writings in this collection are described as journalism, but they are clearly more than that. Whether categorized as journalism or interpreted as anti-genre, Boochani's writings provide us with an intricate tapestry of images, narratives, ideas and theories; an uncompromising and scathing critique of state power and border violence. His anti-colonial resistance gives us insight into the interlocking forms of violence occurring at the Australian border, in his case the extraterritorial prison located in Manus Island. In particular, Boochani's writing around the time of the 23-day siege is significant because it dramatically increased international attention to and action on the inhumane conditions in Manus. Boochani's journalism proved that this form of creative struggle can initiate transformation when endorsed by and connected to necessary support networks. In 2017 Boochani won an Amnesty International Australia media award for his journalism and in 2018 he won the Anna Politkovskaya award for journalism at the journalism festival Internazionale a Ferrara, Italy.

The contributor essays in this book address the pivotal themes and issues covered in Boochani's work. They can be read as examples of and responses to the new language of resistance that Boochani calls for and which he originally created in Manus Prison. Contributors examine both the writing and translation process in the context of the extreme circumstances of the detention centre (Mansoubi, Part One) and the unique form of journalism produced and the networks needed to disseminate it (Doherty, Part One). They also explore the importance of history and the place of this writing in both Australian history and the modern history of incarceration (Silverstein, Part Two). Contributions engage with questions and concerns relating to posthumanist discourses (Kabgani, Part Three) and the place of Boochani's work in modern Kurdish writing and journalism (Germian, Part Three). Others discuss knowledge production and the political power of aesthetics (McNevin, Part Four), and the ways Boochani's work communicates the experience of systematic torture (Canning, Part Four). The collection includes accounts of lived experience and shared struggle (Kanapathi, Part Five), and reflections on transcending borders through writing (Jensen, Part Five). Also included is commentary about journalism and struggle in the Nauru context (Zivardar and Ghadiri, Part Six), and writing addressing embodiment and the environment (Measham, Part Six). There is exploration of the exploitation of Manus Island and its people (Alimardanian, Part Seven) and political economy and corruption (Davidson, Part Seven). Hope as a political act (Tazreiter, Part Eight) and transcultural imaginaries against incarceration (Ratuva, Part Eight) are examined by other authors. Contributors also explain Boochani's dialogic approach and the power of collective activism (Amiri, Part Nine), and they provide critical reflections on poetics and narrative (Surma, Part Nine) (the collaborative and critical features within Part Nine are also reflected in the co-authored contribution by Boochani and Tofighian). Finally, this collection offers us important analysis about the function of social media (Grasso, Part Ten) and the significance of critiquing colonial legacies (Zeweri, Part Ten). Therefore, this book is more than a collection of articles and poetry written by Boochani during his incarceration. It is also an example of a shared philosophical activity,[27] a testament to collective struggle, and a unique, creative form of resistance that centres the experiences of the displaced, the exiled and the incarcerated.

The prison writings of Behrouz Boochani encompass all the themes, events and topics mentioned in this introduction . . . and more. This book presents the most vital features and factors of Boochani's work and thought from the time he was incarcerated in Manus Prison. The chapters are designed to represent the struggle for freedom from inside the notorious Manus Prison – not only Boochani's struggle, but the struggle for freedom by everyone targeted by Australia's ruthless border politics. Boochani's work from inside and, finally, beyond the detention centre is not just one person's story, or one person's resistance. The selected works in this book demonstrate how narrative and analysis can function as the work of one individual, while simultaneously highlighting a collective plight and exposing wider systemic and global issues, including the experiences of people whose lives have been destroyed, or who have been killed, by a brutal system.

Fighting to take back his identity was an act of resistance for Boochani, but it was also an explicitly creative endeavour. In response to a cruel, violent and ugly system, he found beauty, hope, joy, celebration, pride and love. For Boochani, finding beauty in the face of brutality is a political act, and through this form of creativity he has made cracks in the border-industrial complex. Once cracks began to appear, he invited us to join him in tearing Australia's unjust border regime apart. For Boochani, writing is freedom. He writes to find freedom in every sense of the word.

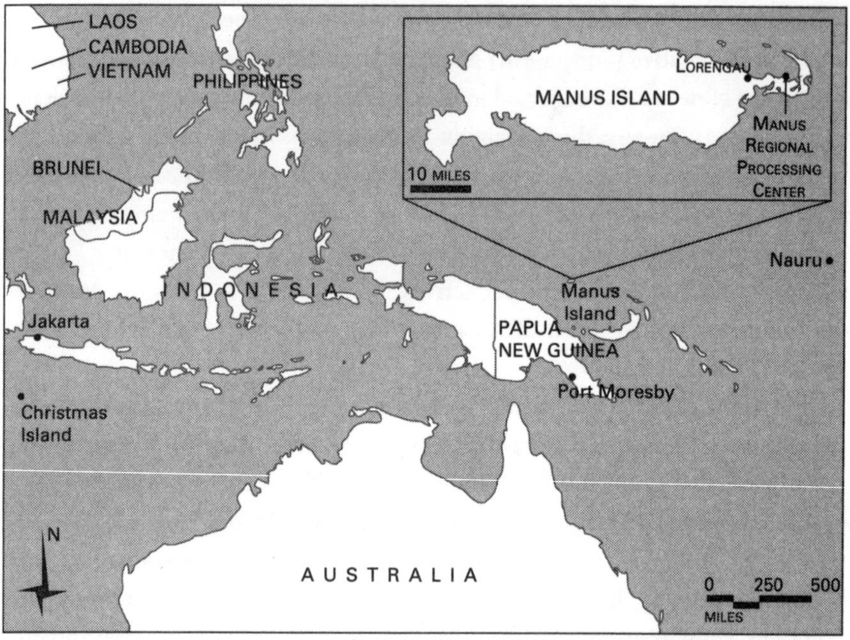

Manus Island in Papua New Guinea (former colony) and Republic of Nauru (former protectorate). Australia has a long history of imperialism in the Pacific which includes the indefinite detention of people seeking asylum. Men travelling alone are imprisoned in Manus; and women, unaccompanied minors and families are imprisoned in Nauru.

Part One

2013–2015 – 'Fighting to Take Back My Identity'

Creating a New Language in Collaboration

Behrouz Boochani was born in 1983 in a village near the border city of Ilām during the Iran–Iraq War. He fled Iran in 2013 after the arrest of his colleagues and because of the risk of his own imprisonment for journalism and cultural advocacy in support of Kurdish identity and language.

On 24 June 2010, Julia Gillard replaced Kevin Rudd as prime minister and leader of the Labor Party and in 2012, Gillard's Labor government began sending refugees to Manus Island in Papua New Guinea (PNG, a former colony of Australia) and the Republic of Nauru (a former protectorate) – the immigration detention centres on these two Pacific islands were first opened in 2001 (under John Howard's Liberal–National Coalition government) and closed by Rudd in 2008 (phase one of the 'Pacific Solution' 2001–8, phase two 2012–13, Operation Sovereign Borders 2013–present). Manus was for men travelling alone, and Nauru for women, unaccompanied minors and families. After replacing Gillard and returning to power on 26 June 2013, Rudd introduced what Boochani calls the 'exile policy' on 19 July 2013, which states that any person seeking asylum in Australia by boat without a valid visa after this date will be banned from entering Australia for life. Boochani arrived by boat from Indonesia four days after this law was passed. Later in 2013, the Liberal–National Coalition defeated Labor in the federal election and Tony Abbott became prime minister on 7 September.

Operation Sovereign Borders (OSB) was then established, led by Immigration Minister Scott Morrison, followed by his successor Peter Dutton in late-2014; OSB is a military-led border security operation that continues today. In particular, it is notorious for its 'turnback' policy which is designed to prevent people smuggling boats carrying asylum seekers from reaching Australia. Morrison visited the Manus Island detention centre in September 2013, that was followed by an uprising during which Reza Barati was killed by Australian, New Zealand and PNG guards on 17 February 2014. Nearly 100 people were injured when the Australian authorities manipulated local Manusians and incited an attack on the prison. Around this time, 12 October 2013, Saeed Qasem Abdalla died after he was moved from the Christmas Island detention centre to the mainland for surgery. In 2013, the United Nations High Commissioner for Refugees (UNHCR) reported on the conditions in the detention facilities in Manus and Nauru and found that men, women and children were being held in 'arbitrary detention in conditions that do not meet international standards' (November 2013). In March 2014, the Human Rights Law Centre and Amnesty International inspected the Manus detention centre, the only time that journalists and advocates have been permitted entry into the facility. Seyed Ibrahim Hussein drowned in Nauru on 22 June 2014 and soon after, on 5 September 2014, Hamid Khazaei was killed as a result of medical neglect in Manus. A mass hunger strike began and the leaders, including Boochani, were held in a local prison during 2014–15. The Australian Border Force Act 2015 was passed on 1 July 2015. The secrecy provisions in the Act stated that if medical professionals, teachers and other employees record or disclose protected information about conditions in the Manus and Nauru facilities, they will be charged and punished with up to two years imprisonment. The Human Rights Law Centre and Human Rights Watch issued a report after inspecting the Manus detention centre in July 2015, highlighting the fact that after two years, more people had died than been resettled. Malcolm Turnbull replaced Tony Abbott as prime minister and leader of the Liberal Party on 14 September 2015. Fazel Chegeni's body was found after he escaped from the Christmas Island detention centre on 8 November 2015.

Boochani began investigating, resisting and writing from the moment he was detained. He mainly used smuggled mobile phones for writing and filing his work and created networks with activists and journalists, sending reports out by WhatsApp text messages. During random and spontaneous early morning raids in search of contraband, his mobile was confiscated twice, but he was able to smuggle in a replacement. Moones Mansoubi was one of Boochani's first translators and supporters, connecting with him in 2014. Most of his early writings remain unpublished, but she assisted him in publishing some of his pieces and began collaborating with him as he started writing his autobiographical novel – text messages that later became *No Friend but the Mountains: Writing from Manus Prison* (Picador, 2018). Boochani also began collaborating with Ben Doherty from *The Guardian* during this initial period of incarceration. In his role as journalist for *The Guardian*, he has been reporting on themes and topics pertaining to Australia's border regime, including the detention industry. Doherty was also part of *The Guardian* Nauru Files team.

Becoming MEG45

Behrouz Boochani

The airport was entirely empty and quiet. There was only a propeller aircraft that was supposed to take us to a far-flung island. I became restless again. I wanted those officers to get on the plane quickly and take us on board so that then the airplane would fly.

I love flying.

The atmosphere was too heavy for me, particularly with the presence of those vultures standing right beside the plane and toying with their cameras. With their crammed backpacks, the officers boarded the plane. They were like soldiers ready to be sent into a battlefield. Some of the officers were shaking hands with the reporters. I felt that they were partners in crime.

F was the first person to board the plane. He needed to walk approximately fifty meters between the bus and the plane's stairs. The officers had parked the bus far from the plane on purpose in order to make us feel deeply humiliated. Two muscular officers put their hands under F's shoulder and took him to the plane in an extremely degrading manner. Although F was a tall person, he was like a fawn, a prey for the two predatorss: the two officers who held him firmly dragged him towards the stairs. Those reporters, too, focused all their energies on taking the last photos of us, so as not to lose those pure moments.

I was confident that they enjoyed destroying our human dignity. It was clear that F stepped reluctantly, however it did not make any difference since those two giants were taking him by the arm. They did not care about him. They took him like a piece of flesh to the plane at a steady speed. When they approached the stairs, two other men took F up the stairs. There was another person waiting for them at the top of the stairs who was filming everything. It was the scene of the day repeated every two minutes. The only difference was that one piece of flesh changed its place with another piece of flesh.

An image of F was flashing through my mind: I saw him sitting on the bow of the boat continually looking to the front and sometimes at his watch. I even recalled his repetitive questions: 'How far is Australia?' I remembered, too, that night, the last night, when he remained grimly silent as the hurricane hit the boat. He was holding me with his two hands in a dreadful darkness. He was frightened. Now, all his agonies had ended here. In that scene, he was being treated more like a dangerous murderer who should be tied up as he was moved by two muscular men. These events were all taking place in the land of Australia. They were taking place in the Australia that F had counted down the minutes until he arrived. He had survived such deep fear because of this ambition.

It was the Myanmarese's turn. He seemed weaker than the others. He was short and skinny. After taking some steps, he was shaky on his feet and was about to fall down. The officers raised him up. He was more like a person who is being taken to the gallows. When I was in Iran, I had seen a similar scene. I wished the man would not reveal his weakness and confusion. He had been a brave person whose courage crumbled. He was the one who had traversed the ocean. He should not have been scared of an absurd tumult and cruel cameras. He needed to try to summon his remaining courage and act in a stronger manner. He took a couple of steps further, turned his head and looked at our bus. It seemed he had left someone or something behind. Or maybe, he could not find anything or anyone to lean on in those debilitating moments, except us. Yes, he did not breathe a word during the half day we had been corralled and we had considered him as a stranger. We had not even offered a puff of the cigarette. We were the only people that he knew in this short time. We had a shared grief. We were all in the same boat. He was about to be thrown into a dark and unknown future; a future which was supposed to continue on an island. During the rest of his journey to the stairs of the plane, he was more like prey being dragged along the ground. There was no determination in his feet. He did not even take a single step. After a while, he was on board.

After some others, my number was called: MEG45. I got used to that number eventually. They regarded us only as numbers, no more than that, and I had to set my name aside for a long time. When I was called, my ears started moving. My name, which was a part of my identity was of no use, and all day long, sometimes, nobody even once called me Behrouz. I tried to attribute a new meaning to the nonsense number with my imagination. For instance, Mr Meg. But there were many people like me: Meg. What could I do with that rubbish number! Throughout the whole of my life, I had always hated figures and maths but now I was forced to carry this number. It weighed on my soul and I had no remedy but to bear its heaviness. At last, I tried to make the number relevant to an important historical event. Nothing came into my mind other than the end of the Second World War in 1945. Still, whoever I was or whatever I think, the number was announced and MEG45 had to follow a route which F and others had taken before.

I confess that I was stressed out, a feeling that combined with anger and ended up as a lump, a piece of sorrow that pressed my throat. What crime did I commit that they wanted to take me by my arms on board? If they had shown me the way, I would have happily sprinted towards the plane and got on it. This situation reminded me of the desperate Myanmarese guy. I thought: I must not appear weak in front of all these eyes gazing at me. I'd had similar experiences in more dreadful circumstances. At least this time I had been eating food for a month; I had a bit of colour in my face and my body did not stink of ooze. However, what could I do with my clothes? A yellow T-shirt which was two times bigger than me reached down to my knees. 'Clack, clack' was heard, when I walked with the thongs. My appearance was like nobody. I had never seen anyone dressed up in that way. For example, the short sleeves reached down to my wrist. It was a terrible combination of colours: a yellow T-shirt, black shorts and bare feet which ended in a pair of thongs. By wearing those clothes, I was degraded in practice, no matter who I was or what thoughts I had.

Put what I just mentioned aside. How on earth could I pass through in front of so many cameras? Particularly, those young and blonde girls who were extremely excited about taking photos, photos closer than close. I must not reveal my weakness. Finally, I took a leap in the dark and got off the bus. Those two giants were waiting for me. All of a sudden, they locked their arms around mine and moved towards the plane. I held my head high and took long steps in order to finish the torturous scene as soon as I could.

I passed the interpreters first. They were dressed in green clothes and were standing watching us without any reason. Maybe they wanted to come to Manus Island with us. They did not look like passengers. I glanced over at the interpreter, who seemed not to intend leaving us. There was nothing in her face. Even her smile which had previously formed as a question in my mind in the first place, disappeared. I was unable to understand her; she was highly ambiguous. She seemed both careless and worried. Perhaps what made her look even heavier was what I felt was a common agony in her black eyes. It was an agony that had caused me to get further and further away from my past and the land that I belong to. There was no doubt that she went through agony like me just because of being labelled as Kurd, being labelled a greedy creature in the Middle East, the one who has always been a fly in the ointment for governments; who is always talking about strange topics like freedom and democracy. Once, she had abandoned everything like me and come to Australia. No matter what means she used to get here, whether a decayed boat or a plane, by looking at her, I felt that I reminded her of a bygone pain. I felt I reminded her of the days that she was considered an extra creature in the Middle East. I felt that this concept evoked in her a feeling of hatred and sympathy towards me.

We approached the reporters. One of the blonde girls took some steps closer and while she was kneeling, she took some artistic masterpiece photos of my ridiculous face. She was definitely able to create a wonderful scene. She would show it to her editor and would be praised by him or her. In a shot from a bottom angle, my thin body was undoubtedly a masterpiece in those loose-fitting and slovenly clothes. I still held my head high and mounted the stairs of the plane with a sense of pride. But those steps were more like the steps of a person who was running away.

I finally got on board. I was directed to my seat and collapsed in a heap. There was no sign of my false pride any more and I kept my head down. A degraded person, someone who had been humiliated and become worthless. Someone who felt all those people either sniggered in their minds or perhaps cried for him. Through looking at my unkempt appearance and seeing those two officers who pulled me like a dangerous criminal, people should hate coming to Australia. I was the one who ought to make them detest the idea of coming there. The piece of sorrow grew several times as much in my throat and was about to suffocate me. I took some deep breaths so that a part of it might find a way outside and make me breathe easier. After a while, the ex-jailer from Iran who was with us also came on board but no longer chattering and laughing like he had been during that day. He sat next to me.

The number of officers on board was the same as us. Two officers sat down on two seats next to the ex-jailor and I. They were watching us carefully in order to avoid us conducting any dangerous activities or misbehaviour. After a while, the plane took off and climbed. We got far and farther away from Christmas Island; the island we had almost died in the ocean to reach.

Unpublished Reports

Behrouz Boochani

Untitled[1]

With a shattered body which was ravenously hungry and deeply wounded, with bare feet and exhausted soul, I made the trip to the soil of free territory, to the soil of freedom, to Australia.

It was exactly four days after the announcement of the 19 of July law. By the implementation of this law, I was exiled to Manus prison, in the heart of the Pacific Ocean; and as a result of this law, I have been under pressure and have been tortured for several months.

The 19 of July law enforced the transfer of people to offshore detentions who arrive by boat and seek asylum in Australia. It is worth mentioning that this law started being implemented when our broken boat with 65 unconscious passengers was lost in the ocean . . . When we reached the soil of Australia, we just got to know about this cruelty.

Whatever it was, the number 19 remains so ominous to me and thousands of people seeking asylum. After many months, this number still tortures our mind and soul with such extreme cruelty. And like a sledgehammer, it perpetually descends into our soul and mind.

One soul, two bodies[1]

I knew those twins from Christmas Island. I met them right before being boarded and banished to Manus prison. Those two brothers were identical twins! It was bizarre and nobody could recognize them from one another.

The twins, on that horrific day, were separated by one brutal and baseless decision. One of them was banished with us to Manus Island and the other remained in prison on Christmas Island.

On that sinister night, the older brother – just a few minutes older – told me, 'My brother and I had never been separated.' He revealed how dependent and connected they were to each other. If one of them had a cold, the other one suddenly would get a cold. Their feelings were entirely the same, senses and feelings were alike in their bodies, souls and mind. Since the separation, that younger brother kept crying and begging, 'Please take me to my brother.'

He knew right from the first moment of the incident, he knew clearly that their separation would have an irreversible and dangerous impact on their life, on their mental health, on their destiny. Something dreadful waited for them. I wish the system was aware of that. Later, they were reunited in Manus, but the scar remained on their soul.

Two nights ago, I saw them again. An extreme toothache led me to the Medical Centre. I was sitting on a chair waiting for a nurse to give me some pain killers. Suddenly I saw several security guards bringing someone in a blood-covered blanket. They rushed into the medical care section where I was.

When they got closer, I recognized him. He was one of them. Yes, he was one of the twins. Oh God, what happened to him?

Bewildered and shocked, I asked the nurse what had happened, she responded: 'He cut his bloodstream with a blade – both his hands and feet. He attempted suicide. He is not well at all.'

It took me back to Christmas Island, to that sinister night. I recalled how the older brother pictured their dependency: 'We are one soul in two bodies.'

A dark thought flashed in my mind and I started worrying about the other body, the other one. Where was he? Was he banished to another compound on Manus? Was he sent back to Christmas Island?

In distress, all negative thoughts occupied my mind. How could I find answers to the thousands of questions invading my mind?

Then, several security guards hurried past me carrying another person covered in blood. It could not be him, could it be? It was him, I anticipated this. He attempted suicide, too. 'They were one soul in two bodies.'

Translating Manus and Nauru

Refugee Writing[1]

Moones Mansoubi

I never imagined a post on Twitter would lead me along a winding road, thousands of kilometres away from Sydney, where I live, to the 'Islands of despair',[2] Manus and Nauru islands. The tweet was the beginning of my work translating letters, poems, and other writings by refugees incarcerated in Australia's Offshore Processing Centres on Manus and Nauru. It was straightforward, posted in October 2014 by Shane Bazzi, a refugee advocate, asking if anyone could help translate Persian letters from refugees imprisoned in Australia's 'offshore processing centres'. I'd already begun supporting refugees in Sydney, in other roles and capacities, but working with people stuck in offshore detention was another story. Though I was never able to travel to the islands, by translating and assisting them with their writing I've felt the inhumane conditions and horrific experiences of many of the refugees. I've worked this way for more than six years now. For me, it has been a long and sorrowful journey.

In 2013 and 2014, as part of Australia's attempt to stop people seeking asylum from reaching Australian shore, hundreds of men, women and children who arrived by sea were transferred to Manus and Nauru islands and imprisoned in utterly inhumane conditions. The deliberate effect of this remote imprisonment was to scratch the human face from the discourse, and dehumanize and criminalize people seeking asylum coming by boat. The policy and the system of offshore detention were designed to strip people of their identities, threaten their existence and cultivate a sense of powerlessness in them. For one thing, these people no longer had names, only ID numbers assigned by the 'processing centre'. Australia's deliberate goal was to break these people so they would choose repatriation despite the horrors they had fled. For many, there was no safe place to return to. They were at risk of persecution, violence, rape, torture and other injuries, stuck between two Hells. The situation created by Australia's 'Stop the Boats' policy was an absolute calamity and a human tragedy.

I first moved from Iran to Australia as a student in 2013. I studied for a master's degree at the University of New South Wales and chose international relations as my focus, since this field plays a pivotal role in our everyday lives as Iranians. Sanctions, war, tension, geopolitical confrontations, threats, international diplomacy and ideological warfare have been central components of living. We grew up with these concepts, and our lives would change overnight because of these realities. To be born Iranian, no matter if you live there or go abroad, is to encounter these concepts every second of your life. Many others around the world are in the same situation, facing conditions that force them to flee, to become stateless, to seek asylum, and many end up becoming refugees.

Before my migration, I had imagined Australia as a peaceful country where I would not encounter warmongering or human rights violations. Australia would be my utopia, where people and their government respect human rights and care about humane values. Not long after emigrating, I became aware of a major political debate in Australia: the fates of refugees and asylum seekers. In disbelief, I watched a humanitarian concern turn into a political question, used for the sake of political gain. I vividly recalled the human rights violations back home, and once again I was perplexed by brutality and cruelty.

I discovered that in Australia, as elsewhere, politicians try to create imaginary 'enemies'. They spread propaganda and fear of others so they can benefit by gaining power. As David Marr, Australian journalist, put it in one of his essays: 'The fundamental contest in Australian politics ... is about a willingness of Australian leaders to beat up on the nation's fears ... panic is a rallying cry for power.' It's the same approach that Theodore Adorno described, in his analysis of totalitarianism, as the use of 'in group-out group differentiation'. In this context, refugees and asylum seekers are categorized as an 'out group', *others*, a threat to Australia's sovereignty. 'They' are criminals, queue jumpers, thieves of taxpayers' money, or so say the politicians. In 2013, the new approach to asylum seekers, 'Operation Sovereign Borders', was passed into law, creating the offshore prisons of Manus and Nauru islands. Mesmerized by politicians, and feeling their own fears of the unknown and of the refugees, the majority of Australians supported the new policy.

The policy was offshore detention of people neither charged nor convicted of any crimes ... During the long and gloomy nights on Manus and Nauru islands, an eerie silence was the only sound; or, more clearly, the groans of a slow but deliberate strangulation could be heard. Men, women and children were imprisoned and deprived of basic rights including the right to speak with the outside world, the right to be heard, the right to be seen, even the right, simply, to have a mobile phone.

It's easy to see how writing could become a means for these refugees to reclaim their identity, escape invisibility, fight injustice and end their isolation. Many of them smuggled mobile phones into the centres, and eventually the rules changed to allow that. The phones became narrow windows through which they could shout, share and bring about transformative change. The fact that their words – in Persian or Arabic, any language other than English – meant nothing to most Australians, opened the space in which translation (my skill) could give visibility to otherwise invisible people. By collaborating and translating, I was able to stand side by side with them in an asymmetrical war.

Australia, the country I had chosen as my new, bright and sunny home, took me into one of the darkest and most twisted passages in its history. I used translation as an act of speaking up, speaking out, and speaking back against this humanitarian catastrophe. As Paulo Freire, a Brazilian educational theorist, wrote: 'Washing one's hands of the conflict between the powerful and the powerless means to side with the powerful, not to be neutral.' I first encountered Freire's work in Iran, when I was doing my bachelor's degree in English teaching (TESOL). His concept of a 'culture of silence', and the ways that it passively impacts the self-image of oppressed individuals, gave me new insight. In addition, his anti-colonial theory explicating how politics can surround and control education, our voices and our thoughts, rang true to me. I related Freire's concepts to the refugee experience by asking how it is that politics can silence the voices of the oppressed, tarnish their self-image, and control public opinion about refugees. With my translation skills, I've tried to correct the distorted image of refugees held by many Australians and to help them recognize that the refugees have power that has been stolen.

In 2013 and 2014, I joined a trusted network of refugee advocates, writers and translators who shared common concerns and values. We encouraged refugees held on Manus and Nauru to write for a number of reasons. First, writing can be a healing process. At the very least, writing can alleviate suffering inside an inhumane system. As Maya Angelou said: 'There is no greater agony than bearing an untold story inside you.' Mary was one of the refugees that I'd been in touch with frequently. She had a creative and sensitive personality, and the harsh situation on Nauru was unbearable for her. She lived with her three-year old daughter, Sara. As a mother, Mary kept blaming herself for putting Sara in this dreadful environment. She had no other choice. She'd left everything behind to escape from domestic violence. If she hadn't left, they would have been killed.

Among the most traumatic and devastating experiences for Mary, at Nauru, was mealtime. Three times a day, they had to go to the canteen at a specific time. Sometimes Sara, her 3-year-old, was sleeping or refused to eat when the time came, like many children. Mary wanted to take some food back to her, but the system, the officers, refused. She wasn't permitted to take even a small piece of bread out of the canteen to feed Sara when she was hungry. The goal was clear: they should suffer. In addition to all of the psychological torture, abuse, and deliberate cruelty that she and others had to endure, the sensation of guilt as a mother hurt Mary the most. Mealtime was a heartfelt pain for Mary. She was begging Sara to eat, and begging officers to let her take food to Sara. If Sara didn't agree, both mother and daughter would be in flood of tears the whole day: Sara out of hunger, Mary out of hatred – hatred of herself; hatred of the detention system; hatred of the destiny that had forced them to flee; hatred of being powerless, unable to fulfil her motherly duties, her only reason to live. Mary didn't speak about it on Nauru; this problem, and worse, were so common. She never revealed her situation to her family back home. I encouraged her to write, and eventually she found solace there. Writing was a respite. She also expressed her feelings in her paintings. Here was a way to have agency in that inhumane situation, by depicting her emotions and her horrendous suffering in writing and in art.

Second, in close collaboration with refugees themselves, we worked to amplify their voices – the voices of those who were marginalized and excluded from public discourse. The 'Operation Sovereign Borders' policy tried to put them out of sight and out of mind. But the combined efforts of many different people, most of them volunteers, led to articles being published in the global media, including in *The Guardian*, and reports by human rights organizations, including Amnesty International, which issued their report, called 'Island of Despair'.

Mary was just one of dozens of refugee writers. Another, Ellie, was a young woman with an independent personality who could not stay passive. I helped by translating her texts about the inhumane situation on Nauru, and these became primary source material for media reporters. Writing is a kind of 'self-representation activism' for people whose suffering has been made invisible, a form of resistance against forgetfulness, against the demand to remain quiet.

Another Manus refugee that I worked with was Behrouz Boochani. He reclaimed his identity as a journalist and a writer through the texts that he sent us via WhatsApp, which led to his receiving the most prestigious literary award in Australia, the Victorian Prize for his book, *No Friend but the Mountains*. Boochani is among the leading figures in self-representation activism, fighting against invisibility and the false images propagated by the government and mainstream media. For five years, I worked closely with Boochani, as the first person to translate his pieces for *The Guardian*, the *Sydney Morning Herald*, *The Saturday Paper* and other media channels, as well as his daily Facebook and Twitter posts documenting the horrifying incidents on Manus, such as self-harm, violence, murder, medical neglect, and the aggressive tactics by guards in response to peaceful protests.

My main contact in this network was Janet Galbraith, who founded and coordinates a group called Writing Through Fences. Hundreds of refugees and asylum seekers developed their writing with help from Writing Through Fences. Janet was receiving poems and other writing from refugees, and helped find translators to bring them into English and edit their work. As Galbraith explained it, 'Most of the [writers] are, or have been, incarcerated in Australia's immigration detention regime. A small group of non-refugee artists and writers resident in the stolen lands now called Australia, are involved in collaborative amplification and resourcing roles.' Many of the collaborators are volunteers, as is Galbraith herself.

Back when I started, Janet used to travel to Sydney more frequently, and we spent long hours in beautiful cafes working on poems and other writing from people incarcerated in offshore detention. It was an exquisite agony, full of paradoxical feelings – the fact that I was sitting in front of spectacular Darling Harbour, reading and translating the emotions, despair, and suffering of people in detention. I felt unbearably tormented, facing unanswerable questions: 'does this all work?' or 'am I just trapped into a spiral of futility?' Galbraith was my first point of contact for most of the refugees I worked with. We both received text messages any time of the day and any day of a week, whenever they wrote and were able to send it through. On many occasions, she would email me and I'd translate the writing on the spot without even asking *what are you going to do with this* or *who's written this*? Promising these distressed people that their writing would be translated and heard helped give them a temporary respite. Janet's selfless support created a reading-and-writing cycle that kept people motivated to write and read. We sometimes sent books to people on Manus and Nauru or 'topped up' people's mobile phone accounts to enable them to keep reading, writing, and engaging.

While sitting in a café, once in 2015, Galbraith and I were working on a piece of writing from Boochani, without having any idea where it might be published. Later, with Galbraith's support, it appeared in Mascara Literary Magazine,[3] which led to the acceptance of his book by a publisher in Australia, in 2017. This was a huge achievement and we celebrated with tears and smiles. If I am not mistaken, that was Boochani's first piece published under his real name. Mine, too. I was still on a temporary visa back then, and Boochani was in detention. The fear of being punished plagued us both and was a normal part of our lives. Janet and our other friends were very concerned, but our deep commitment helped us remain brave and determined on the path we had chosen. Night came, the café was surrounded by darkness, our coffee got cold, and we still had a lot to work on, to speak about, and to be worried by.

On Manus and Nauru in those first few years, prison guards would sometimes invade people's rooms, ripping up papers, confiscating their belongings, including their mobile phones, and vandalizing whatever was there. Imagine the distress, fear, and pressure on these people in detention, and the toll on those outside who were in contact with them. I'll never forget those traumatic moments, when I was receiving pieces of writing from Boochani and all of a sudden, the connection was cut for hours on end; I couldn't be sure if it was an Internet issue or some other invasion. One time, the search lasted almost five hours. Early in the morning, in June 2015, a group of officers raided one of the compounds on Manus. Refugees' rooms were turned inside out, their personal goods and bedding were thrown to the ground. The search wasn't limited to rooms; guards demanded personal searches. One forced a strip search, asking a refugee to remove his underwear in front of everyone else. The impact of the incident was long-lasting and devastating; it took days, weeks, even months, for those who had been violated to recover from this invasion. Boochani managed to hide his phone in his mattress, but during that search thirteen other mobile phones were confiscated.

At that time, in 2015, the Australian Government announced that anyone disclosing the conditions of offshore detention could be sentenced to up to two years in jail. Working closely with Boochani, every day and every night, was an urgent response to a horrendous policy that aimed to suffocate refugee voices and keep the Australian public unaware of the cruelty of offshore detention, imposed in their name. Boochani was writing his book then, *No Friend but the Mountains*, using WhatsApp, and sending the messages immediately. I'd read them as they came and was amazed by the power of his pen. His words allowed me to clearly imagine the situation, engaging all of my senses. I could hear birdsong, smell the stink from the filthy toilets, and be choked with rage, filled by sorrow, then burst into tears in silence. While he was writing his book, he was sometimes only able to write two sentences, while at other times he'd write a full page. I would save all his messages on my laptop and whenever a chapter concluded, I exported them to a PDF. This gave him the assurance that his writings were in a safe place and they wouldn't be lost. I also kept encouraging him by giving positive feedback. It was clear that one day his book would become an influential and important piece of literature, and that has turned out to be true.

When Omid Tofighian started translating the book in 2017, I sent all the PDFs to him. In that process, Sajad Kabgani and I worked as Tofighian's translation consultants. We met up in cafés, going through the Persian original and the English text that Tofighian had translated. The book led the three of us to engage in far-reaching conversations about politics, the system, refugees and migration, injustice, racism, and borders. Every time, during the gloomy winter evenings, I would leave the café with a lump in my throat, and many unanswered questions: What is the use of international laws, treaties and conventions? Who makes governments accountable for their human rights violations? Who is responsible for the lifelong damage the government caused for these men, women, and children? Why should people suffer? When will it all end?

Tofighian worked hard to accurately render Boochani's descriptions of the situation in English, and I think he was completely successful. Every word of the book was carefully chosen by both Boochani and Tofighian, and there are many hidden messages that a reader can uncover. Not only has the book become a seedbed for researchers in many universities around the world, it is now taught in some Australian high schools and will certainly change the viewpoint of the next generation about refugees and people seeking asylum.

These writings make a difference. They're not only acts of resilience or ways to reclaim the identity of incarcerated people, but also, by making them broadly legible, the conditions in offshore detention have seen some improvement and the government has become somewhat more accountable for its actions. While the policies and lifelong damage remain – and many women, men and children still live under the policy's dictates in Australia, Papua New Guinea (where Manus is located) and Nauru – the process of writing and the actions of making it public have birthed a political agency, a kind of polity that was built by hearing and reading those who stand against systematic oppression and human rights violations, no matter if they are detained or not. Together, we have a collective purpose and shared concerns.

Working with people in offshore detention and attending to their suffering has taken a heavy toll on me. It filled me with mixed emotions: rage, desolation, powerlessness, sadness and many more. My close friend in Sydney, Alicia Rodriguez, has always been there to lend a sympathetic ear, and I could never have carried all that pain without her. Reza and Abtin Montazeri, my partner and my son, have also been my patient companions along this path. These three shining stars, who always put humanity first, never left me feeling alone in this dark and twisted journey Their kindness, compassion, friendship and understanding have paved the way for me. Anyone undertaking this kind of collective work needs such support.

Nowadays, I mostly work with people from refugee and asylum-seeker backgrounds, and local community at the Community Refugee Welcome Centre in Sydney Inner West. The Centre was initiated in 2017 by the Inner West Council and its partners to welcome refugees. It's a great model for how local government can step in to act differently from the federal government and welcome those who might otherwise be intentionally excluded or marginalized. I've served as the coordinator of the Centre since its inception. Many refugees and people seeking asylum from across Sydney come to the Welcome Centre to share, to engage, to create, to socialize, to exchange and to build new lives. It's significant that an abandoned old building along a busy bayside walk, can be transformed into an inclusive space full of life and innovation by our incredible participants. The focus here is on wellbeing and community arts and cultural development. I try to change the power relations by encouraging asylum seekers and refugees to co-design and co-lead our projects, rather than enlisting well-established community members to design offerings for the newcomers. People who are mostly marginalized in the society, in fact, successfully run our workshops for the locals. They design public events, run the projects and share their wisdom and culture with everyone. By asking them to actively participate – to lead – the Welcome Centre facilitates their journey towards rebuilding their lives, restoring their confidence and self-esteem, developing skills and knowledge, overcoming their isolation and reviving their belief in themselves. Some of them had been detained on Nauru; they wear many hidden scars as a result of the pain and suffering offshore detention inflicted on them, but creativity and art blossom in them every day. Among the various activities at the Centre, my colleagues and I work with a group of people on a community-based storytelling project called: 'On being.' In this project, we 'evolved an approach that delivers a different kind of literary project that is empathetically against othering, a practice that is dominant in how stories by and about refugees are [usually] formulated, understood and received, guaranteeing a readership, and satisfying a market hungry for tales of misery, suffering and redemption.'[4]

I came to Australia seven years ago, the same as Mary, Ellie and Behrouz. I became an Australian citizen last year, solely because my life was not in danger back home and I did not have to risk my life by jumping on a boat. Mary was transferred to Australia, with Sara, two years ago, after which she fell into a severe depression. With the high risk of self-harm, doctors requested her evacuation from Nauru Island and brought her to Australia to receive medical care. She's in community detention at the moment, still living in limbo with no right to study or to work. Sara goes to school in Sydney, and Mary voluntarily runs art workshops at the Welcome Centre, sharing her tremendous talents and remarkable skills with the wider community. Ellie permanently resettled in the USA, with a job as a community worker, amplifying the voices of those who are marginalized. Boochani's asylum claim was accepted by New Zealand, he is continuing his profession as an author, criticizing the authoritarian regime and its oppressive behaviour.

Fourteen people lost their lives under the offshore policy, so far. There are still hundreds of people stuck in this system, and at the time of publication, there are over 26 million refugees and over 82 million forcibly displaced people worldwide. There's still so much to do. Writing and reading is one way to restore the human face of the refugee condition, to document this history, to bring about transformative change, and to help reclaim an identity for those who had no choice but to exercise their legal right to seek asylum. The leaders of this movement are no one – only the people seeking asylum and the refugees themselves. The path we're on is long and twisted, and every small step we take brings us one step closer to a brighter future.

Collaborating with Behrouz Boochani

Journalists Against a System

Ben Doherty

To begin, I didn't even know his name . . .

Behrouz Boochani was entered as 'Manus contact' in my phone. In 2014, as *The Guardian*'s newly appointed immigration correspondent, I was keen to talk, anxious to learn all I could about the deliberately arcane world of the Manus Island detention centre.

But in his first uncertain months in detention, Boochani was – rightly – nervous about people from outside he didn't know well and he wasn't sure he could trust. While the strictures of life inside the Manus Island detention centre were uncertain and unpredictable, Boochani, by instinct, understood that he was vulnerable where he was.

So slowly, piece by piece, message by message. We built that trust.

Boochani began by offering small pieces of information: 'verifiable intelligence' they might call it in the military. Things that could be checked out, to a journalist.

New procedures inside the detention centre (housed within a military base at Lombrum), new conditions, movements within sequestered camps, another piecemeal step in the bureaucratic process.

I asked questions back. How does the medical system work? What are the forms you have to fill out? What questions are you asked about your claim for protection? Who is asking?

Back came the replies, when the weak signal would work, WhatsApp messages pinging into my phone at all hours of the day and night.

Everything Boochani came back with checked out. Everything.

If he didn't know something, he said so, and with a reporter's dogged determination, he went and found out. He talked: to others in detention; to local staff working on his block; to the guards, his 'gaolers'. He listened and he analysed and he thought.

Rapidly, we at *The Guardian* grew to trust Boochani.

Steadily, he came to trust us.

Growing more confident in his knowledge of the boundaries of his incarceration, Boochani began to offer quotes, attributable to an anonymous 'asylum seeker held by Australia offshore', 'a detainee on Manus Island', 'an Iranian refugee'. Gradually the identifiers grew more specific.

Boochani, from the outset, had an interest in the place that held him far beyond his own punitive incarceration.

He asked broader questions – why had Australia established this offshore detention regime? What did it hope to achieve? Did it achieve that? Was it supported by the Australian public? Did the Australian people even know what was being done with their money and in their name?[1] What of the unfair imposition on the Manusian people, whose beloved island unfairly became a byword for brutality?

Boochani quickly picked up the contours of Australia's wretched political debate over the issue of asylum, and migration more broadly, a two-decades long 'race to the bottom' of demonization and dehumanization, of enlivening xenophobic fears and indulging the basest of instincts. He took prime ministers to task on national TV.[2]

Boochani realized, more quickly than most, that what held him in that place was far more than the high wire walls that surrounded him.

As he grew more sure of himself inside Manus, Boochani became comfortable speaking 'on the record', willing to be quoted by name. He was now unafraid of the consequences inside detention. He was only, he would say to me, 'telling the truth – how can that be wrong?'

He questioned us and our reporting, and asked if we could investigate things on his behalf.

And I remember several key conversations I had with my editors at *The Guardian*.

We had recognized that offshore detention was a critical area of public policy that was desperately under-reported. We understood that what the Australian people were being told about the offshore regime was not the truth, that there was a vital public service in this reporting being done well. And we recognized that the best information was coming from one man.

We knew of Boochani's history and credentials as a journalist in his homeland Kurdistan/Iran. We knew he had suffered for his beliefs, for his writing and for his cultural advocacy. We understood what journalism had cost him already in his life.

'We don't need Behrouz as a source,' I remember saying, 'we don't need him as a quote in our stories, we need him as a reporter. He is a journalist, working in that place right now.'

What was undeniable was that what Boochani was doing from inside the Manus Island detention centre was journalism. And it was very, very good.

Interrogative, unafraid, compelling, consequential.

What better person to tell the story of that place, to bear witness to what was happening within those walls, than somebody living it, somebody standing at its epicentre. His first article in our pages under his own name was published in February 2016, entitled: 'This is Manus Island, my prison, my torture, my humiliation.'[3]

Boochani exhibited such determination to be heard, that his voice would have found its way to the world without *The Guardian*. But I was proud he found a home in our pages. In his work, for us, and for dozens of other outlets, in his autobiographical novel, his filmmaking, he has since demonstrated the dazzling breadth of his talent, the clarion authority of his voice.

He has become the 'Voice of Manus'.

The man who revealed the chaos and cruelty of a secret regime, and made a nation take notice.

Boochani suffered as much as anybody inside the Manus Island detention centre. He was often unwell, he grew steadily thinner, he was twice dragged to the solitary confinement cells of Chauka as punishment, enduring a brutal isolation. But he bore it with a resilience that I think was assisted by his journalism. Writing was good for him.

Boochani was, and saw himself, as a working journalist on Manus. He was a man with a mission every day, a reason and a rationale in that place. Journalism kept him busy, kept him focused, gave him a resolution and a cause.

Boochani had his good days and bad, his quiet weeks and his ebullient ones. But journalism – a sense of mission to bear witness, an unshakeable belief in his 'duty to history' – gave him a purpose that many others held in that place were denied.[4]

Journalism smoothed out the peaks and troughs of incarceration for Boochani, it was a stabilizing influence, a safe harbour to which to return when the calculated cruelties of the regime risked becoming too great to bear.

He dealt with the slings and arrows of detention on Manus with a resilience that was barely believable.

Each time I would see Boochani, I worried for him. His soul was strong, but I feared for his body. Each time I saw him, he was thinner, and he was tired. His shoulders grew more hunched, and his head hung a little lower.

In late 2017, I was being smuggled into the detention centre in the middle of the night – at this point, the centre was decommissioned but there was a stand-off involving hundreds of refugees who were refusing to leave.[5]

With Boochani crouched in the bow of the borrowed fishing boat, illuminated in the moonlight against the pitch dark of the water, I was struck by how emaciated he had become. Down his back, every one of his ribs was apparent, as he huddled over to escape the wind.

But the old Boochani was still there. A joke would bring out that broad smile, and his eyes would sparkle out from under all that hair. Through it all, Boochani was holding on . . . just.

I remember in early conversations with Boochani he had said he would stay until the final person detained on Manus was finally freed. But as the years wore him down, he realized he needed to get out. 'I'm tired, I have done all I can,' he said to me once. 'I can't survive in this place very much longer.' And he meant it.

In the end he did stay until the bitter, bloody end of the detention centre's days.

When the PNG police riot squad stormed the final desperate holdout of defiant detainees, one of the first people they came for was Behrouz Boochani.

They came for the Voice of Manus.[6] Because they knew how powerful that voice was.

Part Two

2016 (February–April) – A New Theory

Examining the Prison, Exposing the System

Behrouz Boochani's network grew. He began collaborating with Omid Tofighian and his voice became more prominent among academics in Australia, especially people specializing in migration and critical border studies such as Jordana Silverstein. At the 2019 Victorian Premier's Awards, she was convenor of the Non-Fiction judging panel, and on the panel for the Victorian Prize for Literature; *No Friend but the Mountains* won both prizes. Boochani began working with Iranian Dutch film-maker Arash Kamali Sarvestani to co-direct the film *Chauka, Please Tell Us the Time* (2017). After the PNG Supreme Court ruled that the Manus detention centre was illegal and unconstitutional, the prison doors were left open for the first time. Australia was obliged to close down the facility but it remained in operation. Also, mobile phones were no longer banned from April/ May 2016. With the help of Kamali Sarvestani and other supporters, Boochani obtained a more advanced phone so he could shoot better-quality footage. Drunk PNG soldiers shot at the refugees on Good Friday in 2016. The High Court of Australia decided that it is legal to detain asylum seekers offshore in Manus and Nauru and rejected challenges on 3 February 2016. Omid Masoumali was driven to suicide by self-immolation in Nauru on 29 April that year. Boochani began publishing with *The Guardian* under his own name during this period. Hodan Yasin, a woman held in Nauru, was evacuated in a critical condition after attempting suicide by self-immolation.

This is Manus Island

My Prison. My Torture. My Humiliation[1]

Behrouz Boochani

Twenty-eight months ago, with a shattered body which was ravenously hungry and deeply wounded, with bare feet and exhausted soul, I made the trip to the soil of free territory, to Australia. It was four days after the announcement of the 19th of July law. Because of the law, I was exiled to Manus Island in Papua New Guinea, in the heart of the Pacific Ocean; and due to this law, it has now been 28 months that I have been under pressure and tortured.

The 19th of July law enforced the transfer of people who arrive by boat and seek asylum to the offshore detentions. It is worth mentioning that this law started to be exercised when our broken boat with 65 unconscious passengers was lost over the ocean. When we reached the soil of Australia, we found out about this cruelty.

Whatever it was, number 19 remains so ominous to me and thousands of people seeking asylum, as after many months, this number still tortures our mind and soul with such an extreme cruelty. And like a sledge hammer, it perpetually descends into our soul and mind. The threat of being resettled on the island, which is devoid of security, causes a severe and ongoing mental pressure in the camp.

Every day, the immigration officers remind us of the presence of this sledge hammer over our head in different ways. They come to the prison every week and announce that we will be resettled on the island very soon. There are short films and classes are held in relation to the PNG local culture and language – various methods and tricks are used in order to maintain the severe mental pressure, yet no one yet has been resettled on the island.

The main policy here on Manus is to put asylum seekers in a time tunnel. In other words, none of the asylum seekers are aware of the stage of their own application and others'. They have no idea about the period of time they will be kept in the detention and what future is waiting for them. They do not even know in which country or city they would live after getting released.

So far, a number of underdeveloped countries with weak economies have been mentioned on the media, including Papua New Guinea, the Philippines, Kyrgyzstan and Cambodia. Being in perpetual limbo has so many destructive impacts on the mental health of every single person. Several times I have witnessed a large number of detainees become mentally shattered due to being kept under such pressure. I have seen many cases of self-harm and suicide attempt. Inflicting torture by the use of time is the best and complete explanation of this situation.

What crime have we committed to deserve detention and torture? It is an anguished question with no answer. I think, one of the natural and basic rights of every prisoner is to know the reasons behind his punishment and the duration of his imprisonment. This natural right is exercised for all prisoners, however it has been denied for people who seek asylum in Australia. Fundamentally, when a charge against a criminal is proven in the court, it is much easier for him to bear the situation of the prison compared to an innocent person being detained indefinitely.

I confess that over the course of my life, I had never experienced such agony. All the personality, dignity and humanity of a person are devastated by this torture. It is a type of profound and annihilating torture. Living constantly under the petrifying sledge hammer, having a destroyed past and imagining a dark future give a person a sense of being crushed.

The heavy feeling of being innocent is also added to the rest of those painful feelings. When a criminal is alone, he usually confesses in the deepest recesses of his mind and heart to the crime he committed before. He would accept that he deserves to be imprisoned. However, when it comes to a refugee who has not committed any crime or sin, it is very tormenting to imagine himself being punished. It is impossible for him to admit that he is a prisoner and he has to be in prison for an indefinite time.

There is certainly a meaningful and important difference between a guilty prisoner and an innocent prisoner. For me for instance, if a trial was held and I was convicted of illegal entry to Australia, I would have a better mental condition, and I would have felt calmer.

Asylum seekers on Manus are caught in a set of daily regulations which are individually able to make a person tense, stressed and broken. Every day, our life is fettered by dozens of big and small laws. The main purpose of these laws is to make people suffer.

The rules in Manus prison are much more strict than the rules in other prisons. The smallest complaint against these rules ends up in various punishment from solitary confinement to filing a negative record on a person's case.

One clear example of these strict rules is that during the first 20 months, nobody was permitted to take so much as a potato out of the canteen. This led asylum seekers to experience extreme hunger during the long nights of Manus. Prisoners slept at night with tension and starvation. This rule was the main cause of the formation of very long queues under the heat of the sun – people had to line up for hours and hours on a daily basis in the hellish hot weather of Manus Island just to get food.

The small shop in the detention centre had been also a source of argument and tension for asylum seekers for twenty months. Every single person needed to wait at least two hours in order to be able to buy a packet of cigarettes. The reason was a rule which allowed the shop to be open only for two hours a day. However, by extending the trading hours of the shop, they could easily prevent all the tension and quarrel. This change happened later and now there is no problem in this regard.

In addition, we have had the same difficulties whenever we want to make a phone call. We need to wait for hours in order to be able to contact our family and talk to them. This situation could easily get better by providing some more telephone devices and letting people talk for longer periods of time. It is another example of being kept under the constant pressure. We are still being told that the rule is the rule and we should respect it.

It is not easy to go to the medical centre. In order to receive medication and see a doctor, we need to fill in a special form. It is another rule which is strictly implemented. Although this situation got better and in the case of requesting painkillers, we are not required to fill in the form anymore, still this rule is unjustifiable. The only explanation for it is to force us to line up and to cause us more pain, discomfort and tension.

For more than two years, I have been suffering from toothache. This rule has been a real torture for me. So many nights I have been racked with pain until morning as I needed to wait for three to four days to receive medication after making a request. Letting the patient remain in pain has been one of the tools to keep people under pressure and it has been clearly one of the main policies. Losing two of my teeth, I finally saw a dentist after waiting for 24 months.

I can confidently say that most patients sleep while suffering from pain. If a person wants to go to the medical centre or the immigration offices, all parts of his body are searched by security officers using a special device. This search happens several times for everyone in detention, even every day.

Consider someone wants to go to the medical centre. His body is checked with those devices about six times until he gets into the place he receives medication he needs. This time consider that a person needs to take three tablets per day. Thereby, his body is checked 18 times.

At the moment, about 300 detainee asylum seekers need to take two or three tablets per day. They have to pass those devices and consequently, their bodies are checked again and again day in day out.

In general, we could say that the combination of these daily rules makes the detention atmosphere unsafe, full of stress and brim-full with pressure. Living for 28 months in a busy and crowded place like a sport club which deafens you with all its noise could easily cause a person to succumb.

In detention atmosphere, we have to tolerate difficulties and suffering even for responding to the most simple and basic of human needs like going to the toilette or lighting a cigarette.

Who could endure such a situation without feeling humiliated?

Life on Manus

Island of the Damned[1]

Behrouz Boochani

18 February, 5.38 p.m.: Here in this prison, everything is abnormal and different from all the villages, cities and continents. The prisoners sleep until afternoon. Life commences with the tumult of noisy queues for toilets. Every day, dozens of imprisoned refugees wake up from their sweaty and sticky sheets as the scorching sun of the tropics sits in the middle of the sky.

These grimy and unbearable toilets are an undeniable part of the identity and history of the Manus prison, and the existence of these toilets is one of the images that, undoubtedly, have been imprinted forever on the mind of every prisoner here. They are a symbol of filth and great cruelty. They have become a centre of insanity and horror in the minds of prisoners. On several occasions, in the dead of dark night, blood has gushed from the bodies of pale young men in the toilets. Fear is struck into the soundless prison by these scenes. Self-harm is a part of life at Manus prison. From time to time, people are found who have lacerated a part of their bodies with blue-handled razors, a result of being kept under intense pressure. Looking at the blood, the extract of their agony, a temporary peace reigns in the minds of these people. In fact, these men endure their pain with a kind of violent and bloody bemusement.

Whatever it is, self-harm has become a horrible habit for Manus prisoners, some of whom have spent 31 months in a space 80 metres by 70 metres. Whenever someone self-harms, all the prisoners gather in front of the toilets and create a situation similar to war-zone front lines. Shouts, groans and swears go up, and for hours the prison experiences a nightmarish atmosphere. These toilets have always been like a tool for torture and agony, whether with the endless lines formed in front of them or when the water inside them is cut off and a nauseating stench hits the whole prison, filth everywhere. The water of these toilets had been cut on purpose in the six months before the incidents of February 2014, when Reza Barati was killed. In the middle of the night, the electricity had been also cut, causing dozens of people to wake distraught and anxious as the fans stopped working and the heat increased. For prisoners, the only relief from the heat was to wander the yard at night.

The difference between the long queues for toilets and the cold showers – there is no hot water for taking a shower – and the rest of the queues is that the prisoners lose their temper and cannot stand still in these lines. Every time there is a person who desperately and urgently needs to relieve himself, he injects his anger and stress into others. The queues are long, tormenting, irritating and humiliating. If we want to describe life in the Manus prison, we could sum it up in just one sentence: 'A prisoner is someone who needs to line up in order to fulfil even the most basic needs of every human being.'

Every day there is a chain of hungry men of various height, weight, colour and age, waiting in curved lines under the sweltering sunshine, which boils the brains. In front of the queue at lunchtime, there are some jailers with indifferent and stern faces. They have one responsibility: to tick off the numbers and then after a few minutes allow the prisoners in groups of five to collect their food. Sometimes shorter, sometimes longer, these queues are constantly repeated: for buying cigarettes, for receiving medication and painkillers, for using the telephone, internet and even for getting a razor or lighter. Life without queues in Manus prison is beyond imagination – inconceivable – although, with the decline of the prisoner population, the situation is better.

When lunchtime is finished, the prison changes to a crowded and deafening club, and everyone tries to keep himself busy with repetitious activities. In corridors, they split into groups and spread out different types of games on the ground. Chess, cards and backgammon are the games that they usually gamble on. These gambles could be called 'betting on nothing' as no one has anything precious or different from anyone else to lose. But a prisoner understands from experience that betting on nothing is more entertaining than a simple and unchallenging game. Many people start playing these games right after they wake up. They do not have anything to entertain themselves with except the games to play the whole day, day in, day out.

In the prison, time is meaningless. However, it is very strange that the prisoners are deeply interested in asking about time. It might also be a childish entertainment for people who always have extra time. There is a constant battle against time here in the prison and an effort to defeat it under the slow pace of life. Time, nevertheless, imposes itself on life on Manus in the shape of history.

Everyone, in his mind, traces a course of the history of the hellish life on this island, from the period before the riot in February, a period prisoners call 'The Great Famine', to the murder of Reza Barati and the death of Hamid Khazaei, or the peaceful hunger strike of 900 people that caused many to be arrested and imprisoned in the dirty jail of the island. All these nightmarish incidents formed the history of our forgotten prison and whenever the prisoners speak about times and dates, they measure it against this three-year course of history. It seems they do not see any point in using an actual calendar. When someone wants to explain, for instance, when he lost his mother or when his wife abandoned him, he puts it in the frame of Manus prison history. He says two months after the riot or three months before the hunger strike. This behaviour might appear strange to many people, but for a normal prisoner, the actual calendar is nonsense and he calculates the events of his life according to his exquisite and anguished pain – according to the repetition of what he has experienced in the prison.

The prisoners constantly talk. Having conversation is a kind of entertainment or amusement for them. They usually divide into groups and speak for hours and hours. It seems there is no end to their stories. Simply put, they intend to kill time with ceaseless talking. In groups, they lean their feet against the fences and let their hearts become calm in the sea of restless waves, the sea that they could just hear its murmur. Behind fences, little local children sometimes pass. They are always the most beautiful entertainment for prisoners in those short moments. I have seen on many occasions that the prisoners, who have kids their age, throw some chocolates to the local children. The children give them a smile and, in this way, the prisoners offer their paternal kindness while their hearts are heavily laden with rue. Then, in some simple words, they mention to the person sitting next to them that 'my son is also six', 'my daughter is as sweet as this little girl . . .'.

Next to this charming scene, some others ignore the children, as they are busy looking for marijuana in order to put it over a Coke can and smoke it with their fellow sufferers at night. As the night wears on, the tumult of this deafening club fades and the prisoners, in groups like weary bees, enter into the two-metre rooms with low ceiling and no window. The rooms are similar to abandoned beehives. Agonies, hopes and nightmares along with the prisoners are piled up in the dark and hive-like rooms. What sometimes shatters the dominant silence of the prison are the bangs of punches made by the fist of a crazy sorrowful man, hitting a rotten punching bag that is hung from 'The Suicide Tree'. Years ago, this name was given to a tree next to the toilets.

Soundlessness and darkness eventually descend over the prison. Dark and forgotten, the prisoners here drift into sleep with the pleasant dream of freedom but wake up with ominous nightmares.

Undoubtedly, no one will forget The Great Famine era, when they sank into sleep hungry and thirsty. Or the murder of Reza Barati, etc.

We still have to live tomorrow but life in Manus prison is limited to the constant repetition of the past three years. Repetition of nightmares, repetition of agonies, vain hopes, little happiness and the repetition of conversations with no novelty.

Further away, a skinny man, while leaning his back against a coconut tree in an outlying corner, deeply smokes, deeply suffers and deeply lives.

A spokeswoman for the Department of Immigration and Border Protection (DIBP) said:

> *There are currently no water or electricity restrictions at the Manus Regional Processing Centre (RPC). From time to time, the water or electricity supply may be temporarily interrupted due to environmental factors, maintenance or other unforeseen circumstances. In the event of unforeseen interruptions to the water supply at the Manus RPC, alternative arrangements are made; for example, bottled water is provided to transferees. Essential services are never arbitrarily shut off at the RPC.'*

Australia, Exceptional in Its Brutality[1]

Behrouz Boochani

The 19 July law caused Australia to be seen, internationally, as a nation that does not respect human rights. According to the 2013 law, people who arrive in Australia by boat after that particular day will never settle in Australia, but instead be sent to Manus Island or Nauru. For nearly three years, this cruel policy has had violent and catastrophic consequences for those of us subject to it.

These devastating consequences mean a critique of this utterly inhuman situation (which supports a budding fascism in Australia) is vital. From this prison, I notice an analytic vacuum amongst many of those supporting us. I hope that this investigation of the damaging impacts upon those of us incarcerated in Australia's black sites will help develop a civil resistance movement that takes into account the crucial need for serious interrogation and insight.

In order to give a deeper understanding of the 19 July policy, I will use Giorgio Agamben's theory, the 'state of exception'. Agamben identifies the First World War as the moment that saw the creation of the 'state of exception' by governmental order. He argues that this has since become a common and essential practice in western democracies. After the First World War, many of the Western democratic states resorted to making exception laws in various crises scenarios including armed conflict, economic recession, natural disasters and intra-state conflicts. Consequently, in the liberal democratic systems, this tendency has been transferred from legislative and judicial powers to executive power, which has resulted in the proliferation and dominance of such power.

To implement the state of exception, Agamben argues, governments frame challenges and subjects in the language of national security or national interest – a political process where the language of war is used to justify an increase in government powers. Issues are represented through a militaristic language and the government is given rights to solve any issues seen as relating to security by any means. The state of exception invests one person or government with power over others, powers that supersede and reject constitutional, human or civil rights. It's a blurry place, and something that we see in our situation incarcerated on Manus, where we are both bound to, and at the same time abandoned by, Australian law.

Through this framework, the 19 July asylum seeker 'transfer arrangement' can be understood not as a law, but as a policy or government order. The government of Australia passed it through special power and has implemented it over recent years with legal support from both judicial and legislative powers. The most recent example of this argument is the High Court decision in regards to the Nauru case in 2016. The High Court found in favor of Australia after the government passed retrospective legislation for the *first time* in the nation's history. Over recent years, it seems that the parliament of Australia has passed whatever the government desires in relation to migration law, extending the powers of the executive and in particular the minister for immigration and border protection. A series of harsh policies towards asylum seekers have been introduced by successive governments and passed by successive parliaments, culminating in the immigration minister being given never-before-seen powers under the state of exception, becoming the most powerful person in Australian politics.

With this extension of powers the Australian Government has employed key terms of national security and national interests many many times in the process of exiling and expelling asylum seekers to the tiny islands of Nauru and Manus. Within what has been labelled an exceptional situation, we could explicitly claim that the content of law, or in other words the Australian constitution, has been suspended; however, the presence of the constitution or its force has remained. Thus, the political system – the borders of law and the pure existence of it – are appearing and acting beyond their defined contents and different from their intended nature. By removing an exceptional element or a part of the constitution, a gaping wound is inflicted on its body.

The state of exception is 'the preliminary condition for any definition of the relation that binds and at the same time abandons the living being to the law' claiming to 'maintain the law in its very suspension' producing violences that 'shed every relation to law'. The nature of this law and its ferocious ramifications are evidenced in the unidirectional way that this law works. It is a law devoid of all forms of mutual respect. It employs language used to manipulate and control not only ourselves – as the bodies upon who the everyday violences of this law are played out – but also the Australian public, who are subject to particular terms such as 'illegal maritime arrivals', reiterated and repeated to produce meanings that will suppress other knowledges – and our voices. Crucially, the law is devoid of any real relevance or relationship to the issues that we who are forced to flee and seek refuge encounter. Further, the law has clearly and intentionally been designed in an ambiguous form. It avoids giving explanations, does not allow for the dissemination of information – so that those who were on the seas as this law was being made and implemented were unaware that it would even affect them – and is devoid of any clear parameters of many factors, such as how the law should be exercised or its consequences. As a result, refugees have remained in detention centres for nearly three years with no end in sight.

Our legal status as individuals has been suspended and we become legally un-nameable beings, transformed into animals devoid of dignity.

If we think of Hamid Khazaei, we can see how his death was used to send a message to the world. He had an infection in his body for six months! Without his requests for proper treatment being acted upon, he became a witness to the poisoning of his own body. One day he fell down and lost his balance. The day after that he had to sit in a wheelchair. On the third day he could not even sit in the wheelchair. On the fourth day he lost his ability to talk. On the fifth day he was on a plane and on the sixth day he lost his life – the doctors could not help him. The message sent to the world was that this is what will happen to you if you try to come to Australia for refuge.

The law of 19 July 2013 relies on such violence and is executed every day, despite the fact that it is contrary to the democratic and liberal concepts and principles Australia professes. It is against all of the principles and standards of human rights and human achievements in the course of history and its violent domination is growing day by day. The nature and essence of this violence in the system is displayed prominently and obviously in front of the Australian political stage. To clarify, the immigration minister occasionally appears as a political figure with the gesture of a dictator, or as a populist representation in the form of a demon, and afterward, he disappears.

The manifestation and the emergence of this violence, which in a systematic form has been one of the ramifications of this law, is devised based on new and profound scientific approaches. It seems to show a resumption of the nineteenth- and twentieth-century violence in Europe, where experiments were enacted to gain scientific insight into and development of other kinds of violence and torture. These island camps on Manus and Nauru can be conceived similarly to the wheel cages that criminals, those accused and those sentenced to death, were put in and taken to cities to represent and advertise the power of violence.

I should mention that all journalists, human rights defenders and politicians against offshore detention have unintentionally been in line with this policy and the government's purposes as they are playing a critical role in advertising the violence and exporting it to the globe. As they discover and come to understand the violence in these two wheel cages, Manus and Nauru, they advertise it on a regular basis. The government, in this tremendous advertising and political game, discerns what type of violence to examine, to produce and to export. Certainly, the most eye-catching headlines are the little children and women who have been raped, the burned body of baby Asha and the crushed body of Abyan, with their bodies the objects of debate in political dialogues in the Australian Parliament.

Somewhere beyond its borders and on the accursed Manus and Nauru Islands, Australia is currently producing and examining violence and advertising it to the world. Simply put, Australia wants to tell the world that for anyone who comes to Australia by boat, the destiny that awaits them is life in a hellish prison on one of these islands.

Those of us stuck between are refugees, who remain bleak and defenceless, our lives exposed to the unconditional power of death in an indefinite form.

Testifying to History

Jordana Silverstein

Two of my grandparents were Jewish Holocaust survivors who came to Australia as displaced people, refugees, or stateless in the words they chose to use in their landing documents and naturalization applications. And I thus find myself drawn to thinking about Behrouz Boochani's project of writing the histories of Manus Prison as being part of the same project of history-writing as the writing about the ghettos, camps, and bureaucracies of violence that made up the Holocaust. This is not to say that the two 'events' are the same, but that our understanding of one can inform our knowledge of the other. The historical insights and languages from those who were there in those places echo through time, across generations.

How to put into words on the page an understanding of *what happened* permeates. As Hayden White has written, the point of this history-writing is to get at the "historical reality" through literary writing, not 'the truth' through a set of facts.[1] 'Historical truths' come in many shapes and forms: in the depiction of emotions or the set of feelings that accompanies an event. In the way in which one testifies to the extraordinary or the ordinary.[2] The task in reading testimony from the hellsites of the world – of which Manus Prison is one – is to be alert to the many historical truths which are being spoken.

We can see this in Boochani's historical approach. His writing is quite plainly literary, testifying to the ruptures (and continuities) in form and knowledge that a moment like Manus Prison produces. The historical impulse is highly visible in his writings from Manus Prison published in *The Guardian* newspaper: they carry a profound historical consciousness. In each piece he locates himself, his words and his readers in time and place, and as part of longer and larger trajectories. The histories he writes are also testimonies of breakage.[3] He testifies from a space and place.[4] He testifies of people, of bodies, of the effects and markings of trauma. He testifies that – in the words of psychoanalytic theorist

Shoshana Felman – *something happened*.[5] That is, he provides the telling which testifies that something happened, that creates a knowledge of this happening, even as the full depth of understanding of what that was remains potentially elusive to readers.[6] There is something in the violence of Manus Prison and the Australian border regime that could be impossible to capture in words, even as the representation and narration of those histories remains vital. Boochani's writings undertake this precise task of locating Manus Prison within a history of camps and of colonialism, as well as of those people who live, and die, in these places and through these processes.

His writings are multilayered, drawing on and further telling diverse histories to different people. The historical reading which I present in what follows is but one reading of these texts, which I (and all of us) read in English translation. In these articles, we read histories of space and place and people. We read stories of violence, trauma, resistance, and endurance; of the complexity of the human experience, endured at the coalface of the depth of human violence and depravity. These things happened, they have a history, a politics, an ethics, a past, a future. Boochani points repeatedly to the force of history on people's lives, to the histories that individual people carry within them, and to the currents of history which produced the circumstances of his imprisonment in Manus Island. This is, it is made clear, a colonial history.

The language of testifying

Primo Levi, an Italian Jewish Holocaust survivor, famously wrote in his autobiography *Survival in Auschwitz* of the need for another language to articulate the feelings that people in the camps felt, given that '[j]ust as our hunger is not that feeling of missing a meal, so our way of being cold has need of a new word. We say "hunger", we say "tiredness", "fear", "pain", we say "winter" and they are different things. They are free words, created and used by free men.' Only a new language that could account for this radical difference could properly articulate what happened in the camps.[7]

I find these words, this sentiment, playing in my mind as I read Boochani's writings. Like Levi, Boochani is a profound writer who testifies from the camp about what he has seen, experienced, and known, and who in doing so creates new theorizations and new modes of expression. Through Levi we must understand that words fail in the face of the profound violence which these men endured. Manus Prison is not Auschwitz, but they need to be remembered within a continued historical trajectory.[8] And in both cases, those of us who were not there can read, and we must read. But the task of reading cannot be to know, for true knowing is an impossibility. Instead, as both Levi and Boochani make clear: they testify to history in order to do work, in order to make clear the workings of the world.

In February 2016, Boochani began his piece 'This is Manus Island. My prison. My torture. My humiliation' with the words:

> Twenty-eight months ago, with a shattered body which was ravenously hungry and deeply wounded, with bare feet and exhausted soul, I made the trip to the soil of free territory, to Australia. It was four days after the announcing the 19th of July law. Because of the law, I was exiled to Manus Island in Papua New Guinea, in the heart of the Pacific Ocean; and according to this law, it has been 28 months that I am being under pressure and tortured.[9]

In this short paragraph, these three precise sentences, Boochani testifies to his readers of the physicality, the embodied nature, of trauma. Of the ways that Australian policy tries to dictate peoples' lives. He locates his readers in time and space, in bodies and emotions. In this piece he testifies to the horrors which are produced by the guards, the ways in which daily life, access to medication, and the ability to live without pain, is controlled, made impossible. Boochani gives language to the violence and trauma of Manus Prison and of the histories within which he and others lived.

Histories of people

In February 2018, Boochani wrote of the murder of Reza Barati four years previously, during the riot in the prison.[10] In this piece, he tells his readers both of the circumstances of the riot – locating us in that time and place – as well as of the commemorations that happened around Australia on the anniversary of the killing, and of the man who Reza Barati was. Boochani testifies that justice has never been served, for there is no justice to be found within the systems and institutions that Australia uses to persecute people, laden as they are with Australia's colonial history.[11]

Each person's history, Boochani shows, exists within a broader frame of coloniality. Writing in 2002, Suvendrini Perera has shown that 'the Australian camp is the site where the prisoner-of-war camp meets the long-term aims of colonial assimilation/annihilation in the forms of the outstation, the penal camp and the mission'.[12] That is, while the immigration detention centre, or the camp for detaining First Nations people, has been deployed as a technique of rule across the world, in each site it has its own genealogy. Part of that genealogy in Australia, Perera shows, lies in the way governments ensure that 'current policies towards asylum seekers have become *normalised* in Australia'.[13] Writing within a growing movement of refugee and First Nation scholars who link the various aspects of Australia's colonial practices, Boochani provides the eyewitness account which fleshes out the history that Perera describes.[14] In Patrick Wolfe's words, settler-colonial 'invasion is a structure not an event'.[15] In Boochani's words, the prisons at Manus Island and Nauru 'are an extension of Australia; they are an integral part of the state and this connection cannot be denied'.[16] Each time that he writes of the coloniality of the government's border work, Boochani makes clear precisely what is at stake: human lives.

Boochani insists on the centrality of peoples' histories to the stories he writes. Each piece ensures that he testifies to what this experience means for the people, as individuals and as a group. He locates the brutality within bodies and souls, showing how this brutality marks a persons and a collective's history. When he writes of the collective, he never loses sight of the individual in all their complexity and humanity, never loses sight of their individual history, of what makes them them. Of the *somethings* which have happened to create them.[17]

The depth of horror which each of these imprisoned men face is made visible. Horror is of course too simple a word (as Levi taught us), as is pain, trauma and devastation, although they all apply. In depicting that horror Boochani reminds us that none of us are separate people. We are part of families and our existence testifies to the flow of connections which travel around the world. The stories Boochani tells offer 'a window into the lives of men who are experiencing a profound loneliness, the unbearable feeling that they are nothing more than forgotten people'.[18] In response, Boochani writes them into the public historical record, remembers them, testifies to their experience and their humanity. His writings are a project which refuses the dehumanization and dehistoricization which Australia's border regime tries to impose through gross violence.

A memorial archive

Writing in plain view, as the events occurred, Boochani offers a history of the people firstly, and also of the politics, spaces and ethics of the Manus Prison moment. 'Writing is a duty to history,' he says.[19] Writing in a tradition of histories written around the world by persecuted and marginalized groups, people who claim the mantle of writing back, Boochani writes that 'this is history from down below'. This 'down below' testifies to the historicity of the writing, and to the various traditions of history- and trauma-writing within which he is participating. But it also conjures up the monumental violence of this 'down below'. The hellishness of it all, and the people at the centre.

We are reminded of our connections to others, of the ways our lives are inextricably linked to other peoples' lives. This act of memory-making, of remembering across difference, is also a profound act of solidarity.

Part Three

2016 (June–December) – Journalism as Minor Epics

Confrontation, Survival and Death

Rakib Khan was driven to suicide in Nauru on 11 May 2016. Kamil Hussein drowned in Manus on 2 August 2016. On 10 August 2016, *The Guardian* released the 'Nauru files', the largest collection of leaked documents detailing sexual and physical abuse and self-harm in the Nauru detention centre. The Human Rights Law Centre and GetUp! published the report *Association with Abuse: The Financial Sectors Association with Gross Human Rights Abuses of People Seeking Asylum in Australia*. Australia–United States Resettlement Arrangement – essentially a 'refugee exchange' – was agreed between Prime Minister Malcolm Turnbull and President Barack Obama on 13 November 2016; President Donald Trump later referred to it as a 'dumb deal' but continued the agreement. Faysal Ishak Ahmed was killed due to medical neglect in Manus on 24 December 2016. After Moones Mansoubi's early translation of Behrouz Boochani's narrative about being exiled to Manus, 'Becoming MEG45' helped Janet Galbraith and Arnold Zable acquire a book contract for his autobiographical novel (still in progress at the time). Omid Tofighian began translating the writing that became *No Friend but the Mountains* in December 2016 (the final draft was completed in December 2017). Mansoubi and Sajad Kabgani (a scholar of literature, education, psychoanalysis and posthumanism) worked with Tofighian as translation consultants for this project. Boochani also collaborated with Kurdish Australian radio producer and journalist Roza Germian.

What It's Like in Solitary Confinement on Manus Island[1]

Behrouz Boochani

The captive refugees in Manus prison have witnessed too much violence and torture, but for them, the taste and intensity of violence and torture in the horrendous solitary confinements of Bravo, Chauka, The Green Zone and MAA, have been much more profound.

The Manus prison has secret corners with solitary confinements.

For those people who follow the changes of Manus prison, Oscar, Mike, Delta and Fox are familiar names – four prisons in the heart of a bigger prison that has accommodated nearly 1,000 male refugees for more than three years.

Given that these prisons are controlled under high-security conditions, the four prisons have been completely separated from each other for about three years, and captive refugees have not been able to know what is going on in the prisons next to them.

Each of the Manus quadrangle prisons has different architecture, shapes and facilities. The 300 refugees incarcerated in Oscar prison sleep under tents divided into groups of 40 or 50 people. Delta is the smallest and most suffocating prison among the others. Refugees live in claustrophobic rooms with no windows at all. Fox is the largest and the hottest one – dirty and dusty ground and hot rooms. Sleeping in them is torture. Finally, Mike prison, the two-story prison with adjoining whitewashed rooms. Over these three years, it is the white colour that has become the main factor of torture.

But the Manus prison also has secret corners with solitary confinements. In those rooms, many captive refugees have been harassed and tortured for many days by Wilson security and Broadspectrum.

In the first few months, G4S, which was responsible for the security of the prison, placed refugees in Bravo solitary confinement in order to punish them. Bravo solitary confinement was located in the north-east of the prison attached to the fences near the ocean. It consisted of two rooms in which many people were persecuted. For about five months, Bravo was the most horrendous part of the prison, and whenever someone was sent there, no one would hear about him for several days. Kept under difficult conditions, with no cigarettes and not enough food, if the captive refugee complained about his condition, he would be threatened verbally or harassed physically. For instance, two Iraqi refugees were persecuted for a week until, at last, they were left in the small medical centre of the prison, covered in blood. Afterward, one of them immediately returned to his country.

Chauka was another solitary confinement. At the moment, Chauka solitary confinement is not operating, however its name still causes fearful shaking in refugees.

Many refugees have spent some nights in Chauka during the past three years. Chauka was a combination of eight windowless, white rooms. The length of each room was eight times larger than its breadth with an ever-open door in the middle of the rooms. The behaviours and movements of every person in Chauka were under surveillance by four cameras installed in the rooms. The rooms were attached to one another and prisoners were not abandoned as the cameras were on constantly. They were not able to put themselves at ease even for a second without being watched.

Next to each dirty toilet the officers were present to observe the behaviour of prisoners. Chauka was a separate part of the main prison with its own regulations. The most bad-tempered officers worked there and they formulated rules for prisoners. If you ask people who spent one or more nights at Chuaka, undoubtedly they will describe them as their most torturous nights in Manus prison. Under intolerable torture and pressure, they were beaten by officers.

The Green Zone, which used to be another solitary confinement, is placed between Fox and Mike prisons. The Green Zone was the most violent place for a few months. It consisted of four rooms that were used for two different purposes. One of the rooms was used for keeping those who had contagious illnesses such as diarrhoea and the others were used for punishing any person that the prison system dictated. The Green Zone has the longest story among the history of Manus solitary confinements, as it has been used for punishing people for more than two years.

The Green Zone is now called SAA and the domain and severity of its violence is reduced. People with physical or severe mental issues are kept there. During the past two years, groans and shouts of prisoners who hit themselves against the walls of The Green Zone, due to the pressure of feeling lonely and isolated, have been heard by many who live in Fox or Mike compounds.

Fixed in their minds are the yells and moans of those persecuted there over the years. It is the most recognized and famous solitary confinement as it is located inside the prison. Once, a Pakistani man who had lost his family was left alone there for twelve days without psychological support – instead, he was forced to suffer the mental torture of being kept in The Green Zone.

In recent months, some rooms have been built in the medical centre located in the prison to place people who resist the violent system that operates the prison. Those rooms are called MAA solitary confinements. MAA is created inside the mass of a huge number of multilayer fences, which causes a person to experience absolute hopelessness. This solitary confinement was under the control of Wilson Security, but after the Supreme Court decision on the unconstitutionality of Manus prison, it was handed over to the local police. Now, it is the duty of the local police to retain those refugees who are supposed to be punished. In one case, an Iranian refugee who once suffered from serious mental instability was injured as a result of punches and kicks by local police. Another refugee was taken and incarcerated in the local prison, spending 35 days locked up there.

The captive refugees in Manus prison have witnessed too much violence and torture, but for them, the taste and intensity of violence and torture in the horrendous solitary confinement centres of Bravo, Chauka, The Green Zone and MAA have been the most profound and impactful. If one day there is an independent and comprehensive investigation conducted on Manus prison, the existence of these solitary confinements and their bitter incidents need separate and independent research.

For Refugees Kidnapped and Exiled to the Manus Prison, Hope is Our Secret Weapon[1]

Behrouz Boochani

Why is hope dangerous?

Central to the policy of exiling refugees to remote islands is the shattering of hope for a future, it is the breaking of people.

Hope is like a secret code enabling refugees to be resilient and to resist the ever-mounting pressure to return to their country of origin, even as life there is impossible.

To achieve this goal, the Minister for Immigration and Border Protection, Peter Dutton, appears on TV screens every now and then reiterating that refugees on Manus Island will never come to Australia and will be settled in Papua New Guinea.

The governing system of the prison on Manus and the companies working to implement this are focused on impacting the mind and spirit of refugees in a systematic manner to destroy our hopes for a future.

During the past three years, they have endeavoured to shatter our hopes by any means and to carve into our minds that there is no way ahead, there is no safe future for us.

The immigration officers arrive in the prison every week and repeat: 'You have to live in PNG.' This is reinforced by security officers, case managers and through notices attached to the bulletin boards inside the prison.

In recent days, the immigration officers have frightened us again as after the Supreme Court hearing that says that the prison is illegal, they have officially declared that we have to live in PNG or return back to where we came from.

They have declared that we will not have any future. However, what is different is that this time they have said to us that we can obtain a visa for another country and leave here.

We understand that this choice is simply more propaganda.

This is one of those choices that, in practice, is not a choice because none of the refugees have the ability to apply for a visa for another country when they are kept in the Manus prison.

We ask the Australian Government: 'If a country like New Zealand accepts us and we are granted a visa, will the Australian Government permit us to go there?' When New Zealand offered previously, Australia refused.

During the past three years, despite all the pressure imposed on me by immigration, I have not submitted my protection case to the PNG government. But it was suddenly announced to me that I had been conferred refugee status and that I have no choice but to live in PNG.

When I asked for reasons as to why and how they concluded I was a refugee, they responded by saying that they had collected my personal information from media and PNG had agreed with Australia that I would receive a positive refugee finding.

What becomes glaringly obvious in this is that any claim to this being a real refugee assessment process is false. My rights to offer my case for refugee status have been taken from me, my human rights to make decisions about my life have been stolen.

It's clear that the Australian Department of Immigration and Border Protection (DIBP) monitors the Facebook pages of refugee advocates, as revealed by the department's head, Michael Pelluzzo, to Senate estimates. Such monitoring is followed up by investigations and the information collated is recorded. Those records were provided to the Senate in an attempt to back up the department's routine accusations that advocates are giving 'false hope' to refugees on Manus and Nauru.

I came across my name among the names of other advocates in these records provided to the Senate, along with a copy of one of my Facebook posts that detailed the time I climbed a tree in Foxtrot compound in the Manus prison in protest.

I do not want to respond to the monitoring of my Facebook page, rather what shocks me is the fact that the social media accounts of refugee advocates are monitored – they are spied upon.

One of the fundamental and basic rights of a free and democratic society is respect for freedom of speech; that every citizen has the right to express their political thoughts and views, whether it be on Facebook or in any form of media.

When DIBP accuses advocates of providing hope to 2,000 refugees incarcerated in Manus and Nauru prisons, they are indicating that giving hope to prisoners is wrong and is against a law.

If we ask why the DIBP spends money and time on investigating those who provide hope, we can understand that the concept of hope itself is seen as dangerous.

The Australian Government, accompanied by the PNG government, has kidnapped us and kept us in limbo, acting against international laws, and denying us access to any court that may bring us justice. The High Court of Australia legalized our exile, and the PNG court has not been able to bring justice to us.

We are people effectively deemed outside of any law.

During the past three years, the only 'laws' applied to us have been force and dictatorship. We are like people smitten with plague, exiled from a civilized society and left on isolated islands.

For us there is no way ahead towards the future and no way behind to the past.

From the Australian Government's point of view, we merely and solely have two choices, but we are human and our rights as human beings tell us there is a third choice as well, the choice of resistance against torture.

Untitled[1]

Behrouz Boochani

Here, in the neighbourhood of the people who stare for twenty-four hours solely at walls and metal, the presence of animals is a virtue; That flock of birds gliding at night under the dramatic moon creates a magical and striking scene in our minds; So too the orchestra of frogs that have no home except a lagoon that clings to the ocean; Shunning the ocean as they grow old, the eldest crabs sink into the damp mud under the fences and after a while drift into a deep sleep; Slithering under the fences curious snakes sometimes enter the prison like strangers and usually lose their lives for their innocent trespass; When the unique fish-eating eagle with a white neck dives into the ocean bed it catches a big fish; Colourful parrots love to hold their family, gathering on the tallest coconut trees. Here animals are the finest elements in the mind of a lonely prisoner who has no interests but the sky, the ocean and the jungle, all beyond the fences.

Manus Island

The Day My Friend Hamid Khazaei Died[1]

Behrouz Boochani

It was a gloomy sunset in the Manus prison. We, a group of refugees from the Foxtrot prison, were heading towards the corridor where the mourning ceremony was held by Iranian refugees for Hamid Khazaei. The news of Hamid's death had been confirmed in the morning when his friends contacted his family in Iran. A deathly silence filled the prison, and the faces of captive prisoners were full of sorrow, frustration and agony.

Hamid's death was totally different from any other death. It was beyond human nature. It could have been easily prevented and was the result of incalculable cruelty, and so our emotions were beyond those a person usually experiences as the result of losing a friend.

Great fear gripped each of us in Manus prison. Was our destiny the same as Hamid's? Was it to be that sooner or later everything would be destroyed and finished by a simple infection? This fear was most notable in those who were sick.

We were about to arrive at the mourning ceremony when a couple of officers came to me and told me there was an urgent meeting being held at a room near The Green Zone (the solitary confinement area) and that as a community leader I needed to be present. Without delay, I went with them.

The room was next to the Foxtrot prison and we were able to hear the movements and happenings of all the people attending the ceremony.

The community leaders of Oscar, Mike and Delta compounds were also invited to the meeting. The atmosphere was full of pain and sorrow. The officers present told us there was no hope for Hamid's life and that he had passed away. They had no response to our questions: why had Hamid passed away? Why should a person lose his life as a result of a simple infection? Why were we not informed of his death sooner? Why was his death announced exactly when there was a mourning ceremony in front of Hamid's room? Why was it announced when all the refugees had already known about his death?

After a while, I left the meeting, which had been full of dispute. Without saying anything to anyone, I headed to the ceremony. I was thinking about the suspicious behaviour of the prison authorities during the ceremony and trying to find a reason why they were evading the truth about Hamid's death: why had they ignored all our questions about his health condition when we had been worried about him during those previous days?

It was completely unacceptable that even when everyone had been informed of Hamid's death, the authorities were still afraid of telling the truth, and that as the ceremony was happening, they took the community leaders to the rear room of the prison and announced it to us.

Everything was suspicious.

Faysal Ishak Ahmed's Life Was Full of Pain. Australia Had a Duty to Protect Him[1]

Behrouz Boochani

'They're trying to kill me, if they kill me take care of my son.'

These were the last words of Faysal Ishak Ahmad before his death on Christmas Eve. The Sudanese refugee uttered these words during his last visit to his friend Walid Sandal. This is not a scene from a tragic film or novel. This is the reality of the prison on Manus Island, hundreds of kilometres from Australia and in the middle of a silent ocean.

Faysal was born in Darfur, Sudan – a region associated with war, genocide and displacement. A symbol of affliction in western media. In other words, Faysal was born into war. In 2004, at the age of 13, his family was displaced and moved to the Kasab refugee camp north of Darfur, a camp managed by international organizations. No refugee from the camp had the right to work and once every few months the organizations would distribute food between the families. It is a place full of hardship, suffering and hunger.

In the month of July 2013, after nine years living in a camp for displaced people, Faysal left behind his nine-month-old son and wife destined for Australia. First he arrived in Egypt and then Indonesia. He spent two months displaced and hungry in Indonesia until, on 1 September 2013, Faysal travelled to Australia on a decaying boat with 90 other people.

The journey was difficult and dangerous and they encountered waves that may have destroyed the boat at any moment. However, after nine days Faysal arrived in the Australian city of Darwin.

In my interview with Omar Jack Giram – who was on the boat with Faysal – he told me:

> *After five days we had consumed all our water and food supplies. We were starving for four days and practically unconscious – as close to death as possible. Faysal*

vomited many times along the way, however he was mostly worried about his family and was always thinking of his son.

The boat was intercepted by the Australian navy, and without attending to the sick people the navy immediately transferred them by boat thousands of kilometres to the west of Australia, to Christmas Island – a trip that would take approximately five days and nights.

After roughly one month, Faysal was forced onto a plane and exiled to another island prison, a flight nine hours north of Australia. From a refugee camp in Darfur to Manus Island; from the Western Hemisphere to the Eastern Hemisphere in something like four months.

First, Faysal was taken to Delta prison together with his friend, Walid, and put in a small cage with dimensions of 70 × 70 meters. After three months he was transferred to Mike prison with a cage of 80 × 80 meters. The transfer to Mike marked the beginning of Faysal's physical ailments. It was there that, for the first time, he became sick with stomach aches.

Walid shared with me the following: 'He had severe stomach aches and the only medicine we received were pain relief tablets such as Panadol. He couldn't sleep most nights because of the intensity of the pain.' When I asked Walid about the attacks on the prison by locals in February 2014 he replied:

That night Faysal and I didn't leave our room and we secured the door using the bed. We heard the sound of shots fired and then everything went dark. That's when Faysal hid under the bed for one hour – he was more afraid for his family than himself. The next day we found out that Reza Barati was killed by officers just meters away from us – it was a horrible night.

Faysal was lucky, this was the second time that he escaped death. But with the stomach pains he was now experiencing his life was to take a different turn. Faysal spent over two and a half years in Mike prison waiting in the queue to use the telephone, otherwise on his way to the medical centre to receive his pain relief tablets.

Regardless of this state of affairs, Walid tells me: 'Faysal was a very warm and cheerful man. On most occasions he would make us laugh and/or he would analyse current news reports. He was so clever that we would call him "The Honourable Minister".' It was in this very prison – Mike prison – that he would eventually receive a response to his asylum case.

His case was accepted, meaning that he was officially recognized as a refugee; a person who the government must treat as someone in need of protection.

In April 2016, the responsibility for asylum seekers who received positive assessments as refugees was transferred to Oscar and Delta prisons, and Faysal was moved to Oscar. In the same month, the Papua New Guinea courts ruled that Manus prison was illegal, which meant one step towards freedom.

But entering Oscar prison was marked by two terrible incidents in Faysal's life. First, he lost his mother who was living in the same refugee camp he left in Sudan. And then Faysal began to experience severe heart problems. He was able to tolerate his stomach aches with pain relief tablets, but heart problems were a dangerous issue and he realized, quite rightly, that this time he needed to fight more seriously for his wellbeing.

For the next six months he would visit the medical centre every day and would stand in long and slow queues for medication. Walid recalls:

> *Faysal became unconscious and collapsed over and over again but every time he visited the medical centre the doctor would tell him he was fine. On every occasion he returned empty handed and angry.*

For six months he wrote more than 20 letters to the medical centre but every time he received a patronizing and dismissive response. This continued up to the point when even Walid asked Faysal to be honest and tell him if he was really sick or not. Faysal responded: 'I swear to God I have pain in my chest (heart), I swear to God I'm sick, I'm not faking.'

In the face of all the indifference from the doctors, he continued to write to them, he desperately begged them for assistance; he sought help from the medical centre but returned unsuccessful every time.

During his final encounter, his situation was so critical that the other refugees wrote a collective letter to the doctors describing his crisis. There was no reply.

A few days later, Faysal collapsed for the last time. After 24 hours they finally transferred him to Australia. The next day, news of his death was published in the media.

He was a man whose life was full of pain; he spent more than half his life in refugee camps. Faysal's brother Salih shared his feelings on the loss. Salih said:

> *When we were told that Faysal died we were shocked! Because Faysal was the only person we were counting on to transform our lives from the refugee camp to a safe world. We don't actually know how he died and the only thing we know is he was sick. He told me so many times that he was sick but I have no idea how he injured his head.*

On the day of Faysal's death, a picture was shared on Facebook of the immigration minister and his smiling son. It was Christmas: a time to celebrate, a day to be merry.

Time and Borders, Policy and Lived Experience

A Posthumanist Critique

Sajad Kabgani

A detainee is *not* just confined within the suffocating, sullen and morbid walls of a prison. Detention, particularly when it happens outside of one's own borders/frontiers, achieves a temporal dimension. A detainee's life is reduced to a dichotomy of before and after: before the detention when s/he is dreaming about freedom and after it when this very ironic afterness harbours a past time that never passes. How can a detainee forget the pain they endured during the seemingly never-ending imprisonment of indefinite detention? The present is never immune to the scars of the past for someone who has experienced the walls of a prison. Although there is an intermediate space between the two previous states that one may interpret as living in *limbo*, it is hard to link this space to any temporal dimension. In these circumstances time is depleted of its familiar, linear and predictable meanings; one is confronted with a mirage of time that evaporates before one's eyes. The detainee, particularly when they are not given a specific release date, does not count days anymore because counting belongs to the world of *countable* people. A detainee does not exist anymore; hence the ominous sense of living in limbo.

If detention has a temporal dimension, then the borders in which you are confined can also be seen as outside of tangible, physical reality. Borders leave you in a world where you are responsible for finding and defining, albeit in vain, *your* time. You not only do not belong to the land whose borders you have entered, but you also feel alienated when you lose track of time in the new society, as in the detention centre. You belong to another time, to the time of your past memories. The new time demands you, urges you to experience flashbacks. A flashback, with all its pain, is the only way through which you can, however temporarily, settle in the present time of the new society, the detention centre. Paradoxically, the detainee resorts to the past in order to navigate the present. And this is the only way through which you can return to so-called 'normal' society. This normal society is one in which people can speak about and live in a particular time and space as though it were natural or given. But what can be said about a person who does not fit into a society's established, normal/normative spatio-temporal dimension? And what is normative spatio-temporality? Spatio-temporality is considered normative when it moves on a linear trajectory, when it is understood as the pathway towards predetermined goals.[1] This is a humanist conception of time which relies on a humanist definition of space where some spaces are privileged over others, some are more beneficial than others. In this sense, time turns out to be progressive yet exclusionary, goal-oriented but a cause of schism.[2] A detainee does not have a place within this strict, predetermined and exclusionary frame of time and space. S/he is in a kind of limbo: timeless, uprooted.

This violence inherent in the conception of modern/humanist time/space is reflected in Behrouz Boochani and Arash Kamali Sarvestani's co-directed film *Chauka, Please Tell Us the Time*.[3] The Chauka bird for Manusian people has multiple meanings,[4] among the most remarkable of which is the way it reflects the natural current of time. Chauka calls out in the morning and afternoon; it tells the time and informs the turning of seasons. But with the introduction of the detention centre, it found its name on a prison: as the film reveals, Chauka was the name given to one of the solitary confinement cells within Manus Prison. While Chauka helps mediate the Manusian people's relationship with nature, in the detention centre this role and ability was ignored or disparaged by Australian authorities. The name thus became emblematic of a rupture on the island. A sacred symbol for the Indigenous people, Chauka also came to represent a conflict: nature against the prison. This is truly reminiscent of 'Manus Island's colonial history and Australia's neocolonial machinations',[3] where the colonization of a land affects all its beings, humans and non-humans, living and non-living. In *Chauka* Boochani and Kamali Sarvestani show how humanist notions of time are adopted when a society is in neocolonial hands, a technique for dispossession that can be intimidating and damaging to the point of paralysis. Neocolonialism, as Boochani and Kamali Sarvestani depict it, is no longer necessarily tied to geographical control; rather, it achieves a spatiotemporal dimension much more manipulative than its earlier versions.

This particular critique of humanist, neocolonial spatio-temporality is a pivotal feature of Boochani's critical discourse pertaining to modern border policies. Whether in *No Friends but the Mountains* (2018)[5] where he unravels a 'Kyriarchal System',[6] or in his journalism,[7,8,9] Australia's border regime is exposed as the realization of an unprecedented form of violence that weaponizes time and targets the identity of asylum seekers. In reading Boochani's writings we come to understand the alienating impact of normalized notions of social time. In this sense, his work forces us to imagine and make sense of conditions where time is interrupted, to inhabit in some way the sense of alienation that Australia's border policies – particularly indefinite detention – inflicts on people by violating their sense of the confluence between space and time.

Kurdish Identity and Journalism

Reporting to Record History

Roza Germian

I was born in Kurdistan and grew up under the brutal dictatorship of Saddam Hussein. I experienced continuous war and oppression until the age of 12; I had no choice but to grow up very early.

I realized what I witnessed in the reality of my everyday life wasn't what we were told at school, or what we saw on Iraqi state television.

My reality was very different to what the state propaganda forced us to believe. I grew up speaking Kurdish, a tongue which was forbidden at school. I ran home several times during my first days of primary school, terrified because the teacher spoke in a strange language. My mother tongue was too intimidating to be spoken or taught at schools or at any other formal/official setting; according to one of the most ruthless dictatorships in the modern era, my language, culture and identity were a threat.

When I asked for clarification from all the adults around me, including my parents, I was never satisfied with the answers I got. Why? Because they were too afraid to explain the truth to me, because 'the walls had ears', and because their child could've gone off and told the truth to other people, and that could have had tragic consequences.

I consider myself a storyteller. I decided to tell stories at the age of nine – it was 1991 and during the mass exodus of the Kurdish people from south Kurdistan (Iraq). This was an event in my life (and the lives of millions of Kurdish people from one part of Kurdistan) that to this day, decades later, still feels surreal. It was then when I experienced and observed the most extreme cruelty and most atrocious crimes. It was then when I asked myself: 'how can this go on?', 'where is the rest of the world?'

One day as my family and I sat helplessly waiting for death to catch up on us, I saw a couple of men asking my mother if they could take photos of our family. They were journalists.

I realized there and then that at least the world could be made aware of this cruelty. I thought maybe the only way was through the lens, microphones, and pens/keyboards of journalists. On that day I decided I wanted to become a journalist. I wanted to become a voice for the voiceless. I wanted to put names and faces to numbers in news stories. This collection of Behrouz Boochani's writings is a testament to the power of journalism, and part of a tradition of journalism by Kurdish writers.

My story and Boochani's story are just two versions of the reality lived by millions. However, for me, as negative, as chaotic and as traumatic as it was being amidst hellish circumstances, it was also enlightening. My experience of resistance helped answer all my questions. And the answer to all my questions was *identity*.

I have interviewed Boochani many times over the years (more than I can remember). In the early years of his detention on Manus Island I tried probably for close to a year to reach him, but it was in 2016 when I finally managed to get in touch via social media.

By then I had gathered that he (just like myself) was a storyteller. Despite his unimaginable situation, he was working day and night to put faces and names to the numbers that were reported in the media. Boochani did not only make noise in order to raise awareness of his own story. In all his pieces, no matter how political, how philosophical, how creative . . . he painted a picture, he introduced us to everyone around him while in Manus Island. An example is when he wrote about Faysal Ishak Ahmed's life to honour him after he tragically died in the detention centre:

> *In the month of July 2013, after nine years living in a camp for displaced people, Faysal left behind his nine-month-old son and wife destined for Australia. First he arrived in Egypt and then Indonesia.*[1]

In another article about the fourth anniversary of Reza Berati's tragic death (in Part Six of this collection), Boochani again takes us on a journey into his best friend's childhood, and his personality:

> *Due to his kindness friends would call him 'the gentle giant'. Reza was born in a small town called Lomar in Ilam Province, part of the Kurdistan region of Iran. This town is located along the river Seymareh and the ancient city of Sirwan. He*

> *was born in the same year that the Iran-Iraq war ended. He took his first steps in this world on the ruins of war, which means that he experienced years of hardship and affliction.*[2]

As a Kurdish person and a former refugee, I know what it means to be stripped of my identity. Everyone should be free to identify themselves as they wish to be. No one, and no system should have the right to take that away from anyone.

Kurdish people know very well what it feels like to be forcefully identified as something that you're not or don't choose to be, and to be called a minority (to say the least) even if your people number in the tens of millions. The suppression of Kurdish identity is not something new in any of the four parts of Kurdistan (Iraq, Iran, Syria and Turkey). But for over a century, the majority of Kurdish people have never given in to assimilation, even though it most certainly is the easier option in comparison to resistance.

The legendary, 'once in a century', Kurdish poet Şêrko Bêkes (1940–2013) who has published dozens of poetry books is an enormous influence on writers like me and Boochani. In almost all his poems he refers to the Kurdish struggle; the struggle of being denied, being dismissed, of being stripped of life itself because of who you are and where you come from. In his poem 'Qesidey Koç', ('The Ode to Migration'), he describes this and the plight of the Kurdish people very powerfully:

> *I don't know which god owns me,*
> *I don't know which Satan owns me,*
> *The heavens don't listen to my blood, nor the world, nor justice, nor laws.*
> *Not church bells, nor mosque domes and minarets,*
> *I don't know, what, and who do I swear to . . .*
> *I don't know, who's my refuge, my saviour, or my friend, I don't know . . .*
> *I am a mountain without an oath now,*
> *My oath is smoke,*
> *My words are ashes*
> *My screams are my frozen blood, and a downhill migration . . .*
> *Ever since there was migration, I'm migrating*
> *Ever since there was blaze, I'm burning*
> *Ever since there was water, I'm drowning*
> *Ever since there was razor, I'm sacrifice*
> *Ever since there was land, I'm landless*
> *Ever since there was mountain, I'm tumbling*
> *Ever since there was stick, I'm being beaten,*

I, before Moses, am a refugee
Before Jesus, I'm a crucified
Before Quraysh, I'm being buried alive
Before Hussain, I'm being beheaded.[3]

my translation

Therefore, as a journalist I believe it is the responsibility of all ethical journalists, politicians, and academics alike, to tell the human stories of all marginalized and oppressed peoples, rather than follow the mainstream narrative which dehumanizes, falsely labels and stereotypes. In this fast-paced world of information overload, journalists and media organizations should not strive to be first in breaking some news, but to tell it better, to give life to that piece of news story, to turn statistics and numbers into mothers, fathers, sons and daughters . . . or poets, writers, doctors, musicians, engineers, teachers, artists.

We should never underestimate the power of truth-telling, we should never give up on telling truth to power despite the challenges. Again, as a Kurdish person who has been labelled with many other names before – and rarely the way I prefer to be identified – I treasure the power of reporting the truth, of telling it as it is, of covering the suppressed side of a story.

Part Four

2017 (May–September) – Introducing the Kyriarchal System

Knowing Manus Prison

Chauka, Please Tell Us the Time had its world premiere at the Sydney Film Festival. Hamid Shamshiripour was driven to suicide in Manus after suffering from mental health issues and failing to receive necessary support in August 2017. Behrouz Boochani published his first piece in an academic publication (*Charles Town Maroon Annual International Conference Magazine, Jamaica*) and introduced the 'kyriarchal system' for interpreting events in Manus. Transcript of phone conversation between Prime Minister Malcolm Turnbull and President Donald Trump was leaked during which they discussed the exchange of refugees incarcerated in Manus Island and Nauru. The first group of refugees from Manus and Nauru left for the USA as part of the 2016 resettlement deal on 26 September 2017. Boochani's work became more visible internationally. Scholars based in the USA such as Anne McNevin and in the UK such as Victoria Canning took interest in his writing and resistance. McNevin was one of the first to write a review of *No Friend but the Mountains* in which she read the book in the context of Boochani's journalism and other forms of activism; her critical analysis and teaching have highlighted the importance of such writing and resistance in differentWestern countries, and the urgency for scholars from different fields to centre this work in their research. Canning has collaborated with Boochani and Omid Tofighian in the context of academic events and publications; engaging with issues such as time, torture and the kyriarchal system, her support helped create more conversation with scholars in the UK and Europe.

A Kyriarchal System

New Colonial Experiments / New Decolonial Resistance[1]

Behrouz Boochani

From the first day here in Manus Prison, as soon as I entered, I wanted people to know about this place. From the first moment I knew it was a kyriarchal system – dictator like – against refugees and asylum seekers.

I have been writing here as a journalist for four years, with and for *The Guardian* especially, and I have made some short documentaries. I expected journalism – work done in collaboration with the media and on my own – to effect some change and open the system to scrutiny from outside. The government propaganda was much too strong and my voice was lost. Now after three years I realize that the Australian people still do not know exactly what is going on here. It seems no one recognizes the situation as a form of systematic torture; they do not see the reality. Journalism is a very weak and superficial form of communication; it's an ineffective language. So I have turned to creative expression. I have been collaborating with artists. One example is a theatre troupe from Iran whose play is currently on the stage and is called *Manus*, directed by Nazanin Sahamizadeh. And I have a book project with the working title *Manus* which will be published very soon by Picador. The style and approach are really different to journalism or academic writing. I use a unique form of literary language to describe and critique the kyriarchal system of the prison. But the most important work I have created so far is the film *Chauka, Please Tell Us the Time* which I made with Arash Kamali Sarvestani. It was made under extremely difficult circumstances. I filmed using my mobile phone and smuggled the raw footage out of the centre after which it passed through a number of people before it was sent to Arash in the Netherlands. When we were making the film, access in and out of the prison was restricted and it was really hard to send the footage out. I initially did not even have a camera.

The people who speak in the film are people who have suffered psychologically and physically.

It was extremely hard bringing them in front of the camera to talk about their experiences. A number of them quit in the middle of the project. The film discusses colonialism because the kyriarchal system of the prison is rooted in a colonial ideology. The Australian Government is using the Manusian locals against the refugees and asylum seekers; they are being sacrificed here, too. In the film we used the symbol of the local bird, chauka, as a concept since it is profoundly significant for the Manusians. The solitary confinement cell within Manus prison is also called Chauka. A horrific concept for refugees and asylum seekers, a beautiful and symbolic concept for Manusians. The Australian Government put that name on the solitary prison and tortures under this name.

There are two narratives running parallel in the film. One is an ugly chauka which exists in the minds of the asylum seekers, the other a beautiful chauka present for the Manusians. The film ends when they come together and it turns out Australia has been behind all this. I made this film after being imprisoned for three years, when I realized I cannot change anything, cannot change the kyriarchal system through journalism. I started foundational work, working for systemic change that will last the test of time. I wanted to make sure the crimes of the Australian Government were recorded in history. This could only be done using the language of art and I am pleased with the results. So there is now a play, film and a literary work. Many things have been written before by asylum seekers and ex-detainees. But my three projects together will secure a special place in history – they document the torture in the camps. They will not let anyone forget the propaganda and the kyriarchal system created by the government.

Journalism is not very powerful – it is just a kind of daily report. The lifespan is only one to two years and then it is forgotten. But film, theatre and literature will secure their place in history. The government cannot torture people with this kyriarchal system and project its propaganda. And then, after four years, say it is all over now – wash its hands of it.

No.

The history of Manus Prison has now been documented in Australian history and the history of migration to Australia.

The play *Manus* has been on stage in Tehran, Iran. I am a prisoner and I do not have the power or opportunities to support a tour of Australia. It is important that this troupe comes to Australia and performs this amazing and high-quality show for people, to help people realize exactly what is going on – it is a documentary-style play.

Art projects of this kind require support, important messages such as these need to be heard, they need support to communicate with Australians and the rest of the world. This is important to me and vital to dismantling the kyriarchal system. The film is an enormous achievement and a powerful statement, there was no influential company or significant organization backing it. It is simply the work of a few creatives, people who felt a sense of duty and created it. These are foundational works; they are new forms of decolonial resistance. They challenge and expose the kyriarchal system of the prison; they contribute to the history of art in Australia; they confront and uncover a part of Australia's colonial legacy; they counter this particular manifestation of coloniality.

Unpublished Report

Untitled[1]

Behrouz Boochani

Stop deporting people after four years of suffering . . . Today a Lebanese guy was deported from Manus prison. Yesterday the Australian Border Force (ABF) invited him to a meeting. His meeting with ABF only took a few minutes, then he was taken by force to Lorengau police station. He was surrendered by Wilson officers during his meeting with ABF.

Their plan is to send him back to Lebanon. There is a flight organized for Friday morning which will land in Lebanon Friday night. Two days ago, six other Lebanese 'voluntarily' went back to Lebanon, but the truth is it was not voluntarily at all, because they were under such pressure for a long time, they signed the paperwork under this unrelenting pressure.

Yesterday, the ABF also had a meeting with three other Lebanese and told them, 'You don't have any other choice, but to sign this and get $25,000 or we will deport you just like what we did to your friends.'

The ABF also had a meeting with two Vietnamese and threatened to deport them in the next few days. Already about 12 people from Bangladesh signed under similar pressure and ABF told them we will send you back in the next month. The ABF is threatening other people to force them to go back, too, saying 'you don't have any choice'. Australia is obviously breaking international laws and the refugee convention that it has obligations under, a big crime by a government that has tortured people for four years. It shows how values no longer exist in Australia. The Australian Government is criminal and cannot wash its hands of this. Why are you deporting people after four years of suffering?

An Island off Manus[1]

Behrouz Boochani

The torturous system of Manus prison sometimes catapults a person into distant and stunning places. Following this country's High Court decision regarding the illegality of the incarceration of refugees on Manus Island, we have gained some freedom, albeit limited in time and scope. During the past nine months, this partial liberty has become a part of my life, a source of restricted freedom. Whenever the tension intensifies in the prison, I take refuge in the jungle, the sea, and in some of the far-flung villages of Manus Island.

When Sudanese refugee Faysal Ishak Ahmed lost his life on Christmas Eve, and later on New Year's Eve, when two Iranian refugees were beaten badly by immigration authorities and local police, I took refuge in nature. The violence and injustices of these incidents cut deep.

I put some bottles of water in my backpack, grabbed my cigarettes, caught the morning bus and followed the jungle road. After 40 minutes, I arrived at Lorengau, the main town of Manus Island. I took to the sea in a small boat, heading for Mendirlin Island.

It was foggy and the ocean was calm and smooth. The route took me past other small islands. First, Rara Islet, 500 metres from the main island, then Hauwei, twin to the famous Hawaii of the United States. According to locals, American soldiers gave this name to the island during the Second World War, due to its resemblance to America's Hawaii. All over Manus and its tiny islands, there are dozens of signs, marking the bitter history of colonization and war.

After an hour, we arrived on a small, green island in the middle of the ocean. Mendirlin is the size of a soccer field and covered in dense jungle. Its economy is dependent on nature. Rubbin Malachi and his family of 35 people live there. Rubbin is a strong, muscular man with a heart of gold.

The story of his life is as incredible as the beauty of Mendirlin Island. He lost one of his hands on a fishing trip, due to a dynamite blast. Rubbin thus became the victim of a war that occurred 70 years ago, a war in which Manus and its surrounding water were transformed into a battlefield.

During the past 100 years, Manus has been a theatre of war in two separate conflicts. The only lasting outcomes of those wars for the people of Manus are about 800 shipwrecks left around the island, along with explosives and toxic materials. Those materials not only pollute and harm the environment, but also the economy of an island that is completely dependent on nature and seafood. People of the island occasionally fall victim to the deleterious impact of the leftover materials.

When the Japanese and Americans fought against each other in the jungles of Manus and its surrounding waters, the people of Manus were slaughtered without even being aware of the reasons for the conflict. This is one of the bitter realities of our planet. People on an island at the furthest part of the globe have become victims of a battle between the world's superpowers. It appears as if nowhere on this planet is there a place that has not yet been affected by war and the competition between superpowers.

But the life of Rubbin and his family presents us with a very different story. He has made a small shelter for refugees out of leaves and wood on the shore of this small island, to allow people to take a rest from their ordeal.

When I told him I was curious to know why he helps refugees, he smiles and says:

> One day, when I was in Lorengau, I saw a few Iranian refugees wandering aimlessly around town. Something flashed across my mind about them. I realized they have no father, no mother and relatives: they are like aliens here. I felt they were afraid of being in Lorengau. I told them that you are my brothers and introduced my island to them. I invited them over and asked them to come and visit me whenever they liked, and to spend some time with my family.

Rubbin has a poetic way of seeing things. He placed a small notebook under the shelter he had built for refugees. When refugees are about to leave Mendirlin, Rubbin asks them to write something about their motherland and about the feelings they experience on his small island.

When I was browsing the notebook, I found many notes written by refugees about war, homelessness and their dreams of a peaceful world. In addition, there were lovely words about Rubbin, his family and the island that reflected how deeply impressed the refugees were by his kindness. Many said they would never forget being there.

I ask about the notebook, and Rubbin replies: 'I like to hear about the experiences of people who have been exiled from distant lands, because I learn from them. I'd also like to know their thoughts about my island as I plan to have many tourists visit my island in the future.'

A strategic question about the future comes to my mind and I ask if he knows anything about climate change and the possibility that his small island may go under water. He replies: 'Yes, it is a reality that my island may go under water one day. I'll become extremely depressed. However, I'll still believe in nature and I'm confident that nature will allow me time to gradually transfer my family to a safe place.'

Mendirlin, a small island, in all its beauty and innocence, is a centre of gravity for many complex matters at the heart of our global crisis: war, environmental pollution, climate change and the refugee crisis. To be more precise, the crisis of people who happen to have nowhere to live, people who have no other way, no remedy but to risk their lives and seek asylum in other nations. It is not difficult to imagine that in the future people like Rubbin and his family who have welcomed refugees to their island may need to seek asylum in other countries.

After a few hours, I returned to Manus Island and its prison. On the way, I was thinking about the images and questions parading in my mind. Questions such as: What has happened to our world when a tiny island such as Mendirlin embraces refugees with open arms, and a huge continent such as Australia throws them thousands of kilometres out into the middle of the ocean?

The Tortuous Demise of Hamed Shamshiripour, Who Didn't Deserve to Die on Manus Island[1]

Behrouz Boochani

I knew Hamed Shamshiripour through music. He was inspired by music; he loved to play the guitar and write lyrics. On one occasion he rushed over to see me eager to share a new song. But, over time, Hamed the musician began to disappear, he was becoming a different person. His mental health was deteriorating rapidly.

The refugees woke me in the morning with the news that 'someone killed Hamed today'. These words totally crushed me.

I was reminded of the time I saw him a month ago, sitting on the main road in Lorengau town. He was weary and emaciated. He was delirious, but he recognized me and asked: 'Brother, when will we leave this island?'

I answered: 'I don't know.'

He looked sternly and repeated with more intensity: 'I asked you, when will we leave this island?'

And so I answered: 'Very soon, we've already been here for four years. We'll be leaving very soon.'

Then he smiled.

I found out that he died near the Transit Centre, which is a camp close to Lorengau town. It was particularly difficult for me as I knew him well, and I know the details of his story.

During the period he was in Lombrum detention centre (RPC) he had an argument with a local Wilson guard. He notified the police who beat him in SAA (Special Supported Accommodation compound; also referred to as VSRA, for isolation due to mental health issues) – the confinement room for sick people. They took him to the police station for a few days before sending him back to the detention centre. Upon his return IHMS injected him with a tranquilizer. A group of refugees wrote to IHMS about his mental health, clearly indicating that they had a duty of care toward him.

Back at the detention centre he had another argument with a VIHICKEY officer (a branch of Wilson). The officer was trying to force him to go to bed by pushing him into a room, but he resisted and pushed the officer back. As a result, they sent him to court.

The court sentenced him to 36 days of prison because IHMS refused to confirm he had psychiatric problems. This is despite the fact that they had full knowledge of his condition. Therefore he was sent to the CIS jail (the Manus jail in Lorengau), after which they wanted to send him back to the detention centre. However, they could not find a room for Hamed and, due to his bizarre and disruptive behaviour toward other refugees, they transferred him to the East Lorengau camp.

In East Lorengau he continued his disruptive behaviour which began to develop into conflicts with other refugees. Everyone who encountered him in East Lorengau saw him to be a huge problem; the refugees were angry because he talked a lot and did not allow them to sleep. He also bothered local people and was causing trouble in the town. He sometimes stripped naked and walked out onto the main road in Lorengau only wearing boxer shorts. Most of the time he was hungry and homeless. The small children mocked him and annoyed him. Some refugees, local people and police would beat him because of his mental health condition. Most would run away from him because of his behaviour.

After another incident with a Wilson guard a complaint was made against him for pushing back. Again, they took him to the police lockup, this time for about a week, and then again to CIS prison. He was there for a month.

Hamed's case is another example of Australia trying to shift its problems to PNG. Refugees in Manus prison have been under systematic torture for a long time and find it hard to maintain hope. But instead of protecting them, Australia has released them in Lorengau town without the necessary support.

Despite there not being any adequate facilities and protection in PNG the Australian Government wants to leave refugees to live on the island with trauma and among a local population who are antagonistic to their presence. It is obvious that this situation will create major problems for both refugees and the local people.

Also the police, as a security structure with a duty to keep society safe, have their own problems with the existence of refugees in the town. The system puts people in danger. Hamed was a refugee who needed psychological care. His situation was an example of how Australia neglects the needs and concerns of both the local people and refugees. Instead of providing medical treatment Australia abandoned him in Manus society where he created problems for locals, police, the court, other refugees and himself.

The Hamed I knew was a kind person, capable of being a creative musician and someone with the capacity to make a valuable contribution to society. He was worthy of respect and dignity. He didn't deserve to be neglected and abandoned the way he was.

HuffPost Australia contacted Wilson Security for comment and were told to contact the Department of Immigration, which in turn said to contact the PNG Government.

'The Man Who Loves Ducks'

The Refugee Saving Animals on Manus[1]

Behrouz Boochani

'The man who loves ducks.' This phrase describes Mansour Shoushtari with poetic resonance, this is the epithet by which he is known in Manus prison. Shoushtari is a 43-year-old man from Iran who has become a well-known personality in Manus prison. He comes across as someone full of joy and with a sensibility particular to the way children engage with the world.

He is someone whose presence in Manus prison is a paradox; that is, his very being conflicts with the prison in fundamental ways. Shoushtari's personality projects beauty, he projects tenderness, he projects kindness; his existence is in opposition to the violence of Manus prison, in opposition to the power of the prison, in opposition to the barbarity of the prison.

Four years ago, Shoushtari managed to reach Christmas Island but the Australian Government exiled him to Manus Island straight after, where he has been detained ever since. He has now been granted refugee status and has been waiting to be resettled in a safe country for years.

Shoushtari is an animal rights activist; a strange role to take for an imprisoned individual. He continues to support animals in the same way he once did back in Iran.

At sunset he puts the leftover food from the dining area onto a plastic dish and gives it to the crabs that live underneath the containers and tents. When I asked him why he feels obliged to feed the crabs he gave me a look that made me feel embarrassed for questioning him. He said: 'The crabs have been living here on this island for ages – they were here before the prison was built. However, by constructing this prison we humans have violated their territory. They have every right to eat our food.'

He not only fed the crabs; for years he has also been a kind companion to the stray dogs that prowl around the outside of the prison. He has been trying his best to provide food for these abandoned and hungry dogs from behind the fences.

As a result of his actions some of the refugees and guards would complain; his activism resulted in the hungry dogs of the island gathering all around there. They claimed that Shoushtari was causing difficulties and making problems for them. But he continued to treat the dogs with affection, living by his simple philosophy that 'dogs also have the right to eat well'.

After the supreme court of Papua New Guinea declared that Manus prison was illegal, he had the opportunity to bring one of the dogs into the prison.

He brought in the most emaciated dog and took on the duty of taking care of it in the prison. Its name is 'Leopard' and when I asked why he named it such he answered: 'This dog was extremely depressed and malnourished. It was frightened of humans and when I offered food it become shy like a leopard and would take the food I gave it out of sight and eat behind the tents. From the day I witnessed that I named it Leopard, I named it that because it was so thin and frail.

'And now it's grown so fat, it's become so cheerful, now it's as healthy as can be. It's become just like an actual leopard, just like a powerful leopard.'

Shoushtari smiled as he conveyed this account. I asked him about his journey across the ocean and his thoughtful response again referenced animals; in particular, he referred to his pet duck, the one he left with a friend back in Iran.

> I had a five-year-old duck. I had left it with a friend back in Iran to look after. Our boat had gone missing out in the ocean for five days. Just when everyone else thought we would die very soon, a feeling came over me that signalled to me that I wouldn't die. I had that feeling whenever I thought about my duck – I felt that my love and kindness toward it would help me, my feelings toward my duck would stop the boat from going under, I felt my emotional connection to it would end up saving my life.

I asked Shoushtari why he loved animals. He answered: 'It's love. In my opinion one does not need to give reasons for love. Love is a personal matter, love is an existential state. But in my view if a human being does not love animals they are incapable of loving human beings.'

For the short time I was in his presence I forgot about all the violence and hardship associated with this prison.

I asked him: 'Do you love animals more than humans?' He smiled once again. He responded in a humorous way: 'You're asking some really tough questions today! The question you ask is similar to asking the question: do you love your father more than your mother? It's an extremely tough question to answer. I love human beings and I also love animals. But I have a special affection for birds.'

Shoushtari is not only popular and well known among the refugees in the prison, the guards even acknowledge his personality. Everyone shows him respect and admires his character and dignity.

According to Shoushtari there are some guards who even call him 'Duck Man'. Acquiring this moniker has been a cause of happiness for him because he believes it is an honourable title; especially in circumstances where those same guards call the other refugees by number.

Shoushtari has a remarkably affecting personality, he has an extremely poetic nature. So much so that I dare to ask him the following question: 'You love animals and you also love human beings. But do you also love [Australian immigration minister] Peter Dutton?'

This time he lets out a boisterous laugh and replied: 'My God, now this is really a tough question.'

'Today is a good day, so why are you asking these extremely difficult questions? I know, it would be hard to believe if I admitted that I love Peter Dutton, as well.' He laughed once again.

Shoushtari has plans for his future and he is determined to put those plans into practice once he is freed from Manus prison. He has a desire to work as a mechanic like he did back in Iran, and he also has hopes to read English literature. Another one of his dreams is to establish a centre for stray animals one day; you see, he has a simple philosophy: 'Animals also have the right to live life well.'

Getting to know Shoushtari has been a blessing and inspiration. For the short time I was in his presence I forgot about all the violence and hardship associated with this prison; my love for life increased after I spent time with him. I was reassured by the fact that there were warm people like Shoushtari in our close company. I think I'll keep these memories of him with me for years to come, memories of 'the man who loves ducks'.

Epistemic Violence and the Man Who Loves Ducks

Anne McNevin

The power of language is in many ways the centrepiece of Behrouz Boochani's sustained critique of Manus Prison. Across his oeuvre, Boochani shows that the reduction of language about the prison to a bland administrative form serves to disguise and banalize the violence at stake. Language becomes part of a structure of violence – what philosophers call epistemic violence.[1] In order to resist this violence, Boochani adopts a literary and poetic form. He does so most notably in *No Friend But the Mountains*, but a poetic style also runs through his short-form writings which refuse the conventions of journalistic prose. In his documentary film about Manus Prison, *Chauka, Please Tell Us the Time*, Boochani centres the Chauka bird, whose regular calls mark time on the island, alongside the sinister appropriation of the same bird's name for the prison's solitary confinement cell. Together, these works reveal a quality of truth that exceeds what can be captured by facts alone and compels a confrontation with the forms of moral atrophy bound up with bureaucratic obfuscation. More than deconstructive in intent, Boochani's literary method is an invitation to enliven forms of knowledge with which to break with the prison's brutal logic and with that of the wider carceral regime of which the prison is a part.

In 2016, Boochani staged a protest in Manus Prison by climbing a tree. He remained in the tree from the early morning until the afternoon, while those below, fearing he would jump, attempted to coax him down. What happened that day was later narrated in very different ways that speak to the kinds of epistemic violence with which Boochani is concerned. When the protest was reported in *The Guardian*, journalists cited an Australian spokesperson for the relevant department saying they were 'aware of the incident and that Manus authorities were onsite "to ensure the ongoing safety and welfare of the individual concerned"'.[2] Sometime after 'the incident', Boochani wrote an account of exactly what he had been doing in the tree:

> When I was on top of that tree I found I was a crazy actor, a crazy poet . . . I was completely crazy. But philosophical crazy . . . [That day] I wrote a letter saying that today I am a free man because I have enough power and I am outside this system. On top of this tree I was above the fences, and I was outside the prison . . . If I come down I will lose my power and you don't have enough power to tell me to come down.[3]

In Boochani's account, climbing the tree is an escape of sorts – into madness perhaps, but also a wilful refusal to comply with the prison system and a stunt to attract attention. Atop the tree, he literally sees beyond the prison walls and is free from its enclosures for a day. Atop the tree, a rebellion is in play and the prison's weak points are exposed. 'When I climbed up that tree I did it with the spirit of a theatre actor,' he later recalled, 'I was enjoying myself up there'.[4]

Attempting to avoid the reduction of his protest to the ravings of a madman, Boochani insisted that the climb be reported as 'a political protest and . . . not because of mental problems'.[5] The day before his protest, he had been informed that he would be transferred from one prison compound to another, where refugees would be separated from those amongst the prisoners whose asylum claims had been rejected. But Boochani had never submitted a formal claim for asylum. He and 60 other men had refused to do so, anticipating that the process would be used to divide and control them. In a Kafkaesque turn of events, the men nevertheless received decisions on their status. Boochani was amongst those declared a refugee; 45 others faced deportation or indefinite detention. These crucial details are missing from the bureaucrat's response to the tree-climbing protest. The bureaucrat's words intimate that a ludicrous gesture by a nameless man is best understood as a sign of mental illness. The difference between these two accounts gives us a sense of the battle to control what can be said, in truth, about what happens in Manus prison.

This is the context in which one can more fully appreciate the subjects Boochani engages in his writings. The same intuitions that compelled Boochani to clarify the meaning of his tree-climbing protest are in play in his account of the unusually zoophilic qualities of fellow refugee and prisoner, Mansour Shoushtari – the man who loves ducks. Like the view from the treetop, Shoushtari upends the logic of the prison: 'his very being conflicts with the prison in fundamental ways' Boochani explains. In Boochani's account, Shoushtari reveals what the prison has displaced and erased, including the crabs who now live underneath the containers and tents, and to whom he feeds the prison's scraps because the crabs, too, 'have the right to eat well'. Boochani describes a certain kind of suspension of the real that Shoushtari invites, even for the prison guards, who address Shoushtari as 'Duck Man', in breach of the rule that otherwise compels them to call the prisoners by numbers. 'For the short time I was in his presence,' Boochani explains, 'I forgot about all the violence and hardship associated with this prison; my love for life increased after I spent time with him.'[6]

Boochani conveys a seductive quality that exudes from Shoushtari's love for living things, describing it variously as 'character and dignity', a child-like simplicity and a personality projecting 'beauty ... tenderness ... kindness'.[7] But the brilliance of Boochani's essay lies in what it leaves unsaid and in what remains equally essential to the story of Shoushtari precisely because it is unnameable, unfathomable, sublime. Here, Boochani signals that part of the human condition that exceeds linguistic capture. It is this *something else*, this immeasurable surplus, that persists in the face of violence and resists its normalization. Boochani invites his readers to connect with those affective and relational qualities that resist reduction to the formulaic words of fact-based forms of knowledge.

Why does Boochani take the time to find poetic words for the man who loves ducks? Why does he tell a story, instead of accumulating evidence for the violence of the prison that might contribute more directly to the case for the prisoners' release? Something of Boochani's method is captured in the statement by the philosopher, Jacques Rancière, that '[t]he real must be fictionalized in order to be thought'. By this, Rancière means that there are forms of intelligibility in which the border is 'blurred ... between the logic of facts and the logic of fiction' such that '[w]riting history and writing stories come under the same regime of truth'.[8] What is real in history, including what is real in histories of the present, is only partially illuminated and frequently concealed by facts presented as evidence. Facts can be overwhelming, compiled in order to document the real by virtue of scale and repetition. But accumulated facts also banalize their constituent parts: irrevocable loss, for instance, or a man's depth of feeling for a creature with whom he shares a form of displacement. In fiction and in stories, paradoxically, the real becomes visible more precisely for what it is.

Boochani tells us that Shoushtari draws on his emotional connection to animals to steel himself against the threat of death: 'my feelings toward my duck would stop the boat from going under', Shoushtari recalls of his journey across the seas; 'I felt my emotional connection to it would end up saving my life'.[9] As Boochani describes the sustenance Shoushtari takes from his acts of kindness to the crabs and stray dogs in the prison, he confronts us with a question: what else could sustain us, in the face of the most mundane and obscene forms of violence, *other than* connections to what is living? What else could hold our attention against those who would distract us with petty rules, strictures of law, measures of compliance and tests of worthiness beyond the simple fact of life that matters, only because it is life.

It turns out that this simple claim on behalf of life that matters is also the basis of a radical political philosophy driving what has now become a global social movement. The Movement for Black Lives is distinguished by the fact that it is not centred on rights that are owed to humans in law, but on practices of care for life that matters, by virtue only of its existence.[10] And just as that movement's political philosophy has general implications, beyond the lives of those directly affected by racialized violence, Shoushtari's intuitions as rendered by Boochani have relevance beyond the prisoners on Manus Island. It is in this sense that Boochani's writings take the form of a provocation aimed at those with little direct influence over prison life, but everything at stake in ongoing relations of violence – material and epistemic – that condition the prison's possibility. Boochani writes, he says, 'as a duty to history'.[11] The prisoners rise up, he tells us, not only to secure their own freedom, but 'in order to return something valuable to the majority of the Australian public, to return what it has lost, or what it is in the process of losing'.[12] As Australians, and especially settler-Australians, come to terms with our own implication in denying rights to others, in extinguishing life and in decimating systems that support life on the planet, we also confront our interconnection with multiple forms of life from which we distinguish and elevate ourselves only at our peril. It turns out, that Shoushtari's acts of care for life other than his own taps into a collective realization that such acts are also acts of self-preservation.

These two ideas – that life demands care, including epistemic care, and that care for the other is simultaneously care for the self – are linked to another minor detail recorded by Boochani in his account of the 23 days in 2017 when refugees occupied the prison. When food became scarce, the stray dogs who had also claimed the prison as their own, were included in the count of those amongst whom rations would be divided. 'In our meetings,' Boochani explains, 'we were adamant about the fact we had to show even more compassion to these dogs than before. Feeding them was imperative'.[13] He says no more, leaving his readers to muse on why this decision was made. Was it because the dogs engaged with the men as humans, even if the prison guards did not – a dynamic noted in other reflections on animal encounters in the midst of prison violence?[14] Was it that the act of dividing scant resources amongst *all* the life that would otherwise be exhausted was itself a source of nourishment?

Boochani invites reflection on what it is to be human and what it means to be in relation with a more-than-human world. The signalling is mixed, frequently emphasizing what is distinctly human as the source of freedom pertaining to the men detained. Yet the mere inclusion of crabs, dogs, ducks and the island's Chauka birds as companions worthy of care and poetic attention resists their assimilation into forms of knowledge that would treat such creatures only as instrumental to human ends. Perhaps Boochani takes this approach because, in the words of Shoushtari, when questioned on the reasons for his feeling for ducks, 'one does not need to give reasons for love'.[15]

Exposing 'Incalculable Cruelty'

Writings on Border Harms and Atrocity as Resistance

Victoria Canning

Behrouz Boochani's collective writings while indefinitely detained in Manus Island expose the utterly dystopic realities of exiled life on an island used by the Australian Government as an immigration prison. He speaks of the 'repetition of nightmares, repetition of agonies, vain hopes', all things which would drive anyone past the brink of despair. And although despair emanates from the scenes that unfold across the articles in this book, their very existence is testimony to the strength of spirit and determined resolve which culminates into an emancipatory form of resistance – his freedom from Manus Island in 2019.[1] So much of what we come to see aligns with the views of people who have been held in immigration detention the world over: a sense of loss, confusion and life disrupted, a place where 'time is meaningless'. The experiences are all individual to each person that faces the violence of detention, and yet curiously shared across continents as collective histories. Manus Prison – like other offshore detention centres – is shown as a space of social death, necropolitics and, as we have seen, for some even physical death.

A key value of Boochani's perspective is that it draws on the structural, institutional and individual; the personal and the political. He uses clear and uncompromising language: naming the lack of intervention in his friend Hamid Khazaei's death 'incalculable cruelty'.[2] In later referring to detainees as 'captive refugees',[3] he leaves no sense that there is choice or autonomy. There are no illusions that Manus Prison is a space of colonial captivity – juxtaposed with the freedom of the indigenous bird that so heavily features in his writings and films, Chauka. 'Captive' conveys a sense of stuckness that one might equate with the degradation of caged animals, of pacing and anxiety, and the cruelty inherent in the stealing of freedom. He names the tormentors – states, corporations and medical officials co-opted into his confinement (see *No Friend but the Mountains*[4]. Boochani goes so far as to call some of this torment 'torture' and 'systematic torture'. Indeed, numerous texts reveal multifarious forms of physical and psychological violence that are too often hidden, leaving gaping voids in justice and accountability. Torturous conditions are both deliberately inflicted, and architecturally designed into the functioning of offshore and onshore immigration detention.

In 'Island of the Damned'[5] and 'What It's Like in Solitary Confinement on Manus Island'[6] we are introduced to a litany of abuses that are otherwise recognized as torture when inflicted in confinement: water deprivation, starvation, sensory deprivation, and sensory torture through high heat exposures in the 'scorching sun of the tropics'. Boochani exposes the brutality of solitary confinement 'in claustrophobic rooms with no windows'. We are also shown the deprivation of dignity and autonomy that comes with detaining humans based on Othering and racialization and xenophobic exclusion. The structural violence of the systems include invisiblization, human rights deprivations and the endemic stealing of human time. And time is no secondary issue here: time is unlike any other capital. One may lose money or friends, and work to claim them back; lose a sentimental object that, in essence, cannot seem replaceable, but with which another can replace its function. But no matter how rich we are or what cultural capital we accumulate, we can never, ever re-accumulate time.[7]

Exile in Manus Island, like immigration detention globally, is *life theft*.

Atrocities at the border can no longer be ignored or denied

The articles in this collection highlight the ways in which some harms have been wholly preventable, again exposing the lack of accountability for those who did not intervene while there, and the bystander states that have allowed Manus and other offshore/onshore detention centres not only to exist, but expand and proliferate.[8] If we know such endemic state/corporate harms and crimes exists, how can we continue to deny atrocities and allow them to continue?

This is what makes these writings unique: that words were able to reach us from an island in the Bismarck Sea – opening a window that was otherwise closed and to which we could no longer close our eyes – is one such element of uniqueness. That he did so with unparalleled insight into the Manus Prison regime, and that it was done through poetry, rigour, and unrelenting humanity is another. However, what arguably makes much of this work transcend other experiential accounts of detention is the way in which brutality is counteracted with tales of dignity – the very dignity that detention seeks to strip. The painful, untimely and ultimately avoidable deaths of Faysal Ishak Ahmed – a young Sudanese father who survived half his life in a refugee camp, only to die in exile on Manus – and Reza Berati – a young Iranian Kurd murdered by Manus guards – are etched in our consciousness by Boochani's determination to keep their memory alive through words.

The dignity that is shattered by the Manus regime is carefully reconfigured through tales of friendship, community and mutual aid. This is a thread which traverses many articles, as well as *No Friend but the Mountains*, but is most present in 'The Man Who Loves Ducks'.[9] In the same way that Boochani does not allow for memories of his friends to die, neither does he allow memories of innate humanity to wither. Reflections on Mansour Shoushtari, whose love of animals transcends bordered spaces, epitomizes this. It is a story of beauty, tenderness and kindness, one where 'his existence is in opposition to the violence of Manus prison'. Shoushtari comes to life not as a detainee, but as an animal rights activist whose actions in feeding a roaming dog and looking after animals around the island are a link to his life in Iran, and the 5-year-old duck that he left with a friend when he left his life behind. He encapsulates what Biko Agozino terms a 'discourse of love'.[10] In conversation with Boochani, who asks why he loved animals, Shoushtari answers, 'It's love. In my opinion one does not need to give reasons for love.' This is an answer that many of us should strive toward. It is also a reminder that everyone held in detention is part of a human temporal trajectory: all complex beings with a past, a present and for those who survive, a future. Even for those who have not survived, Boochani's articles keep their memory alive in our own present, an act that itself is a discourse of love.

In this way, Boochani's collective writings, and indeed his wider work with Moones Mansoubi and Omid Tofighian, not only allow us a window to unmitigated suffering, but a way of thinking and being which brings with it a lens that is otherwise closed off from those of us who have not experienced such torment. It is an emancipatory lens, one that encapsulates collectivity, resistance and liberty. Indeed, as he argued, 'We are determined to never settle for anything less than freedom'.[11] It is the reader's role to take this message forward, lest we become bystanders ourselves.

Part Five

2017 (October–December) – The Siege on Manus Prison

23 Days of Collective Resistance

Chauka, Please Tell Us the Time had its international premiere at the London International Film Festival. Rajeev Rajendran was driven to suicide on Manus on 2 October 2017. The official closure of the original detention centre (Lombrum Naval Base) was announced and soon after, the refugees experienced the beginning of the 23-day siege on 31 October 2017. Other refugees who resisted alongside Behrouz Boochani during the siege such as Shaminda Kanapathi worked with him to develop their skills as writers and activists, acquiring a stronger social media presence. Boochani won Amnesty International Australia 2017 Media Award. Mohammad Jahangir died in a motor accident in Nauru on 2 November 2017. Boochani was arrested by the PNG police for his journalism and released on the same day on 23 November 2017 – the same day the siege ended. Refugees were forcibly evicted and moved to three new detention centres in the main town of Lorengau. At this time there was a dramatic increase in worldwide attention of the plight of refugees in Manus due to journalism and social media activism by Boochani and others in the prison. Erik Jensen, editor of *The Saturday Paper*, published Boochani's poetic manifesto written in the aftermath of the siege. Australia rejected another offer by New Zealand to accept some refugees from offshore detention. Minister for Immigration and Border Protection, Peter Dutton, was appointed minister of the newly-created Department of Home Affairs (with Michael Pezzullo as secretary), an interior ministry referred to as a 'super-department'

Days Before the Forced Closure of Manus, We Have No Safe Place to Go[1]

Behrouz Boochani

Only a few days remain until the Australian Government meets its self-imposed deadline and closes the prison that it created on Manus Island. On 31 October 2017, the imprisoned refugees are supposed to be transferred from the regional processing centre (RPC) to the small town of Lorengau. It is a place that reminds the refugees of violent attacks. They have memories of being confronted with knives, memories of theft, memories of threatening encounters. It is a place without safety, where just a year ago refugees experienced myriad forms of aggression, a place that symbolizes violence against them. In every instance, the police never conducted an investigation and the people who had attacked the refugees were not held accountable; no arrests took place and no one was put on trial.

The Australian Government, in collaboration with the Papua New Guinea government, has employed various strategies to force refugees out of the RPC and into the East Lorengau camp. However, until now their efforts have been futile. Over the last few months large sections of the RPC camp have been demolished.

They started with the telephone room – a bulldozer annihilated it within a few hours. Then they destroyed a tent where a number of refugees had been living. They cut the power and water there, forced the refugees into Oscar and Delta camp and then bulldozed the place.

For four months now the power and water have been cut in a large section of Fox camp – the biggest camp in the RPC. During this time half the population from that location have had to move to the other camps. After four months of work by the bulldozers the result is the destruction of practically half the camp. As a result, Delta and Oscar camp have become extremely crowded. Also, the supply of food in the prison has been halved.

Clearly, these actions were done with certain intentions in mind. Demolishing parts of the prison and causing overcrowding in other parts were consistent with the plan to evict refugees, leaving no choice but to accept going to East Lorengau. This plan to move them there meant that refugees would have to go to a place where they would be attacked and where they would never feel safe. It was that exact place where, over a period of just three months, two refugees were found hanged in suspicious circumstances.

The machinations of Australia's Department of Immigration have come down to these tactics. The services within the prison have been reduced to a bare minimum.

The gym area has been disbanded, the sporting equipment taken away and English-language classes have been cancelled. Cigarettes, tea, sugar, coffee and fruit have not been available for a long time. The quality of the food served to refugees has been so poor that it is practically inedible, and what food is provided is never enough; many refugees end up going without.

The situation is such that the basic needs of the refugees in the prison are not being met, and there are no possibilities for finding alternative ways to meet their needs. Life has become extremely difficult for everyone in the prison.

In addition, the local people of Manus Island are vehemently opposed to the transfer of refugees to Lorengau. Over the last two weeks they have held more than four meetings and invited representatives from the Australian Immigration Department and the local police force. But after no representatives turned up on those occasions, they made an announcement at the fourth unsuccessful meeting that the Immigration Department is adamant about transferring refugees to Lorengau.

The local people oppose the presence of refugees in their community because they do not feel safe with 800 foreign men among them. Their feeling of insecurity is understandable if one considers the circumstances characterizing the Manus Island society: one must account for the cultural framework of the local people, their economy and demographics. The population on Manus Island exceeds 40,000 people, most of which live in villages nestled in the jungle. Only a small number – just over 3,000 people – live in Lorengau. This is a tribal society, living according to traditional cultures unique to Manus Island. Also, the island's economy is totally based on a traditional system that is connected with the natural environment. With the closure of the RPC more than 2,000 jobs will cease to exist in a small traditional society that does not have the capacity or the readiness to accommodate hundreds of refugees; not to mention that a high percentage want to settle down with their families.

The local people are extremely angry and think that the Australian and PNG governments have no respect for their needs. One must realize that they have been humiliated as a result of this situation.

With the conditions being as they are refugees have been receiving threatening messages from people in recent days. 'If you come to Lorengau we will be forced to attack you.' This is the reality faced by refugees: neither the refugees nor the locals feel safe in any way, and forced removal of the refugees in order to move them to Lorengau will therefore be extremely dangerous. Another point to consider is the fact that once Wilson security guards leave, the refugees are left with no one to protect them in Lorengau.

On 19 October, the Australian Immigration Department distributed threatening documents throughout the camp. Two points were emphasized: (1) after 31 October water, power and food will be completely cut and the fences surrounding the prison will be taken down, and (2) the PNG Navy will enter the prison and occupy the space.

These are threats in no uncertain terms. Clearly, they are telling the refugees to get out of the camp. The refugees are even more worried about the presence of the navy than about the termination of food and water. They are extremely frightened, and they have every right to be if one remembers events involving the navy in the past. In February 2014, local people attacked the camp and killed one of the refugees, injuring 77. Also, on the evening of Good Friday last year the navy attacked the camp, firing bullets in the direction of the refugees, with most of the shots hitting their rooms and tents.

These two incidents remain vivid memories of the refugees; one can predict a similar occurrence if the refugees do not evacuate the camp by the end of October.

So on the one hand, refugees are facing the threat of the navy and on the other hand, if they go to Lorengau, it is certain that danger awaits them.

For some time the refugees have been conducting peaceful protests every day in front of the main gate of the prison. They are determined not to leave the camp. The way things are at the moment the refugees must decide between one of two choices: attack from the local people or attack at the hands of the navy. The whole situation is volatile and unpredictable.

Last night the refugees held a large and decisive meeting, and everyone agreed that no one should leave the camp. Not one person has agreed to move to Lorengau over the last two to three weeks.

Diary of Disaster

The Last Days Inside Manus Island Detention Centre[1]

Behrouz Boochani

Wednesday, 25 October

I woke up from a nightmare today. For a long time now I have been experiencing regular nightmares, and it is these nightmares that get me out of bed, nightmares that wake me as I sleep inside one of the warm tents within Oscar camp. Before I have even had the chance to consider my immediate surroundings, I have a vision of myself outside the tent. Nightmares are a significant component of our reality here, an important part of the life of a refugee in Manus prison. I am used to sleeping until just before noon. During this period, and under these conditions, the heat of Manus has been somewhat more tolerable. For this reason, the nights have been a bit easier here in the prison.

As soon as I awake, I have to grapple with the images from last night's nightmares, then immediately I approach the dining area to have breakfast. A few local guards are there, but the breakfast trays are empty. Furious, I just stare at the guards. They respond by saying they are sorry and that there is nothing left here to eat. These days, with the impending closure of the camp, there is never enough food to eat for breakfast or any other meal. At noon I go over to join the protest. For more than 80 days we have been protesting every day with the hope that the government will be dissuaded from sending us to Lorengau.

During the protest all the refugees decide that we should chant slogans at the top of our voices in support of Phoebe Crane. Phoebe is the Australian women who has engaged in a hunger strike over the last 25 days in support of us. We also decide to gather for a meeting at 9 p.m. in Delta camp to determine what strategies of resistance we plan to employ after 31 October. The central question is: what should we do when water, power and food have been cut?

For the whole day I am engaged in interviews with a number of people. Among us there is a Rohingya refugee whose whole family is in danger of their lives back in Myanmar, a refugee from Pakistan who has an infection on his head and who needs to be sent to Australia for medical care and other refugees whose role it is to write slogans on placards. During this time in almost every part of the camp, refugees are consumed by discussions about the situation next week. Some men are playing cards or backgammon. Life inside the camp has become extremely mundane . . . just like all the prisons throughout the world. Night falls, and I am waiting in a long line to get some food. After dinner the meeting begins. This morning I woke from a nightmare, and now I have to go to bed with the fear of another nightmare. I expect another tough day tomorrow.

Thursday, 26 October

As usual, I wake up around noon. In contrast to previous days it is raining. When the weather is like this one feels that the prison is more tolerable. A large crowd has gathered in the area between Delta and Fox camp. A tree with a large and robust trunk has fallen down onto the prison, damaging the fences. These kinds of unexpected occurrences always attract a lot of attention among the imprisoned refugees.

This isn't the first time that the overpowering tropical ecosystem of Manus forces its way into Manus prison, reclaiming its space. Reflecting on the incident, I entitle it 'The Victory of Nature Up Against Steel' . . . a smile emerges on my face. I have a theory based on the idea that had the ecology of Manus not been so pristine, if it had not been so pure, perhaps all of us incarcerated here would have succumbed to the torture by now . . . we would have broken under the regime of torture and died. During all these years Australian immigration has been destroying the nature on the island; the desecration of the natural environment has been relentless. Australia has violated the sanctity of nature by disrespecting the habitat and constructing a prison. Today is another instance of nature's struggle against the prison.

I don't eat lunch and go to join the protest. It is a peculiar protest because it is raining and everyone gets wet; regardless of the conditions a large number has turned out. An Australian guard is recording the number of people in the crowd using a counting device. This is their daily task: to measure the degree of support for the protests and send updates to Canberra. During the protest a discussion ensues about a report published by Human Rights Watch regarding the violations of human rights against us, in which they condemn Australia. Everyone experiences a fresh burst of energy.

The rest of the afternoon ends like every other day. I meet a few of the refugees, while some of the others occupy their time with cards and backgammon again. At sunset a few are playing football while an audience of 200 look on. Sometimes the refugees take the game so seriously that one can't imagine that this is a prison. It's remarkable how these people forget that they've been incarcerated for 51 months.

I am starving when dinnertime comes around. Like always I wait for the queue to reduce in size – I don't have any patience for long queues any more. When it is my turn all the food is all gone. I get so angry that I swear at Peter Dutton a number of times. I swear out loud on purpose so everyone can hear. This manner of swearing is commonplace in prison; even the guards smile when they hear it. A guard sticks a document on the door of the dining area; it writes: 'Manus RPC will close Sunday. All mess facilities will cease & 2 days worth of food packs will be handed out.' This is distressing, but I am pleased to read it. It will no longer be necessary to wait in the queue, and at least I can be certain that I will get something to eat.

One hour later the police broadcasts a statement that they are prepared to help close the camp after the 31st. Everyone is terrified again. What is going to happen next week? I smoke cigarettes the entire night and contemplate this question. I hope I get to eat lunch tomorrow.

Friday, 27 October

The agony of extreme hunger wakes me up early in the morning today – I'm out of bed early today so that I can make it to breakfast. The weather is cool. Whenever I'm able to find something to eat I feel a sense of calm. It's been more than one month since cigarettes have ceased to be issued and I've been smoking local tobacco. Straight after breakfast I go back to sleep until noon again. I go to Oscar, Delta and Fox a number of times until I find some Kurdish refugees who lend me some tobacco. In a prison such as Manus being able to count on the kindness of those who share the same language as you is always something to be treasured.

The protest has begun. We discuss the court case involving the deputy prime minister which led to him being disqualified from office. When something occurs in Australian politics everyone thinks that it might somehow lead to our freedom, but I explain to a few people that we shouldn't forget the political climate in Australia and the fact that both major parties loathe us. Don't forget that until now we have encountered three prime ministers and three immigration ministers and so far nothing has happened.

I go over to Fox camp. The whole place is littered with garbage and the toilets are full of filth. Even cleaning services have been almost completely disbanded. I take a cold shower right next to a stinking toilet. I've become used to the filthy toilets, but still after more than four years I've yet to get used to showering with cold water. In this place a shower with hot water is an impossible dream.

I do some interviews and do what I usually do up until night time. These days a lot of European news reporters are getting in touch. I feel that this place has become like a battlefield, and I've become a war reporter

I get in touch with the locals. For some weeks now many have been furious with the Australian Government, and they are constantly threatening the refugees, saying that we have no right entering their society. Their interaction with me is all right, and they say that they have conducted a few meetings and have planned to protest against Australia's political machinations in the next few days.

Experts from Amnesty International and a few news reporters are also on the island. I speak to them on the phone and we plan to meet tomorrow.

On Fridays Lorengau is a really dangerous place. Most of the attacks on refugees occur on this day.

It is more or less a tranquil night. But one can sense the fear on the faces and in the behaviours of the refugees. And one can sense even more that we are now one of the most forgotten groups of people on earth. More than anything else, it is this feeling that torments me.

I'm anxious about tomorrow. Anxiety and stress are the most pernicious feelings one can experience here. I'm anxious about tomorrow. We're anxious about tomorrow.

Saturday, 28 October

Again, I awake from nightmares. The sun isn't up yet. It is the worst time to wake up because on the one hand, I am starving and I don't want to miss out on breakfast, and on the other hand, I am extremely sleepy. I go back to sleep. When I wake up again, it is 11am and I have to wait another hour until lunch.

Just a short distance away from my bed an Iraqi refugee, who lives with us inside the tent, is highly distressed and suffering. For years he has had pain in his eyes. It is harrowing to witness this middle-aged man lamenting in pain; he has been utterly degraded. He is an engineer.

The bed over on the other side is occupied by a Sudanese refugee. With high-spirited enthusiasm, he calls me over – like he always does – to show me a picture of his daughters. A feeling of joy comes over him for a moment – he laughs, recites their names, recounts that the eldest daughter is eight years old and the youngest is six – then drifts into sorrow.

Three years ago his wife has been killed. He has shown me their picture dozens of times by now; sharing his memories makes him smile and helps address the anguish. Then he asks me: 'When will we be free?'

I reply: 'We'll be free really soon, it won't be long before we're free again.'

After lunch I call some people outside the prison to cancel the appointments I have made with them. These days no one can really leave the camps because the security situation is dire.

The protest is simple today, it takes place without anyone engaging in any discussions, in an atmosphere of silence and heightened anxiety and stress.

For the rest of the afternoon I am on the phone. Many major media outlets are waiting in anticipation to see what happens next.

The situation in the toilets has become a disaster. The prison is full of rubbish and filth. The people who were contracted to clean this place have discontinued their services and there is no trace of any cleaning products.

At sunset the refugees try to clean the camp as best they can.

In the middle of working away, some of them are making jokes. It's always the case that when the refugees are gripped by fear they end up joking around with each other. It's a good strategy to forget the terror and stress.

The bastards don't give many of us any dinner, but I am one of the lucky ones who get to eat.

All through the night the refugees discuss the days to come and the threats from the police.

No one can sleep until really late due to the fear. Hundreds of people gather in the prison yard to talk. The prison has submerged into a state of terror, the atmosphere is full of fear and anxiety.

The Refugees Are in a State of Terror on Manus[1]

Behrouz Boochani

Tuesday, 31 October

Last night the refugees were up until the early hours of the morning. You see, the Department of Immigration posted a document on the fences in the prison warning us that we only have until 5pm to exit the camp. If we remain we will be confronted with soldiers from the navy.

This is a serious warning. It is a warning of impeding danger that has sent the refugees spiralling into terror. This is what has impelled the refugees to stay up until the morning. At 5 a.m. all the local and Australian guards have abandoned the camp. For the whole day there has not been a single person inside or around the parameters of the camp to protect the refugees. The situation has descended into an even worse crisis. At the same time we are receiving news from outside that the soldiers and police have armed themselves. The whole precarious situation has been militarized in a terribly perverse manner. However, no one knows for sure if the police and navy want to attack the refugees, or if they want to set upon the locals who have stolen everything from around the rim of the camp.

Many of the locals have now entered the camp and are taking away whatever they can. The situation is perilous, it is volatile to such an extent that the refugees have been forced to lock the gates from the inside because of the possibility of an attack at any moment. The refugees are in a state of terror, but they have announced that they refuse to quit and leave the camp for Lorengau.

After a few hours Senator Nick McKim and an ABC reporter enter the camp. Their presence here has instilled a sense of safety among the refugees. A number of refugees represent the drama that is unfolding here; they shed tears as they stand face to face with the ABC cameras. The other refugees feel that those few are reflecting the anguish felt by everyone else, those few shed tears that channel the sorrows of hundreds of refugees.

The senator and ABC reporters have now left the camp, and the refugees once again have to grapple with the isolation. As I write, the refugees are engaged in a large meeting inside Delta camp; they have all decided not to leave the prison and continue resisting through peaceful means. The situation has reached a critical juncture, right now there is not enough food and water here – at 5 p.m. they will also cut off the power. The hours that await us are going to be extremely harrowing, intensely dangerous.

Right now, the atmosphere in the camp is particularly unstable – an attack by the police and navy is imminent. The refugees are drawing on all their resources, their ingenuity and their sense of brotherhood to protect themselves from danger. Everyone realizes that they have been abandoned and that this system, and this system alone, will dictate their fate. Constant anxiety, constant terror, constant aggression, constant affliction, unrelenting affliction. There is nowhere to go and various threats encircle the incarcerated refugees – we sense the malignance of the navy, the fury of police, we sense the unpredictability and volatility of the locals.

We're facing all these threats at the same time as feeling a deep sense of abandonment. Recently the refugees have repaired the fences that had been destroyed by the fallen tree in order to restore some security. But the fear of locals entering the camp has become a reality now with numerous people entering the prison and looting it. Security is the greatest danger that we face right now – no one feels safe in any way whatsoever and the threat of an attack looms over the prison and is deteriorating the fortitude of the refugees. Everyone here has gathered in Mike camp to discuss options and strategies – there is no choice but to gather here and find ways to support each other. The only thing left to do is find ways to resist if something were to happen suddenly.

We have heard that around 200 locals have also gathered in East Lorengau outside the camp. They are protesting against our transfer to this new facility. They are shouting and protesting against removing us out of the current prison and into their community.

A Merciless Fear Provoked by Last Night's Events Has Gripped the Manus Island Camp[1]

Behrouz Boochani

Wednesday, 1 November

Last night the refugees were in a state of absolute exhaustion, starvation and thirst. They drifted into sleep as they wasted away. We have not been able to sleep well during recent months; the possibility of sleeping at night has been completely disrupted, particularly in recent weeks. Nightmares have been an inseparable part of our sleep and our lives. After the generators in Oscar compound have been shut off, many have left their hot tents and moved into other camps. As people are moving to other camps I observe this horrendous scene playing out before me. Their movements resemble people who are left wandering due to war, but it is people seeking refuge in a neighbouring country.

Rooms and tents are crammed with people, and the atmosphere is filled with tumult and a deafening ruckus. It is a tropical ecosystem out here, full of insects and oppressively hot. Without the benefits of having power, insects chew into the skin. The constant, unbearable fear is provoked by the events last night. This relentless fear continues to haunt us, a merciless fear has gripped the camp. Fear of being attacked, fear of being murdered. We decide to assign some people to watch the camp and inform others in case something suspicious happens or police attacks us.

Nevertheless, if any incident occurred last night, would there have been a place for us to take refuge? Surely not. And this is the reality of Manus today. If we are attacked, we will be nothing but a group of defenceless bodies. It took a long time for everyone to fall asleep, or maybe they were just pretending to sleep. Sleeping with absolute exhaustion, sleeping with starvation, sleeping with thirst. This is the most disastrous situation ever.

At 7 a.m. in the morning, the generators suddenly shut off. Subsequently, all refugees wake up at the same time. After a few minutes, dozens wander around the camp again. The heat is unbearable out here. This is hell out here. Hunger makes everyone angry, the atmosphere is full of tension out here, and there is struggle and tumult. In these tragic circumstances, a refugee has cut his wrist and his chest using a razor. It has agitated the situation even more for a while. It is like throwing a match into gunpowder, adding fuel to the fire. Shouts come up and tensions rise. It takes a while until the situation becomes stable again. But the fear remains.

When the power is cut off the water in the toilets is also automatically cut off. This means the toilets have become even filthier. They stink to high heaven, it is extremely annoying and debasing. It is so humiliating. I have witnessed with my own eyes how a human being can degrade another human being, using toilets as a technology of torture. It is utterly disturbing when one comes to the realization of the cruel machinations of a human being, of what a human being is capable of.

At 9 a.m. PNG immigration officers come and tell us: 'You have to leave this place, there is no way you can stay.' However, it is very dangerous outside. In the past, refugees have been attacked several times, even the police cannot guarantee their safety. We are stuck here, no way to go forward, no way to go back.

Senator Nick McKim comes to see us again. He tries to enter the camp, but immigration officers threaten him in a manner that resembles a form of faux respect: 'If you do not leave here within five minutes, you will be arrested.' He has to go. It is like a war zone here and people have become refugees all over again. They have become homeless in the detention centre; their faces are frightened, distressed and weary. Their eyes ... their eyes are looking up at the sky, they are looking up at the clouds. Looking forward to rain. If it rains, the weather will cool down. Also, they can save water. They have trust in the Manusian ecosystem. It is a tropical ecosystem out here; it will rain in the evening for sure. Nature will not abandon us. Right now, there are hundreds of men out here with their clothes stripped off, they are wandering around.

We have no idea what will happen tonight. It is both horrific and surreal when the threat of an attack and abandonment is fused with extreme starvation, thirst and instances of self-harm. The worst part of this oppression and debilitation is the humiliation. Throughout this whole ordeal we have been utterly debased. The situation in the toilets, the lack of food and water, the insulting visits by Australian and local representatives and guards, the looting of out belongings, the abandonment ... the abandonment ... It is humiliating to be thrown into this prison space for years and now left to deteriorate.

There is a rumour in this camp that the navy is ready to attack. The fear is unbearable. We have taken control of the camp and refuse to be forced into a place we are not wanted and where we do not feel safe at all. However, even though we have experienced a glimmer of autonomy by deciding to stay here against all odds, it is like we are now living under the sword of Damocles. The blade of the sword is looming over our heads.

I am worried about my physical health. I have become very weak over this past week. I have not slept. I am extremely concerned about my whole state of being. I am no longer afraid of experiencing nightmares as I sleep. I am now undergoing a surreal experience where the horrifying reality of my waking state has taken on the characteristics of the most harrowing nightmare, and this nightmare is more horrendous than I can ever imagine.

Manus is a Landscape of Surreal Horror[1]

Behrouz Boochani

Thursday, 2 November

Yesterday was an unbearably torturous day characterized by 'the survival of the fittest'. The day ends, nightfall begins. Under the cover of night the bond between the refugees becomes even closer. This sense of brotherhood is stronger than any other time. This is a strange feature peculiar to human beings. Groups of a few dozen are divided throughout the prison, across Delta, Oscar, Mike and Fox camps, throughout the corridors and prison yards. I am with the Kurdish refugees in corridor M. But because of my work, I have to visit all the other camps.

There are bedsheets hanging right throughout the corridors and hallways of the prison. Those who are more worn-out than the rest are lying down on them. And many people are sitting along the fences and hanging their feet up on them, just like they have been doing for the last fifty-one months. They rest their feet on the fences and engage in conversation.

Those who have local tobacco share it with the rest. And a few find pieces of wood to start a fire. They have gathered a few litres of rainwater during the half-hour period when it rained earlier today and have brought it to boil. They mix the water with sugar and offer a portion of it to everyone. These actions reinforce our community spirit and inject badly needed energy into our bodies.

I must admit that this was vital for me; my bony body desperately needed something sweet. There are others who have been able to cut down a few coconuts. It is always the case during times like these that someone takes charge and manages these kinds of tasks.

The corridor where I am staying has now developed into a kind of family environment and a feeling of brotherhood has taken over.

Starvation.
Thirst.
Terror.
Starvation-thirst-terror.

Starvation, thirst and terror slowly but surely dominate the prison. Gradually these factors impose their power over the incarcerated refugees. Bodies are weak, muscles are fatigued, spirits are weary. It has been nearly five years full of anguish – anguish that has ground everyone down. During this last week in particular, no one has slept properly. Everyone is weary out here, but the one mantra continues to reverberate:

> We will never retreat and leave this hell of a prison. We will never move to another prison. We will never settle for anything less than freedom. Only freedom.

This is the scene here in Manus prison. These words are the soul of Manus prison. To you people who are looking on from outside the prison and think you understand exactly what is happening here, this landscape, which is replete with affliction, is totally incomprehensible. But I can only write about the environment here in prison. The words I write are starving, the words are thirsty . . . just like me. The pain of dozens of human beings all around me, with their clothes stripped off in this oppressive tropical heat, human beings with their bodies crushed, ravaged by mosquitoes – there is no end to the barbarity of the merciless mosquitoes . . . all this affliction is channelled through me in these words. Only those who have had to endure tropical condition will have some idea. The heat is a relentless attack, the mosquitoes conduct relentless attacks, the terror is amplified by the agonizing heat and the tortuous mosquitoes. The trauma of Manus prison. Never forget that this place is Manus prison.

It is night here. I have moved around from Fox to Oscar, and then to Delta camp. In these locations there are also dozens of people lying down under the illumination of moonlight. I must say, I am lucky in this respect. That is, I am lucky that the moon is out. At least with the guidance of moonlight I can determine the way in front of me and identify the bodies lying down and left broken before me.

I can hear some commotion in Oscar. A group has gathered over there in that compound. A few individuals are digging up the ground. They are shovelling away using two metal poles. It is hard work but they persist with quick and vigorous movements. The presence of others around the men is empowering for them. When one finishes making his contribution, another one fills his place immediately. They just continue to dig.

People always speak loudly in these moments. The sound of the crowd is muddled together; the sounds have fused into one.

The human being is a strange creature. When one has to fight to survive one's strength is multiplied. The will to survive is running through the biceps of those young men, one can sense the desire to stay alive. The ground is being dug up, the dirt thrown aside. One person digs, another one empties. Those young men are determined to keep digging until they reach water.

They keep digging until the middle of the night. I swear, digging up the earth using a pole is extremely gruelling labour.

The time is now after three. We are tired. I have to return to Fox. I know the way back quite well. It has been more than four years that I have been living alongside these fences and travelling this route. Even if the moon was not in the sky I could certainly find my way back. The prison is quiet now, the prison is silent.

I arrive in Fox and right there in the middle of the camp lay the exhausted bodies of dozens of weary men, starving men, scattered all over.

I look up at the moon. The moon remains kind. The sound of the sea floats in. The prison is terrified. The prison is silent. The prison has an extraordinary power. I am sure those young men will reach water by the time morning comes.

The Breath of Death on Manus Island

Starvation and Sickness[1]

Behrouz Boochani

Friday, 3 November

The refugees wake me up early in the morning. When this happens, it's like suddenly entering a nightmare. The last time I experienced this was two months ago when they woke me up to news of the death of Hamed Shamshiripour. Hamed's dead body was found hanging with a noose around his neck one rainy morning in the East Lorengau camp.

No one has died today. However, the news is that death is on its way to take someone else from us. It's a Rohingya refugee who is known to have been suffering from an illness. For years this middle-aged man has been battling against epilepsy.

I hurry over to Oscar camp. The refugees have laid him out on the floor. The rim of his mouth is covered in foam and it seems his eyes have doubled in size. What could one possibly do in this situation? There is no medicine here. Everyone is perplexed and in a state of panic. One person pours water over his face. Everyone wants to do something, even though we all know too well that our efforts are in vain. He's lying there for an hour before he finally starts to feel better. Everyone is frightened. Manus prison can no longer tolerate the death of another individual. There is a mood of death, climate of death. And for a moment the presence of death has completely disrupted the equilibrium in prison.

Death is always ever so present.
Death.
The breath of death.
The scent of death.
The reign of death over Manus prison. This is the reality of living out here.

I return to Fox prison. On the way I see a few people drawing up water in buckets from the well that they have dug up within Oscar camp the night before. For a moment my mind captures the image of a well inside a strange and faraway prison. I pass the middle of one of the corridors in Delta. A group of men are still sleeping, all laid out and their clothes stripped off. They are sleeping in a manner that resembles people who have been knocked unconscious. The mosquitoes on Manus have no mercy. All throughout the night they are at work, busy trying to suck our bodies dry. It is supposed to rain today. After all these years I have really come to understand the ecosystem here on Manus.

Managing all this media attention has become a difficult task. I receive calls from every point on the globe, in every language. The situation is so very critical.

I receive news that one of the refugees, who had gone to East Lorengau just days before, is spotted walking back here along the road. For a moment I picture him, even more afraid and even more weary than the men who I see around me here. I picture him alone, nowhere to turn to for protection … I picture him there, walking alone on an unknown path through the jungle.

Throughout all the corridors within Fox I witness the same scene that I have encountered in Delta. Men with their clothes stripped off lying down on the ground. A group of refugees is running about and searching for something. Some of them are preparing the garbage bins in order to collect rainwater. They are like men from a rescue team; a great spirit of collective action.

All the sounds.
All the shouts.
They all saturate the prison landscape.

A few individuals get up onto the roof of the bathrooms to sweep up the leaves so that if it is going to rain the water can flow into the tanks and the bins with ease. Two news reporters and photographers from the *Australian* have arrived by boat. I am worried. A few moments later they enter Oscar. When the refugees see their cameras, they circle them like a swarm of bees. The photographer gets excited. The place is full of subjects for him to hunt down and capture. Although he seems to be anxious, he still photographs the sick Rohingyan refugee, another man whose eye is infected, and one who had shown him a letter. He also takes shots of the whole community of bewildered and worn-out refugees. They are there for less than 10 minutes. They do what they have to do in a hurry and leave. I pursue them the whole time they are here. I shake hands with them and request that they report fairly and stand up for justice. They say: 'Of course, that's exactly what we plan to do.' I am still worried. I hope that is what eventuates.

The rain suddenly starts to pour. Thunder and lightning comes from the sky. Until now I have never seen the Manus sky so furious – it unleashed its anger with hammers and fire. The garbage bins are filling up with rainwater delivered from the tropical heavens. This rain is such an enormous blessing – it is delivered with perfect timing.

In the afternoon we receive news that the refugee who was making his way back from East Lorengau has arrived. I see him. He has walked for more than 30 kilometres. He is exhausted – even more fatigued than the incarcerated refugees. And he is starving – hungrier than the refugees.

A missionary on Manus wants to bring food for the refugees but is prevented by the navy. The Australian Government insists on starving everyone. I have to eventually make my way to Delta prison. The silent protest begins at five. The mosquitoes of Manus are again ruthless and barbaric. Another tough night awaits.

All We Want is Freedom – Not Another Prison camp[1]

Behrouz Boochani

Manus prison has reached a historic landmark. It's a culmination of years of premeditated violence and affliction. For more than 10 days, hundreds of refugees have been refusing to leave the prison camp and, as a result, the situation has morphed into a large-scale humanitarian crisis. If things deteriorate further, we will witness a disaster beyond imagination.

For many who are watching from Australia or other parts of the world, particular questions have arisen, including: why are the refugees refusing to leave the camp? From the perspective of someone who has lived in this prison for more than four years and who has been critically analysing the politics of offshore processing throughout this time, I am certain that there is a misconception of the main reason behind our resistance – a misinterpretation of the principle driving the stand taken by the refugees. This mistake has both been made by people who are actively supporting the refugees and by individuals who have been indifferent toward the events in Manus and Nauru prisons all these years. And it also pertains to those who have supported the government's political strategy.

The misreading of the issue is reflected in government officials and the Australian prime minister attacking Senator Nick McKim, refugee advocates, the Papua New Guinea immigration minister and a few incarcerated refugees, saying that they are encouraging and motivating the other refugees to remain in the prison camp. First, the PNG minister responded by explicitly stating that a few individuals who were 'leaders' inside the prison were forcing the refugees to stay inside the detention camp.

These kinds of accusations are facile and unacceptable. It comes across as a form of degradation because it strips the refugees of agency, reducing them to children who cannot make decisions on their own. It represents them as humans who lack a decent understanding of what is unfolding around them. It degrades their dignity by assuming that the refugees cannot assess the situation.

On the other side, the refugee supporters announce that the alternative accommodation units in Lorengau, Hillside Haus and West Lorengau, are not ready yet. They also claim that Lorengau is not safe to accommodate the refugees and that the new camps do not provide medical facilities and are unsuitable for housing refugees.

All the claims made by the refugee activists and human rights organizations, such as Amnesty and Human Rights Watch, are accurate and significant. However, the central point that must never be forgotten is that for more than four years the refugees of Manus prison have been detained for no reason, incarcerated without committing any crime. During these years lives have been destroyed and many families torn apart.

The reality inside Manus prison and the reasons for the refugee resistance are totally different to what is stated in some media and claimed in official public statements. When the refugees engage in discussions, all their dialogues have one thing in common: 'We won't put up with being incarcerated anymore. We have no energy left to go from this prison to another prison. We haven't committed any crime and we can't tolerate prison any longer.'

All the conversations are driven by one thing, and one thing only, and that is freedom. Only freedom. Perhaps from all statements and all speeches published over the last week none of them hurt and angered the refugees more than the one by Peter Dutton where he said, 'The only difference in the new centre is that where we serve three meals a day at the [detention centre], we're asking people to prepare their own meals with food supplied.' Talking about the refugees in this way is a perverse manipulation of the human dimension. Dutton is basically saying that if he were to build a prison fully equipped for comfortable living, and he incarcerated people there for years, then no one would have the right to object.

This is not about the prison itself and the conditions of imprisonment. It is about freedom, and it is this point that is always forgotten or ignored. In order to understand this issue, one does not need to complicate things. It is plain and simple.

It is enough for people to imagine themselves, only for a moment, in the place of a refugee imprisoned in Manus; enough for people to imagine themselves as someone whose human dignity has been debased over these years; enough to imagine the torture this refugee has had to endure. Imagine there is nothing positive to look forward to in the future for this refugee; possibly his partner has left him; or his children have been left alone; his dreams have been shattered. He has become a mere subject for the media, a mere subject for reporters, a mere subject for photographers, a mere subject for politicians, a mere subject for human rights activists, a mere subject for intellectuals and researchers. Over these past years, they have all been reinforcing a huge industry that is built on the indefinite imprisonment of this refugee. And after four and a half years they now decide to transfer him to another prison and, according to Peter Dutton's promise, provide him with three meals a day.

The issue is plain and simple. We did not come to Australia to live in a prison. The peaceful protest by refugees is not because we want to remain in this prison. We are resisting because we want freedom in a safe environment. The core concern is freedom . . . only freedom. The rest of what you hear are just peripheral issues.

I Write from Manus as a Duty to History[1]

Behrouz Boochani

Last week the *Guardian* requested again that I report on what is happening on Manus. It had been two days that I had not eaten a thing, two days that I had gone without sleep.

The situation had reached crisis point.

I contacted Omid, who translates my work, immediately.

Omid answered my message. Like always, he was worried about my wellbeing.

'Behrouz, I know that this reporting is historically monumental, I know that this is a duty toward history and those people lost to history, and I know that the two of us are totally committed to this work … but I'm worried about your wellbeing. You need to sleep.'

'But we need to write,' I replied. 'It's no time to sleep. I promise that nothing is going to happen to me. This'll be the last article. I promise I'll sleep then. I promise you, Omid.'

A central part of Australia's history relates to its forgotten people.

This is an excerpt from the dialogues that took place between Omid and me, and an insight into the situation underlying those days when a humanitarian crisis was unfolding in Manus prison.

Those days and those articles are over and finished now, but one question still remains: why do I write continuously right here in this prison?

It is a difficult question – why does Omid pay more attention to the work related to Manus than to his research and other academic work? I must admit that Omid and I have come to a mutual understanding regarding an interpretation of the Manus and Nauru phenomenon. It is that writing is a duty to history.

Only a meta-historical and transhistorical approach can unpack the peculiarities associated with the issue of Manus and Nauru. Only a rigorous analysis of a colonial presence in Australia and its tactics in the region can disclose the reality of violence in these island prisons.

This issue must be understood as the annihilation of human beings, the incarceration of human beings within the history of modern Australia; it is a long history, a comprehensive history, it is intertwined with its colonial history.

This form of affliction, inflicted on people in similarly vulnerable situations, has always existed in the history of modern Australia. Pain and suffering systematically inflicted on defenceless and vulnerable bodies.

People who are not recognized as humans, not recognized as embodying human dignity. People who are debased, people who are subject to discrimination.

Australia is a developed country. Australia has invested significantly in the arts, in intellectual life, in cultivating culture. Australia is generally known for being a country of goodwill.

But one aspect of the history of this country has always been associated with violence and affliction. Modern Australia must not always be interpreted in terms of its successes, its beauty and its achievements.

A central part of Australia's history relates to its forgotten people.

This writing that comes out of Manus is the unofficial history of Australia, a history that will never be authorized by the government.

This writing that comes out of Manus is history from the viewpoint of people who have been subject to systematic violence.

This writing that comes out of Manus is the suppressed history, the marginalized history of Australia.

This writing that comes out of Manus narrates a significant part of Australian history, it narrates a feature of Australian history that continues to manifest time and time again.

We are confined to the task of writing, we are confined to the practice of creativity so that generations to come have resources at hand, resources rendered by those who have always been violated by the official historical narrative of Australia, violated by the beautiful image projected by Australia, violated by the image of a compassionate Australia.

This is history from down below.

Certainly, this writing that comes out of Manus does not only pertain to the articles I have produced, it not only pertains to the film that I co-directed. Soon my first book will be published – an autobiographical novel. In the future I will continue to produce more writing. The history of these prisons, here on these islands, must never be forgotten.

A Letter from Manus Island[1]

Behrouz Boochani

For many months, the refugees living inside Manus prison have had to endure extraordinarily oppressive conditions orchestrated by the Australian Government. During this time, the Department of Immigration used various strategies in order to force refugees out and transfer them into three new camps: East Lorengau, Hillside and West Haus.

They announced 31 October 2017 as the deadline for refugees to leave the place.

That date signalled the beginning of extreme force and dictatorship. The government believed 31 October would be the date its vision would become a reality and its plans would be put into practice. When this date arrived, 600 refugees refused to transfer to the new camps. Instead, the situation transformed into a humanitarian crisis that lasted 23 days.

For many watching the events on the island and in the prison from the outside, some central questions have arisen. How could we continue resisting without food, water and medicine for three weeks? How did we keep the character of our protest peaceful throughout this period? How did we continue resisting without ever resorting to violence?

From the standpoint of someone operating at the core of the resistance for this long period of time – that is, the whole three-week period – and privy to everything that was happening inside the prison and the details of the resistance, I think the only thing that helped us persevere for the long stretch of time was our dedication to principles of humanity and human values.

In the community meetings we held every day at 5 p.m., we stayed true to the principles of love, friendship and brotherhood.

There was nothing greater for us than respect. There was nothing greater for us than equality and camaraderie.

We have reminded a majority of the Australian public that throughout their history they have only ever imagined that their democracy and freedom has been created on the basis of principles of humanity.

In reality, it was a resistance that was completely democratic. By democratic I mean that every day, right at 5pm, at one fixed location in Delta prison, we gathered and everyone had the chance to express their opinion with the group and discuss. If anyone had a new suggestion, they could outline it and then we would put it to a vote; as a group we would consider whether the suggestion should be put into practice or not.

Debates surrounding how to manage the tasks inside the prison and the rules pertaining to the prison were also resolved by voting. This was in addition to deciding on other methods we should incorporate that could help stand up to power and continue our struggle.

Throughout these three weeks, the gates were completely open and anyone could leave the collective resistance at any moment. They were totally free to go to the new camps and acquire food and water. We were particularly committed to the following point: no one had the right to reproach another for leaving us. In fact, we all had to thank anyone who left the community because they stood with us for as long as they were capable, and we were all grateful for that.

Sometimes, during this period, we smuggled into the prison a limited amount of food in the dead of night, and this food would be distributed equally among the prisoners. This principle also applied to the dogs that live among us: we factored them in. In our meetings, we were adamant about the fact we had to show even more compassion to these dogs than before. Feeding them was imperative. These principles applied to the sick, too; we cared for them now more than ever before.

And so the emotional connection and collaborative work began to take shape between special groups of people in Australia, numerous local Manusians, and all of us detained here. This collective sentiment developed into an important partnership in support of our struggle. During that three-week period, special people in Australia united with many people on Manus and made attempts to deliver food inside the camp. Ultimately, this meant that the Papua New Guinea police and navy intensified their strategies as the boats carrying supplies got closer to the main prison camp.

The local Manusians also organized a protest in Lorengau to support us. The protesters, both in Australia and in Papua New Guinea, are not the majority, but they are representative of the conscience of their societies. They are among the people who are socially and politically aware.

In any case, these interrelations between the three communities, all with different cultures and nationalities, proved that there exist people with a sincere understanding of other people, no matter where they are in the world. It proves that there always exist significant people who transcend government ideologies.

I imagine the rallies that were organized can be nothing more than messages of friendship and humanity. But apart from these spaces of solidarity and the alliances formed between societies, the question remains: What are the conditions and the framework that give rise to a resistance constituted by half-naked men on a remote island known as Manus? And what are the messages that this resistance is attempting to convey?

The refugees are overpowered.
The refugees have had extraordinary pressure imposed on them.
The refugees have resisted an entire political system; they have stood up to the power of a whole government.
From the very beginning right through to the very end, the refugees only used peaceful means to stand up and challenge power.
The refugees have asserted their authority.
The refugees have claimed power.
The refugees were able to reimagine themselves in the face of the detention regime.

The refugees were able to re-envision their personhood when suppressed by every form of torture inflicted on them and when confronted by every application of violence.

According to its own logic, and consistent with the character it has moulded itself into, the detention regime wanted to manufacture a particular kind of refugee with a particular kind of response. However, the refugees were able to regain their identity, regain their rights, regain their dignity. In fact, what has occurred is essentially a new form of identification, which asserts that we are human beings.

The refugees have been able to reconfigure the images of themselves as passive actors and weak subjects into active agents and fierce resistors. The concept of the refugee as a passive actor was an ideal instrument in the hands of power and could be exploited by Australia's political machinations; it formed the refugees into something that could be manipulated and leveraged for the Australian Government's own purpose.

The refugees have established that they desire to exist only as free individuals. They desire only an honourable existence. They have established this in confrontation with the proliferation of violence in the detention centre, one that is implemented by a mighty power structure. Up against the determination of this monolith, the refugees have, ultimately, vindicated themselves.

The refugees have been able to refashion the image of themselves as the 'Other'. We have reshaped the understanding of us as politically inept and have been successful in projecting an image of who we are. We now present the real face of refugees for a democratic Australia to discern.

The refugees have found the responses and reasoning provided by the government regarding the hostage situation and our incarceration to be absurd. There have been ridiculous fabrications. We have exposed this as a form of political opportunism, as a politics driven by economic mismanagement and incompetence, policies that benefit bloodthirsty financial investors, a politics that experiments in order to further ingrain a system of border militarization and securitization.

The refugees have identified and exposed the face of an emerging twenty-first-century dictatorship and fascism, a dictatorship and fascism that will one day creep into Australian society and into people's homes like a cancer.

The refugees have been resisting with their very lives.
Against the real politics of the day.
With their very bodies.
With peace as a way of being and as an expression.
With a rejection of violence.
With a kind of political poetics.
With a particular style of poetic resistance.
These features have become one with their existence.
Refugees pushed back.
Risking their lives and bodies.
Just fragile humans risking everything.
Risking everything that is beautiful.
Risking the only things of value left to them.
Risking what nature had bestowed upon them.

They never gave up these things to become mere bodies subject to politics. In opposition to a system of discipline and the mechanization of their bodies, the detained did not surrender. In reality, they proved that the human being is not a creature that can be entirely and completely consumed by politics.

From another perspective, this mode of resistance and the messages communicated by the imprisoned is nothing more than refugees asserting and putting into practice their values and their standpoints. They took this stance in order to return something valuable to the majority of the Australian public, to return what it has lost, or what it is in the process of losing. We formulated a schema of humanity that is, precisely, in polar opposition to fascist thinking – the kind of thinking that created Manus prison.

We have reminded a majority of the Australian public that throughout their history they have only ever imagined that their democracy and freedom has been created on the basis of principles of humanity.

If a majority of Australians were to reflect deeply on our resistance and sympathize with us, they would come to realize something about how they imagined themselves to be until now.

They would undergo a kind of self-realization regarding their illusions of moral superiority.

And they would be forced to self-analyse in relation to the principles and values they hold dear at this point in time, and realize that they are not connected to a mythical moral past.

Our resistance is the spirit that haunts Australia. Our resistance is a new manifesto for humanity and love.

In any case, our resistance and the three weeks of hardship we endured produced a new perspective and method that was remarkably transformative, even for us incarcerated within Manus prison. We learnt that humans have no sanctuary except within other human beings. Humans have no felicitous way to live their lives other than to trust in other humans, and the hearts of other humans, and the warmth within the hearts of other humans.

Our resistance enacted a profound poetic performance. This persisted until the moment we were confronted with the extremity of the violence. We found that the baton-wielding police had killed one of the dogs we had adopted into our community. At that moment, we descended into sorrow and wept,

in honour of its loyalty,
its beauty,
its innocence.

This profound poetic performance was implemented on another occasion when we were facing off against a group of police officers. We linked our arms to create a chain and told them that we only had love for them. We recited this as a poem that then became a collective expression:

A poem that united us.
A poem that we chanted in unison.
A poem of peace.

A poem of humanity.
A poem of love.

When the police chief stood in front of the community of half-naked refugees and named the leaders over the loudspeaker, asking them to surrender themselves, everyone called out:

'I'm A . . .!'

'I'm Y . . .!'

'I'm B . . .!'

This was the scene that emerged in Manus prison.

On the same day that we were brutally bashed, a number of individuals placed flowers in their hair. A sick Rohingya man put two red flowers behind his ears and smiled even as his body was emaciated and in the worst shape possible.

Our resistance was an epic of love.

In any case, I think that our resistance, our strategy of defiance, our message of protest, are the product of years of captivity, of a life of captivity, all produced by captives of a violent governmentality in Manus prison.

Resistance in its purest form.

A noble resistance.

An epic constituted by half-naked bodies up against a violent governmentality.

All this violence designed in government spaces and targeted against us has driven our lives towards nature.

towards the natural environment,
towards the animal world,
towards the ecosystem.

It has pushed us in this direction since we hope that maybe we could make its meaning, beauty and affection part of our reality. And coming to this realization is the most pristine, compassionate and non-violent relationship and encounter possible for the imprisoned refugees in terms of rebuilding our lives and identities.

We built profound relationships with the indigenous people, with the children, with the birds, the interaction between elements of society, even with the dog that was killed under the brutality of the system.

But the prison and its violence will never accept this, and in every situation the imprisoned lives and spirits have to reconfigure themselves in the face of death; they avoid projecting the malevolent dimension of their existence as the most dominant.

Ultimately, they beat us down and with violence put an end to our peaceful protest. But I think we were able to communicate our humanitarian message to Australian society and beyond. This sentiment is what all people, whether in Australia or elsewhere, need more than anything else these days.

Feelings of friendship.
Feelings of compassion.
Feelings of companionship.
Feelings of justice.
And feelings of love.

23 Days of Resistance Alongside Behrouz Boochani

Shaminda Kanapathi

We were around 450 men stranded in Lombrun detention centre (officially called Manus Regional Processing Centre) on Manus Island PNG in October 2017. Behrouz Boochani and I were good friends having known each other since I was banished to Manus Island from Christmas Island in Australia. He was a very quiet guy when I first met him and I knew that we would be good friends and work together. Boochani is the one who introduced me to many people and encouraged me to write and to be active on social media.[1]

Following the PNG Supreme Court ruling in April 2016 that our detention was unconstitutional and illegal, the Australian Government announced that the Centre would close on 31 October 2017 and gradually withdrew all services to force us to leave on that date. We were left in extreme tropical heat without any basic facilities such as food, water, power and medicines, but were sustained by our resilience and the strong bond of brotherhood built up over many long years. We had to organize our water supply by saving rainwater in garbage bins and digging wells, source and prepare our own food, keep the camp clean and generally maintain sanitary conditions. This was a huge responsibility and challenge, but every person who remained was very courageous and we worked hard to maintain our resistance.

Obtaining food and other essentials for the 450 camp people from what was effectively a small town was a major challenge. Each night at around midnight, we would use a small boat to smuggle the food and supplies from the town and sneak the things into the prison camp. Some local people who lived near the camp and local staff who worked in the camp felt really sorry about our miserable situation. They had compassion for us and took the risk of helping us, despite being fired at by the authorities while doing so. This secret operation was necessary as the PNG Navy was stationed next to the camp and was patrolling day and night to prevent supplies getting into the camp. Both the Australian and

PNG governments were aiming to starve us into leaving and moving us to Lorengau, the main town on the island, where there were supposedly newly built facilities; in actual fact these were still under construction and, as we were to discover, not fit for purpose.

Getting the food safely into the prison camp and then distributing it to each man in each community was extremely difficult but we managed well. I still remember the insulting comments of most of the Australian security guards and the staff who labelled us as indecent and immoral when it came to food, accusing us of fighting amongst ourselves over it, but none of this occurred and all the refugees continued to show their solidarity, unity and extraordinary moral character under these punitive conditions.

Each and every one of the men demonstrated remarkable intelligence in order to maintain our protest and shouldered their individual responsibilities without complaint. Even the government officials were completely stunned to see how we managed to survive. The Australian Government had spent billions of dollars to facilitate the security and inadequate services in the camp, but without any of these we survived for 23 days.

Boochani was one of the leaders, among others, taking on different leadership roles during the siege. Boochani used his diplomatic and journalistic skills to take on the vital task of talking to and writing for the media, both in Australia and internationally. Throughout this period when we were not only suffering the everyday problems of survival but were at constant risk of being attacked, Boochani had the courage and strength to overcome the fear and concentrate on writing and publishing about the camp situation through his work. Without power and limited fuel, we had to use a generator sparingly in order to charge our mobile phones which were our only contact with the outside world. Boochani wisely managed this resource in order to use his journalistic skills to ensure that the world was aware of our plight and thereby shield and protect us as much as possible.

All those who could took on individual responsibilities. My day-to-day duty was taking note of each and every incident that happened in the prison camp and taking videos and photos to share with the Australian and New Zealand media such as SBS and Radio New Zealand. I worked with journalists, Stefan Armbruster, who works at SBS, and Benjamin Robinson, who worked at Radio New Zealand. Whenever the police, immigration or the navy entered the camp I took videos and photos and would then send them to Boochani.

Boochani always wanted me to speak to the media and to journalists whenever they visited the prison camp. A group of Australian journalists came to the camp at midnight while I was sleeping. Boochani was looking for me everywhere in camp and it was very hard to find people at night as there were no lights, but eventually he found me while I was sleeping, took me to the journalists and introduced me to them. Through him I came to develop relationships with many Australian and international journalists.

I'm so proud to say that while we were surviving the siege, we still continued to do our work in sending strong messages to the outside world. We filmed short videos, made speech recordings, and Boochani never gave up on writing stories, reports and exposing both the Australian and PNG Government's atrocious and high-handed activities, violating international norms and standards of human rights, particularly during the siege, for Australian and international newspapers. A good example of how far our story reached was when I was contacted by reporters and journalists from Indian local media. Artists and academics all lent their voices to support us during the siege and Boochani's contribution towards making this possible cannot be overstated.

Our strong mutual cooperation and resistance became role models for many refugees to stand up for their rights. For example, those refugees who had been stranded in Indonesian immigration detention centres started to protest. We are so proud that we have developed platforms and pathways for those who want to be heard by encouraging them to raise their voices to the global community.

We were not fully successful, though, as we were finally removed from the camp by force after 23 days and sent to various new detention centres. However, we did succeed in dispelling the secrecy with which the Australian Government had sought to cloak their inhumane asylum seeker policies and tell the world of their true cruelty, which tragically still continues today for those still remaining in detention.[2]

I have no words to express my gratitude to those who stood up for the injustice and courageously united to overthrow it, my heartfelt gratitude to all of my incredibly strong fellow detainees. Among them, Boochani taught us a lot, through both his leadership skills and his clever and persistent advocacy and survival skills. For example, he smuggled into the prison camp mobile phones and technology that would enable us to connect with journalists and NGOs in Australia and around the world, and he skilfully built close relationships with journalists and groups supportive of our cause, such as Grandmothers Against Detention.

Words That Escaped from Prison

Erik Jensen

The easiest comparison is the most obvious: Martin Luther King Jr's *Letter from Birmingham Jail*.[1] It is not just the incarceration and the injustice of it. Nor is it the capacity to see all suffering as connected and alike, to see and understand the patterns in resistance, to know that truth is not always or even often preserved in law.

It is all of these things, but it is also something else special to these two men: they are writers. Their anger is formed in even sentences. Their words are arranged with fierce dignity. King asks that his voice be patient and reasonable and in doing so reminds the reader of a generosity we cannot truly deserve.

King wrote that he was in Birmingham because that's where injustice was. He had travelled from Atlanta not to cause trouble but to end it. The same was true for Behrouz Boochani, although different: he was on Manus Island because injustice placed him on Manus Island, not because he went there to confront it. The injustice was Australia.

*

Boochani's work arrives like post. Sometimes it is commissioned although mostly it is not. The first piece he sent to *The Saturday Paper* was a fragment of diary, a note from a world we had made but were not allowed to see.

'Here in this prison, everything is abnormal and different from all the villages, cities and continents,' he wrote. 'The prisoners sleep until afternoon. Life commences with the tumult of noisy queues for toilets. Every day, dozens of imprisoned refugees wake up from their sweaty and sticky sheets as the scorching sun of the tropics sits in the middle of the sky.'[2]

'A Letter from Manus Island' arrived almost two years later.[3] Just as before, it came without warning. It was a poet's manifesto written as the Australian

Government attempted to close the island's main prison camp and move refugees to three others.

Australia by now knew that its actions were unlawful. It left open the doors of its prison, as if this made the suffering less. There was no legal sophistry because none was available: the best they could do was unlock the gate. Later they commenced the strange shuffling of a person who knows they are wrong and who fears they will be caught. They moved for the sake of moving. They set up new camps, as if they might be different. They turned off the power, as if in darkness people could not see. Food, medication and water was also denied.

Boochani described the shape of the resistance. His piece was a revelation. Six hundred detainees refused to be transferred. For 23 days they denied requests that were arbitrary and absurd. He described people kept alive by their humanity. They were sustained by their character.

Boochani wrote about personhood, about the imagination of identity, about love. He wrote about how in resistance the refugees on Manus Island remade themselves and left it for Australia to discern who they really were. His letter was not just a retelling of these events but a political theory by which to frame them.

The morning Boochani's piece was published, the poet Maxine Beneba Clarke read it in front of the Malthouse Theatre in Melbourne. A few hundred people gathered to hear these words that had escaped from prison.

*

I have written before about the man with no face. I saw him first in a photograph, taken after he died. His name was Hamed Shamshiripour. He had no face because Australia refused to give him one. It is only in the writing of people like Boochani that this has changed.[4]

In the photograph, he was wearing a polo shirt and loose blue trousers. His arms were thin almost to wasting and his head was shaved bald. His eyes were empty and the sockets so large they eclipsed his other features.

For a few days I kept the photograph on my desk at *The Saturday Paper*, deciding whether or not to run it. When people came into my office, I turned it over. This was the point: Australia was hiding these faceless people, and yet when we did see them the images were too terrible to show.

The scene was like that of a lynching because it was. Hamed was hanged from a tree, killed by Australia's refugee policy. His shoulders slumped as if responding to a question for which there was no answer.

Hamed killed himself after he had been assessed as a refugee. He killed himself after Border Force's chief medical officer had been made aware of his dire mental state. He killed himself after Australia had refused to honour his wishes to be returned to the country from which he was fleeing.

Hamed Shamshiripour killed himself because he could not escape the hell Australia had made for him. This was not an accident. He killed himself not because the system we had built was malfunctioning but because the system had worked just as it was intended to work.

Boochani wrote about Shamshiripour after he died. 'I knew Hamed Shamshiripour through music,' he wrote. 'He was inspired by music; he loved to play the guitar and write lyrics. On one occasion he rushed over to see me eager to share a new song. But, over time, Hamed the musician began to disappear, he was becoming a different person.'[5]

Another refugee first told Boochani of Shamshiripour's death. He said: 'Someone killed Hamed today.'[6]

*

Offshore detention is a legal trick. It was conceived of to deny refugees access to Australia's laws. Over time, however, it acquired a new and appalling function: it allowed the extraordinary torture of thousands of refugees to be done in complete secrecy.

Large sections of Australian society are comforted by the punishment of refugees. It makes them feel that what they have – their own comfortable lives – is being protected. In the end Australians will do almost anything to be comfortable.

In the past few decades, this has meant building prison camps on islands off our borders. It has meant taking people's names and their dignity. It has meant spending inordinate amounts of money to ensure that this suffering is absolute and that the people it is supposed to benefit know about it only vaguely.[7]

When Boochani began writing for Australian newspapers, he prised open a crack in this system. His work on Manus Island, and the work of other refugees who also began to write, people like Imran Mohammad,[8] who learnt English in detention and then wielded it against his captors, broke down the multimillion-dollar artifice built to contain it. They ended decades of facelessness. They did so with the most basic of tools: the truth.

Part Six

2018 (February–June) – A Duty to History

Dignity, Time and Identity

Behrouz Boochani was awarded the Liberty Victoria 2018 Empty Chair Award. Salim Kyawning was driven to suicide in Manus on 22 May 2018 and Fariborz Karami was driven to suicide in Nauru on 15 June the same year. The writing and activism by refugees in Nauru is not as well-known as the work produced in Manus and other carceral sites, but the work has been just as intense and profound. Elahe Zivardar, aka Ellie Shakiba, documented footage, wrote and created art while detained. She eventually spent over six years in Nauru – during which she collected the largest available archive of images, videos, interviews and reports – before being resettled in the USA as part of the Australian–US agreement where she now continues her work. She has been supported by Mehran Ghadiri since her time held in Nauru who worked as an economic development worker on the island nation – he left his position after witnessing Australian border violence first-hand. #KidsOffNauru campaign began planning its launch and collaborated with Zivardar and used images she took inside the detention centre. Boochani's writing continued to gain respect from the Australian literary community, especially with the announcement that his autobiographical novel will be released soon. Writers such as Fatima Measham have been engaging with Boochani's work in significant ways for years and her writing has helped amplify the importance of themes and topics pertaining to the ecosystem, settler-colonialism, migration, creative resistance, kyriarchy and Manus Prison Theory. She was also one of the judges for the 2019 Victorian Premier's Prize for Non-Fiction when *No Friend but the Mountains* was awarded the winner; the book also went on to win the 2019 Victorian Prize for Literature.

Four Years After Reza Barati's Death, We Still Have No Justice[1]

Behrouz Boochani

I want to tell you about Reza the man, a gentle giant and my best friend.

It has been four years since the Manus prison riot of February 2014. It led to the killing of Reza Barati. Every year on the anniversary of his death refugee rights activists from different cities around Australia hold memorial ceremonies and join us as we mourn for Reza. Even though four years have passed, the killers have yet to be brought to justice, and there are still no clear answers to the fundamental questions concerning the riot.

Over these past years every violent occurrence in Manus prison has arisen whenever refugees demand an answer to one question. This simple and reasonable question is the source of every brutal event, and it was what initiated that particular peaceful protest. During those days the refugees asked the authorities in the prison: 'For how many more months or years do we have to remain in prison?' They followed this up by staging a peaceful protest for two weeks. They continued until immigration officials requested a meeting with representatives from the refugees in the dining area of Mike camp.

On that day, more than a thousand refugees were hopeful that the immigration authorities would tell them how much longer they would have to remain in prison. When immigration authorities didn't answer this question, a large-scale riot started that very night.

It was obvious that immigration orchestrated this kind of response for the angry refugees on purpose. They wanted to proceed with their plan to suppress the refugees with an 'iron fist'. The refugees were already furious, weary and volatile. And immigration knew this all too well. By being evasive at the meeting, they basically threw a lit match onto petrol.

In addition to that, immigration had fomented hate against the refugees among the locals. For days on end after the riot the Manusian residents and local guards told the refugees that they were just following orders. They claimed they were not to blame and it was all the machinations of the Australians. This was a well organized plan. They wanted to put the refugees in their place; people who only wanted to know how long they had to remain in prison. There was just one objective to their plans: to make the refugees return back to their countries by giving them a severe beating. The politics of offshore processing and the logic behind managing the Manus and Nauru prison camps are essentially founded on one principle: to create a situation so harsh that it forces the refugees to return to their countries of origin.

The riot occurred over two consecutive nights. The first night was 16 February, where the refugees were able to gain control of the prison for a number of hours after struggling for some time against the officers. On the second night, the power was cut and the prison became completely dark. Some local people together with G4S guards attacked the prison. It was then that over 100 refugees were severely injured, one person was shot, one person had their throat slit … and Reza was killed. Over the years that particular riot and the killing of Reza gave rise to many other incidents.

One refugee by the name of Behnam Satah witnessed what had happened with his own eyes, he saw how Reza was killed. As the main witness, Satah was called to appear in court on a number of occasions. After he testified against two of the main defendants he was threatened with murder on many occasions. However, he maintains: 'I was determined to go to court for the sake of achieving at least some justice.'

Now that I think about this issue after years have passed I still feel that justice was not served. You see, two Australian officers involved in Reza's death did not have their cases prosecuted. They were flown off the island immediately. One of the two local individuals who received a more than four and a half year jail sentence escaped from prison in 2016. He is still at large. The other one escaped from prison on 4 January but was captured after nearly three weeks.

For years, Satah has been living under conditions of impending danger. And this is the reality of his life on Manus. He is still struggling with the impact from witnessing the killing of Reza by the officers; he is extremely traumatized.

Just a few months ago we were reminded of that fateful February 2014. In mid-November 2017, when the refugees refused to move out of the prison, the situation became like what we experienced when Reza was killed. We had the opportunity to bring in a few journalists in the dead of night and meet face to face with the refugees. On one of those nights, I walked over to Mike camp with one of the journalists and a photographer. Satah was asked to provide a description of the events from the night of the riot while standing at the very spot where Reza was killed. He went up onto the steps, and as soon as he tried to explain the events of that night, he just stood there for minutes on end and wept. After all of these years, he is still affected by the killing of Reza. It seems that his nightmares are not over yet.

But the main purpose of this article is Reza Barati the man. I met him on the first day when we were transferred to Christmas Island and got to know him well after that. He was a young man with an incredibly broad and powerful physique, so much greater than a regular-sized man. For one month we shared a room, until they forcibly exiled us to Manus Island.

Reza was a kind-hearted and compassionate human being. His huge and strong build was the butt of jokes, and people would forget how gentle he always was to his fellow inmates. He possessed the face of friendship and warmth. However, he also revealed characteristics of youthful naiveté. Due to his kindness friends would call him 'the gentle giant'. Reza was born in a small town called Lomar in Ilam Province, part of the Kurdistan region of Iran. This town is located along the river Seymareh and the ancient city of Sirwan. He was born in the same year that the Iran–Iraq War ended. He took his first steps in this world on the ruins of war, which means that he experienced years of hardship and affliction. He studied architecture at university and was determined to finish his studies. During those days on Christmas Island, he would sometimes call and talk to his mother and little sister. He would share his feelings towards them with me in that childlike sincerity of his. He was essentially nothing more than an ordinary youth with the kind of dreams that every single young man from every single culture has for his future. He died at the hands of people who he requested to provide him protection and in a prison on a remote island.

His death is an utter tragedy. And it is because of this that he has become a symbol; he represents the innocence of the refugees held on Manus and Nauru. The way he was killed, and the violence that left him dead, more than anything else, echoes the level of ruthlessness inherent to the system of offshore processing. Four years have passed since that event and questions are still left unanswered. Why didn't the police force try to stop the attack by the locals and officers on that night? Why weren't those two Australians pursued and investigated? And why didn't they appear in any court? Also, what was the role of the G4S guards who had the responsibility to protect the refugees? And why didn't they carry out their duties appropriately?[2]

It is because these question remain unanswered that the violence of February 2014 continues to repeat itself; it occurred again in January 2016 during the mass hunger strike. At that time the Wilson officers attacked the prison. They beat the community of starving refugees and imprisoned many of them in the local jail. These unresolved matters are at the core of other manifestations of violence. Consider what happened on Good Friday in 2017 when soldiers from the army attacked the prison, firing more than 100 shots. It is also this point that influenced the police and immigration officials to bash refugees who were involved in peaceful resistance on 23 November 2017 and ultimately forced them to shift to the new camps.

Violence is an essential feature of the system that exiled refugees to Manus Island and Nauru. After all these years it still manifests itself in many different ways. Therefore, people such as Reza, Behnam, Fazel Chegeni and others who have been killed and injured, as well as the mothers of all these people, have been sacrificed to this political programme.

Our Mothers, a poem for Reza

My mother, Reza's mother and Fazel's mother are crying together.
I heard the Seymareh river crying with them.
Beneath Fazel's village is Sirwan, one of the most ancient and significant cities in the world.
The city of Sirwan.
Mothers cry upon the oldest city, cry for Reza and Fazel.
I heard all the beautiful mountains in Kurdistan are crying. All of Sirwan is crying. Mountain, rivers, wild flowers . . . all crying.
All of Sirwan is crying, all separated from their mothers.
I hear the most ancient of chants, I hear the mothers chanting in the city of Ilam, in the city of Sirwan, all throughout Kurdistan.
I hear their cries from inside Manus prison.
I hear the most ancient of songs, chanted by mothers. This form of chant is called Mour.
Mour is the oldest of songs, a song the Kurdish mothers chant for their boys and warriors who lose their lives fighting against enemies that attack the land of Kurdistan. It is a song for brave sons.

Fazel and Reza were brave sons. They fought for their lives.
When I was in Kurdistan, I climbed up the highest mountain on many occasions. The oldest chestnut oak trees reside up there. I hear the chestnut oaks crying too. My heart is extremely heavy, as I heard the deepest and most sorrowful Mour chanted by my mother today.
I have never heard a Mour like this, a choir of Mours, Reza's, Fazel's and my mother chanting.

This is Kurdish culture. We are born by song, live by song, fight by song, and die by song.
I feel the deepest sorrow because of Fazel's death, because of Reza's death.
He deserves the deepest Mour to be sung for him.
My heart is heavy because I am crying and listening to a Mour sung for my best friend, sung in a prison on the remotest island in the world.
I never thought I would hear Mour sung for the bravest of Kurdish sons out on a remote island, out in the middle of a massive, silent ocean.
I always think about the Mour my mother will chant for me when I die.
I thought that song would be sung for me in beautiful Kurdistan. I am sure Reza and Fazel had this thought just like me, but their lives were taken in a remote place, not in Kurdistan.
They lost their lives because of injustice.
They lost their lives in a foreign land.
Who was there when their lives were taken?
My mother, Reza's mother, and Fazel's mother,
all together, all mourning, all chanting, the deepest Mour.

Policy of Exile[1]

Behrouz Boochani

It has been more than three months since refugees were transferred from the Manus Island detention centre to new camps in Lorengau town. Refugees had resisted leaving the prison for 23 days and the transfer relied on the dramatic use of force. Ultimately, police and immigration officers invaded the prison and moved refugees to the new camps, beating them physically to make them go. This transfer became a critical stage in the Australian Government's policy of exile, forcing refugees to remain in Manus for a new chapter of violent indeterminacy and brutality marking time in an otherwise uncertain future.

After the transfer, the life of refugees has dramatically changed. We have been moved from a prison with hundreds of big and small rules, hundreds of prison guards who have absolute power and control over us, to an environment where rules and power structures have to be learnt anew. In this new environment, difficulties and suffering are imposed on refugees in a different way.

One significant change is to do with geography. The refugees were transferred from an actual prison to three new camps 35 kilometres away. These are West Haus, Hillside and East Lorengau. The last of these is very close to Lorengau town and sits atop a forested hill. It is the only one of the camps where construction has finished. Nevertheless, there was an issue from the beginning: East Lorengau does not have the capacity to accommodate all the refugees housed there, and it has now been three months since some refugees were forced to set up makeshift beds in a number of classrooms. They face ongoing issues with more difficult access to toilets and showers. They sleep in rooms as a group with no privacy.

Refugees are now able to freely visit Lorengau town. During the day, they walk through forest tracks in groups and take buses that travel twice an hour between Lorengau and the East Lorengau camp. Only a limited number of people take this option to travel to Lorengau, usually to shop at the market or small stores. Mostly, they prefer to spend their time around the camp.

At the end of the forest route, Hillside and West Haus are located side-by-side. They are furthest from the town, but conversely have the closest relationship with locals, thanks to a small village right next to the camps. Both of these sites are still under construction.

Hillside is unique in that it houses those refugees who are not recognized as such by the authorities. These people are under intense pressure to return to their home countries.

There are many people in Hillside who have never submitted their protection cases to determine their refugee status, and the authorities have punished them by giving them negative assessments. The people in Hillside are not being considered for resettlement in the United States. They are the most depressed and hopeless ones. Just last week the Papua New Guinea police sent five of them to a prison in Port Moresby, and every minute there is a possibility more of them will be transferred there by force.

The proximity of villages to Hillside and West Haus is extraordinary, particularly for people who see this scene for the first time. In some ways, the interaction between locals and many refugees is beautiful, sharing a space in the deep forest and dappled light. From another perspective, it has enormous potential for conflict between the two communities who are both thrown into this situation against their will. In the eyes of many locals, refugees are uninvited guests. It has been disrespectful to build the camps without local consent.

Anti-Australian sentiment grows among Manusians, as they believe Australia exploits their tiny island with a colonial mentality that never retreated. This is an important reality in Manus. People in the forest villages beside Hillside and West Haus are kind towards refugees, but they have held demonstrations outside the camps to voice their opposition to this profound disruption to their lives.

On 13 January, people from one of the villages barricaded the main road leading to Hillside and West Haus. They were incensed because sewage from the camps flowed down close to their homes, threatening their health. This protest was clearly directed towards the authorities, who had allowed this unacceptable situation to persist.

Other confrontations have also arisen between locals and refugees in Hillside and West Haus, and have created an extremely unsafe atmosphere. In the most notable incident, on the night of December 10 a number of drunk local men came to the fence and seriously threatened the refugees.

Just last week, about a dozen navy personnel attacked refugees in the middle of the main road in Lorengau town. Three refugees were badly injured. From the refugees' point of view, this attack is rooted in the Good Friday incident last year, when navy personnel fired gunshots into refugees' rooms. Police are now investigating the most recent assault, but local witnesses to the incident place the blame on the navy personnel.

Over the past three months, landowners have raised significant concerns with the Immigration Department and government officials. They have blocked the road to East Lorengau camp a number of times, most controversially on 19 December. They barricaded the main entrance of the camp with trucks and cars, creating a siege-like situation in which food and staff were prevented from entering the camps and refugees were prevented from leaving. Landowners believe that officials have not treated them well, and want to be involved in contracts for security and other services. The political, social and cultural realities here are very complex, but the many pressure points can at any time threaten the life and safety of refugees.

Although these difficulties with the three Manus camps have continued, about a hundred refugees who had been transferred to Port Moresby for medical care have been put under great pressure to return to Manus. This is despite the fact some of them have received no treatment. So far, small groups have been moved to Manus under military escort and sent to West Haus and Hillside. This puts more pressure on residents and facilities in the camps. If it continues, living conditions in the camps will worsen as more people are brought in to these already confined spaces.

For some people, these many years of pressure have become too much. Last week two men in the camps attempted suicide. Despite the transfer to new accommodation, violence and suffering are being reproduced in new and evolving ways. It was always apparent that the small community of Lorengau does not have the capacity to house hundreds of refugees. And it is now clearer than ever that the anguish, both for refugees and local people, will not come to an end for as long as refugees continue to be held hostage here.

Mohamed's Life Story is a Tragedy. But it's Typical for Fathers Held on Manus[1]

Behrouz Boochani

Approximately five years ago Mohamed, a Sudanese refugee, was exiled to Manus Island by the Australian Government. The blow was sudden and significant – this man's life was completely transformed. He had left behind a pregnant wife and two-year-old daughter in Darfur, Sudan.

Mohamed's life story is a real tragedy. He is young, he is a handsome man with broad, penetrating eyes. But as he stares ahead one senses an intense depression deep down in his soul; the lines running across his face flow with intense sorrow. A few months after Mohamed was exiled to Manus his second daughter came into the world. He was overjoyed in the way all fathers are upon the arrival of their newborn child.

That was at a time when the refugees were suffering – they were being brutally punished in an effort to force them to return to their countries. For Mohamed, however, refoulement meant the ultimate end; returning to Sudan meant death.

News spread through the prison a few months after the birth of his daughter: 'They killed Mohamed's wife.' Losing a partner is absolutely shocking for any person, and Mohamed was deeply in love with his wife. The story was like this: a group of armed men sprayed her with bullets as she stood out on an empty farm. This incident elicited a wave of emotional support from the other men – men who were themselves struggling with feelings of hopelessness.

It has been five years since that loss and Mohamed's daughters have turned seven and five years old. And Mohamed remains a captive here on Manus Island. Suddenly, he stares ahead once again, gazes up into the sky and says: 'At the moment they are with my elderly mother living in one of the villages in Darfur. My mother is looking after them. But for some time, I've been thinking to myself that my eldest daughter should have started school by now. However, our village doesn't have any schools.'

No doubt, Mohamed has dreams for his daughters. Throughout all these years their father has only ever been like a shadow in their lives; they feel his presence, but only in spirit. He has many dreams for his daughters, but one of the most fundamental among them is that they go to school.

Mohamed expresses a bitter smile:

> They have been the only thing that has given me hope throughout all these harsh years. They are the only reason I'm alive. Over these years I've been trying my hardest to communicate this feeling to them, I want them to know they have a father, I want them to know that one day their father will hold them in his arms.

There is also Kaveh, who I know well. He is a man with bushy eyebrows and a broad, chiselled face. A visage full of a kind of vibrancy for life – the joys of childhood clearly radiating from his face. His son Taha was born while he was still in Indonesia. He has never laid eyes on his boy. Taha has started speaking now. Taha has started to walk. He calls his father bābā over the phone.

Kaveh is extremely compassionate and a genuine family man. I am sure his situation was extraordinarily difficult that he was forced to leave his pregnant wife and flee Iran. I ask Kaveh if he has ever thought about returning during these last years. He wraps his hands around the crown of his head, he pauses for a moment in reflection, the question evokes feelings of shame, the question humiliates him. He replies: 'Is there any man in this world who wouldn't want to be with his boy and his partner? If I could return, I wouldn't put up with this agony for a second, let alone have to live with the pain for five years.'

Kaveh's story doesn't end with the separation from his wife and child. It had only been a few months since being exiled to Manus prison when he received news that his father had died. Having to mourn the loss of loved ones is part of the reality of being locked up in Manus prison. There is no choice but to confront this reality – it is an integral part of life in this place.

But for Kaveh this incident was incredibly difficult. He is still trying to come to terms with the death after all these years. He sighs with grief and tells me:

> I knew my father was sick. Talking to him over the phone at that time was really tough. We weren't permitted to talk for more than a few minutes every week, calls were restricted. One day, no matter how much I tried to convince them to let me call, the authorities wouldn't allow me to use the phone. They told me I had to wait a few days. When I called after a few days I found out he had died. After all these years I still think if I had had the opportunity to speak to my

father what would he have said. They showed no mercy when they prohibited me from speaking to my father. The whole thing was horrific.

Kaveh's is the story of a father who lost his own father.

And there is Aryobarzan, a 45-year-old man from Iran with two daughters aged 5 and 7. He puts up their photos on the wall in his room. When he looks at the pictures, he describes the sweet manner in which they speak to him over the phone, and he begins to laugh. He says that his youngest daughter's personality takes after him. Remembering this aspect of her character makes him happy for a moment, he laughs again.

I have known Aryobarzan for years. He resided over in the bed opposite me for a whole year. A man with curly hair, a strong man with a broad physique. A kind-hearted human who has respect among all the refugees; everyone can count on his him because of his wealth of life experiences. His personality is such that many of the younger guys look up to him like a big brother. But on many occasions, in the middle of the night, I used to notice he would descend into the depths of sorrow thinking about his little girls.

When I ask him what is the most painful thing he has had to experience in this prison, he just continues smoking and says: 'You know, I love my wife and daughters. The thing that causes me the most suffering is being away from them. But there's another pain within this suffering; that is, Australia didn't let me take pleasure in seeing my kids grow up during the sweetest period of their lives. And this causes me enormous distress.'

But he also speaks of something really beautiful, as well. He recounts: 'Some time ago it was my daughter's birthday. She said to me, "Daddy, I want a kangaroo soft toy." And through one of my Australian friends I was able to post a toy kangaroo to her.'

Moments later he showed me the photo. I can only describe the image in one way: a little girl, dark eyes, hugging a kangaroo, and her thick lips kissing the toy.

These are some short snippets from the stories of the fathers held in Manus. They are just a few examples of dozens of men who have been battling the pain of being separated from their partners and children for years and years. It is not completely clear how many of the refugees in Manus are married. But what is obvious is that the suffering that these fathers undergo is profound, the suffering is compounded with all the other anguish one feels on this island.

It is important to point out that the other refugees totally identify with their pain and sympathize with them. This is nothing other than the realization that the fathers are suffering in ways over and above what every prisoner already goes through.

These stories are exclusive insights, a window into the lives of men who are experiencing a profound loneliness, the unbearable feeling that they are nothing more than forgotten people. Men killed between the cogs of a political machine. However, it is their humanity that helps them endure this system.

Many people try to construct an accurate picture of the situation for refugees on Manus Island and Nauru using statistics: such as 'five years in detention' or '2,000 individuals'. I must say that applying this statistical approach cannot penetrate the depth of the issue.

The central concern is the opportunity to live life well. Only through a profound engagement with the lived experiences of refugees can one realize the extent of the human disaster, only by listening to the life stories of the prisoners can one understand the torture they have had to endure.

The core problem is that one cannot arrive at an accurate picture of the lives of these men by searching between the layers upon layers of newspapers, or within the arguments made by politicians and human rights activists. Perhaps this is the reason that until now Australian politicians have avoided coming to this island, perhaps this is the reason why they do not want to see these men up close. Perhaps this is the reason why they do not want to hear their life stories. They are afraid to look into the eyes of these refugees.

This is the standpoint of the political authorities and leading public figures in Australia, they all see the prisoners as nothing but 2,000 refugees. The only result in this way of thinking is to reduce the character, identity and humanity of these people to a basic category: 'refugee'. They want to simplify them to a one-dimensional being, a one-dimensional construct. They want to render them an object without any capacity to think intelligently, an object without feelings, an object without family.

For me, who has been incarcerated in Manus Prison for five years, this question plagues me: if I was in a situation like these fathers, where I had a little son or a daughter who I could not hold in my arms, could I have withstood the hardship for this many years? I must confess, in all honesty, that when I think about this question, I not only cannot find an answer but I also experience a mix of agony and terror. They are truly inspiring men.

Without a doubt, this suffering is being felt thousands of kilometres away. This suffering is real in the lives of children, in the world inhabited by those little girls who hold their dolls tight in the dead of night. This suffering engulfs the dreams of children. This suffering isolates and afflicts women who have to carry all the burdens of life that weigh down on them. These women have to endure the misery of separation.

The affliction continues to travel far and wide. Without a doubt, this affliction is reproduced in faraway lands and distant places, in remote towns and villages. These families suffer together. This is another side of the world we inhabit. Australia is not only holding 2,000 individuals hostage – Australia is holding many thousands more people hostage around the world.

The Gay, Transgender and Bisexual Men on Manus Are Forced into Silence[1]

Behrouz Boochani

It was five years ago in Fox prison camp. A group of immigration officers accompanied by a number of interpreters burst in. All of a sudden, one of the officers stood on a chair precisely like a king's representative in ancient times, like one of those men reading the king's announcement for convicts. The officer took a piece of paper, and surrounded by dozens of refugees he started to read. The announcement was serious, decisive, to the point and threatening, like his voice. 'Homosexuality is illegal in Papua New Guiana and considered as a crime. If anyone in the immigration detention engages in this behaviour, he will be sentenced to 14 years in prison.' It was a dire warning from the prison's officials and directly targeted homosexual prisoners.

A few months later, Alex, an Iranian gay refugee, stood on the same chair, trembling with rage, and shouted with courage: 'I am gay, and this is my sexual identity, I am gay and that's why I left my country, I announce it loudly and clearly: I am gay.'

Many people gathered to listen to him. What was the story behind this? What made him speak out? Due to the lack of a private place, Alex and his boyfriend had made love in one of the toilets. When they had left the toilet, they ran into some people who started teasing them. It was the trigger for Alex to get up on the chair and give his short speech.

Alex's performance was nothing short of a 'revolution' in a remote prison in front of dozens of refugee prisoners. He rebelled against a system and a community that suppressed and humiliated his human identity because of his sexual identity. His performance was undoubtedly inspired by the immigration performance, but this one was a revolt against law, against discrimination, against the system and the community, which considered him as 'other' and 'different'. Alex announced his sexual identity loudly in opposition to a system fundamentally designed to represent him and other refugees as devoid of human identity.

After his performance, Alex was well-known in the prison community made up of hundreds of people. Some began to call him 'beautiful Alex'. Eventually, this label spread throughout the whole prison, many people, including some guards and refugees, started addressing him in this way. In other words, his human identity was again presented as less-than while heterosexist presumptions about his identity were thrust upon him, leading him to stand up on a chair and give another speech.

Alex became more socially isolated every day. There is no doubt that many refugees still did respect him and his identity and sympathized with the situation he was stuck in. However, many of these people did not have a chance to directly express their sympathy. From Alex's point of view, it was the whole community that targeted his existence.

Another problem came up. Toilets, the last refuge for Alex and his boyfriend, were converted into a public place. In practice, he did not have any privacy in the prison any longer. Those who never had to experience being in prison might not be able to contemplate what I mean by lack of privacy. It is hard to imagine how tough it is living under the heavy gaze of a closed community.

After his speeches, I carried out an interview with Alex. He was 30 years old, with a long history of experiencing suppression, ignorance and humiliation. But he liked life itself, he liked living. At first sight, I could sense the pain and suffering that had been inflicted on Alex over the course of his life, due to reactions to his sexual orientation. Yet, he still liked life and knew himself as a warrior, who had been defending his sexual identity for many years, fighting against the conservative, cruel and heterosexist structures of society.

Right at the beginning, he directed our conversation to his adolescence, the time he discovered his sexual identity. Subsequently, he spoke about his family who banished him. He was trying to provide me with a precise picture of the situation that LGBTIQ minorities live with in Iran, and explain how the society and the government suppress them.

Alex opened up about his experiences in Manus prison. He was raped twice. The prison officials, however, completely ignored his complaints. Covering up rapes and sexual harassments has been the policy of the Australian Government during these years. The most public incident was when three Wilson security staff from New Zealand and Australia were alleged to have drugged and gang-raped a local female staff member. They were immediately flown off the island

and out of PNG; and despite the order of the PNG government and the PNG court, they never returned to justice.

It was an in-depth interview I conducted with Alex, and consequently, his story was published in *The Guardian*. Back then I had to work as an anonymous source thanks to pressure that immigration had placed on us within the tight security arrangements of the prison.

What did happen after the publication of the report? Evidence was leaked, divulging that a special inspector was assigned by the immigration to find the source contributing to the report on homosexuality in Manus. Revealing stories related to gay, transgender or bisexual men in the prison had always been frightening for the immigration because those stories are like a gateway, disclosing other incidents in the prison and showing more systematic and in-depth issues including rapes and sexual harassments.

Alex continued to suffer and was becoming more isolated every day. And as a result of Alex's experiences other gay refugees did not dare to reveal their sexual identity. It got to the point that if they let others know about their sexual orientation, if they moved in line with Alex, they would face further isolation, targeting and social pressure. In the prison, intentionally designed to destroy the human identity of prisoners, where prisoners are nothing more than numbers living a mechanical existence, revealing that matter would cost them dearly, leading them to further isolation and depression. Over the years only a few gay, transgender or bisexual men have spoken out or made their sexual identity public. Many have been forced into silence.

Alex ultimately returned to Iran as a result of the difficult situation imposed on him, and then escaped Iran again via a different route. Sometimes I imagine how it would be if he had stayed. Another chapter of Manus history would have been written, the history of pain and suffering endured by gay minorities. Alex went back and took a part of the prison's anguish with him, a scar on his soul.

No one knows how many gay, transgender or bisexual refugees live on Manus, but what is clear is that the suffering they experienced in their countries has been repeated on Manus in a disastrous way. Fear, humiliation, threat, banishment, rape – these are all concepts and experiences lived daily by these men. Gay, transgender and bisexual men here have experienced even greater torment than other refugees. Alex was a revolutionary symbol for the gay, transgender and bisexual men on Manus. His was a revolution against the kyriarchal system, a revolution against the extremely conservative community, a revolution that seems to have ended in resounding defeat.

Salim Fled Genocide to Find Safety. He Lost His Life in the Most Tragic Way[1]

Behrouz Boochani

It's pouring rain. As usual, the sky tries to wring every single cloud and squeeze out every single drop. A rainy day . . . right after a day full of nightmares.

A rainy day . . . to cleanse, to wash away the sorrow, to eliminate the grief, to stop the inhumanity, to end the viciousness and barbarity. A rainy day . . . after another death on Manus.

Salim died on Tuesday morning. He committed suicide. He was riding the bus that takes the refugees to town. He got up off his seat, he opened the door, and he jumped out. And moments later, the wheels of the vehicle ran over his head. He was left there crushed on the concrete.

Another suicide, another extreme set of circumstances. The third death by suicide on Manus in under a year, the seventh death of a refugee on Manus in total. When I say suicide, I am using the definition that the police use to describe the death.

Salim would at times fall to the ground and begin to tremble. His mouth would foam and he would yell. All the refugees were familiar with his situation. All the staff working in Manus prison, the medical personnel, everyone in the Immigration Department including the immigration minister, human rights organizations, and the journalists reporting about Manus, they all knew about Salim. We introduced him to every authority figure who visited Manus from Australia.

Our hope was that by witnessing this man they would be so moved that they would put an end to the torture, that they would understand what they were doing to us. Everyone could see what he was going through. And maybe this was why immigration officials were determined to keep him there, to help reinforce the ruthlessness and brutality of the system.

I had known Salim for a long time. The first time I encountered him was in Oscar prison. It was the same day that Sudanese refugee Faysal Ishak Ahmed died due to numerous health issues which included heart problems. For six months Faysal had been begging doctors from International Health and Medical Services to help him. Like Faysal, Salim was struggling to stay alive. He approached me, indicating to his heart, to his head, trying to tell me that he was afraid he would end up like Faysal. During our first interaction, he had hope that I might be able to do something for him, he hoped that someone might hear his cry for help. Salim could not speak a word of English. He was possibly the most vulnerable refugee who had to endure the violence of Australia's border regime all these years.

I also remember Salim in other ways. There is one particular feature that remains in our memory. He was always in anguish, but he had an extraordinary love of flowers. He would pick flowers from along the prison fences and playfully place them behind his ears or put them in his hair. There are pictures of him sitting by the fences holding flowers, but it is clear that his spirit had been crushed.

There was a time when he was more vigorous. It was in November when we were under siege for 23 days by Australian immigration and the local police. In the final days when they began to attack with more force, Salim took his flowers and went to welcome them to the prison – he showed compassion and respect to the same people who had come to beat us.

Many, like Salim, have lost all hope in the political system and the medical services.

Salim did not know a word of English but he was fully aware of what was going on around him. He used his body language in powerful ways to convey his message, even though his body had been punished and tortured. He used his flowers to communicate his opposition to the system.

Salim had epilepsy. Two years ago, immigration decided to transfer him to Australia for treatment. He stayed in Darwin for a while but they exiled him back to Manus while he was still experiencing a great deal of suffering.

There is no hope in Manus prison's medical centre, which is run by International Health and Medical Services (IHMS). How many people have they treated successfully in these five years? Salim had nowhere else to turn; he returned to IHMS for help over and over again, at least to collect some pain relief. It was a like seeking asylum from your torturer.

The IHMS has always been under the command of immigration. The institution is part of a predetermined political strategy which smothers sick refugees and tosses them into a horrific bureaucratic maze. They not only leave refugees untreated, they also aggravate the minor pains of healthy refugees and

Plate 1 Behrouz with some local children in front of a shop in Lorengau town, 13 July 2016. Photo credit: Unknown.

Plate 2a P Dorm, one of a number of 'tunnels' used as sleeping quarters. Photo credit: Omid Tofighian, January 2019, during third visit to Manus.[1]

Plate 2b Deportation, 9 February 2017. Photo credit: Behrouz Boochani.[2]

Plate 3a Destruction of Manusian ecosystem. 7 June 2016. Photo credit: Behrouz Boochani.[3]

Plate 3b Peaceful protest in Manus Prison, 25 August 2017, before the siege. Photo credit: Behrouz Boochani. People protesting against their impending transfer to other prison camps.

Plate 4 Boochani taking a selfie with local woman in Manus. Photo credit: Getty images.

force them to return to the countries they fled. All the documents pertaining to the torture of Salim are available now and there is a lot of evidence of his maltreatment.

Salim and many others were driven to death by the application of systematic torture. The death of Salim is the outcome of organized tactics of violence that involve a chain of command and administrative procedures. These are deaths ordered by political actors and a government that knows what it is doing; strategic manoeuvres designed to eliminate people incarcerated on Manus in the most violent way. The deaths that have taken place have had a profound effect on the inmates. Physical violence is only one aspect of the attacks; after all these years the system also plays sick games with tortured and vulnerable souls.

Many, like Salim, have lost all hope in the political system and the medical services. It is not surprising that the first reaction from many of the prisoners was: 'Good for him, at least now he's free.' By sacrificing his life Salim freed himself from the shackles administered by the doctors and nurses, from all the documents and forms, freed himself from registering on lists and anticipating treatment, from hoping aimlessly for aid when there was no intention to help him in the first place.

Salim was a Rohingya who fled genocide. He crossed a treacherous ocean, endured five years of illness in a prison on a forlorn island, and in the end, he lost his life in the most tragic way. He was a father and a husband. He had three children: eleven, eight and five years old. He had never seen his youngest because the child was born while he was on his way to Australia.

The deaths on Manus must be understood in the context of the various interlocking processes that occur here: the never-ending queues under the burning sun just to receive food; the hierarchies constructed to divide people in the prison; the rationalization and control of every decision and action; the humiliation prisoners experience, and the contempt of the staff and authorities; the denial of rights and respect; the demeaning of human life; chains of events leading to death; death via a mechanical process; death as a commodity, for political profit.

For years Salim was like a possessed corpse who would die a number of deaths every day . . . death at sunset, death every night. He would be reborn every morning without any recollection and without resuming anything from his life in the past. He would just walk over to the medical centre in the hope of being healed. Death by a thousand blows; death endured over and over again; death of the body, death of the soul; death silenced by the noise of the tabloids and latest fashions; death covered up by the bride of a royal wedding; death lost among the chatter of celebrities; death that has the lowest value possible.

The rain washes away the blood spill, it cleanses the anguish.
The killers and the victims, the scene of the crime . . .
the rain carries them all away.
Everything returns to nature,
everything that has happened returns to the land.
But the rain cannot fathom the perpetrators, the government of killers. The rain cannot comprehend the blood that has been spilled by using the law as a weapon.
These words are a form of lament in honour of a man who always had a few flowers tucked into his hair.
Just like the falling rain . . .
wash over this jungle . . .
cleanse these plains.

Manus Island Poem[1]

Behrouz Boochani

Forgive me, my bird, as I am not able to embrace you.
But here,
in this corner,
I know some immigrant birds. I smile at them at the crack of dawn
and I embrace them with open arms,
as open as the immensity of the sky.
My beautiful love!
Forgive me, as I am not able to quaff the aromatic scent of your breaths,
but here, in this ruin,
I know some wildflowers which grow every morning in my heart,
and at the dead of the night, they drift into sleep with me, in my place.
Forgive me, my angel!
I am not able to caress your gentle skin with my fingertips.
But I have a lifelong friendship with sea zephyrs
and those zephyrs strum my nude skin here, in this green hell!
Forgive me, as I am not able to climb the green mountains of your body,
but here, at a depth of the darkness, in the middle of every night, I enjoy deep and utter seclusion with the tallest and more vain coconut trees.
My beautiful! I sing you in the profundities of the oldest and the oddest songs,
further away from the world of a man who loves you amongst the deepest oceans and the darkest forests.
Inside a cage,
the man loves you,
inside the cage located between the vastest ocean and the greenest forests.
Forgive me, my love.
Forgive me, my love, as I am only able to love you from a remote island,
inside the cage,
from the corner of this small room.
Forgive me, please, as the only portion of the world that belongs to me is these pieces.

Journalism, Borders and Oppression

The Nauru Context

Elahe Zivardar and Mehran Ghadiri

When all the people seeking asylum first boarded that plane to the nightmare of imprisonment and exile in Nauru, they did not know they were entering a complex spider's web of private corporations, contractors and governments – something we call the border-industrial complex. Its targets are the victims of global Western imperialism, marginalized and targeted people from the Global South. We did not realize at first that there are many thousands of people employed and paid highly to keep about 1,200 other refugees in an indefinite stasis in far-away Nauru, to feed the complex, to grease its wheels with the blood and tears of its powerless and oppressed victims. After a while inside the complex, we saw how the companies that operated within it were incentivized to punish any act of humanity and reward all acts of inhumanity towards the detainees. We saw how they pushed people towards conflict and sowed division to increase their profits. They sowed division and mistrust between the refugees and the Nauruan population by misrepresenting the refugees as bad people bent on destroying the reputation and livelihoods of Nauru and its people.[1] They sowed divisions between the different ethnic groups within the detainee population in Nauru by unevenly delivering services and support to them. Meanwhile the Australian Government sowed division between the Australian population and the refugees with assistance from right-wing media organizations by labelling the refugees potential terrorists and criminals. They also sowed division between the Australian detention centre workers and the local Nauruans, by assuming all Nauruans to be lazy, uneducated and corrupt, while Nauruans deeply resented the colonial attitudes of Australians towards them. The border-industrial complex relied on division, paranoia and conflict to maintain an oppressive system that harmed and stole from all of these groups.

We met in Nauru on opposite sides of the divide, Elahe Zivardar was detained and Mehran Ghadiri was a social worker from Australia, working for Connect Settlement Services in 2015. But it was not until Ghadiri returned in 2018 to work for HOST International, the successor to Connect, that we really met each other. Ghadiri had realized early on just how destructive and deliberately harmful the offshore detention system is and had already come to a realization that to sit silently and accept it, or to work within it, no matter how well intentioned, would only serve to further generate more profits for the border regime. For years, I (Zivardar) had been documenting as much as I could in any way that I could from inside the detention centre. I interviewed and recorded people's stories of how they got there and their personal experiences of mistreatment at the hands of the border-industrial complex. Luckily the Nauruan guards were usually easy to bribe, as their pay was so low that they would smuggle in a camera for cigarettes. We decided to work together to do everything we could to expose the truth of offshore detention from the inside.

After a few years of imprisonment in Nauru, due to public pressure campaigns put on the government over the detention of children, and the undeniable existence of the toxic black mould that covered tents, many of the refugees were moved outside the camps and into prefabricated units around the tiny island. Many of my photos and videos were used by the media to show the condition of the children and the mouldy tents.[2] But the tents were not completely removed until just days before Nauru hosted international leaders and media for the Pacific Islands Forum of 2018, to hide their shame and protect their contracts. Ghadiri returned to Nauru for the second time a few days after the Pacific Islands Forum and together we resolved to continued recording evidence outside the camps where most refugees were now quartered.

As we were now living among the Nauruan population, we began to realize that the Nauruans who we often blamed for some of our poor conditions, such as the lack of electricity and clean water, were also the victims of this border-industrial complex. Corruption had only increased with the influx of Australian money and theft of public funds by government officials skyrocketed. Despite the influx of billions of dollars into Nauru from Australia, the grinding poverty of the average Nauruan, whose population numbers only 10,000 to 12,000, was in no way alleviated nor were any of their basic needs met. All the while what remained of their natural environment was being bulldozed and dug up. Even the once plentiful fish in the ocean were being sold off to foreign countries and overfished. Fishermen could no longer feed their families as they had for thousands of years on what was once known as 'Pleasant Island'. Even the coconuts were contaminated with radioactive cadmium, a by-product of the defunct phosphate mining that once made this island the second richest in the world by GDP. Every man, woman and child on the island has absorbed a huge amount of this heavy metal into their system from simply breathing the dust, drinking the water and eating the fish, including all the refugees who have been held there.

The Nauruans who worked for the many foreign companies present on their island would always complain about the rampant corruption and huge theft that was underway right in front of their eyes. Every adult Nauruan was fully aware of the entrenched corruption within their government and their corrupt dealings with foreign companies. There was no secret in that, and we interviewed Nauruans who opposed their government and lamented the deep corruption that existed, but who felt powerless to act against the corrupt cabal who grabbed power and were busy enriching themselves at their expense. Emboldened by Australian support and funds, they had begun to govern Nauru in an increasingly authoritarian manner, relying more heavily on fear, blackmail and bribery to maintain their hold on power. They routinely blacklisted their political opponents, forced their employers to fire them from their jobs or sent the police to shut down their business, effectively ending their ability to earn a living on the tiny island of approximately 12,000 people.

This was the main difference between being detained in Nauru versus being detained in Manus; while Manus Island is part of PNG which has many other sources of income, the Nauru Government was completely beholden to Australia, which provided a full two thirds of Nauru's annual income since 2013.[3] This not only made the government completely dependent on and therefore compliant with the wishes of the Australian Government in every aspect of their domestic policy making, but it also made them fearful and desperate to keep as many refugees held on the island for as long as possible, without regard to their health or wellbeing. Conversely, the longer the detention of refugees went on, the PNG government increasingly viewed the Manus Island detention centre as an embarrassment and repeatedly requested that Australia close it down, even declaring it illegal under PNG law. Meanwhile in Nauru, the government was busy changing their national laws to accommodate the detention of more refugees in Nauru, even hoping to procure those refugees being held in Manus.

Wanting to shine a light on this aspect of the Nauru detention centre, we began to seek out Nauruans who were willing to be interviewed about the oppression of their own government against the local Nauruan population. We met with Nauruan dissidents who explained in great detail the extremely high level of corruption that existed around the financial arrangements between the Australian and Nauruan governments, including contracts handed out to friends and family of government officials, embezzlement and bribery. They were willing to go on the record to detail their government's role in creating the extremely poor situation for the Nauruan people in terms of healthcare, the covering up of rampant sexual assault,[4] including against minors, the extremely poor state of the education system and the theft of Nauru's remaining natural resources. They risked serious consequences to talk to us in front of the camera and asked that their identities not be disclosed and their faces and voices obscured. They detailed how those who have spoken out against Nauruan government corruption or criticized its agreement with Australia to detain refugees in Nauru, have often ended up blacklisted, in prison or in exile. They also detailed how their government has denied life-saving medical treatment to its political opponents leading to their deaths from treatable diseases.[5] They could have replaced the word 'Nauruan' with 'refugee' when describing many of the issues that Nauruans faced daily – the poor living conditions, threats of imprisonment and denial of treatment.[6] It was at this point in our journey when we realized that the Nauruan's were in the same situation as the refugees – victims of the border-industrial complex that only sought to use them to extract wealth and did not care if they lived or died. It was no wonder then that the first new building that Australians built for use by the government of Nauru was another prison for Nauruans.

As for the Australian victims, they include every citizen and resident. The same systems that Australia set up to mistreat refugees, having gone unpunished so far, will inevitably lead to those same systems being inflicted upon the Australian population. We have already seen aspects of this come into play with Christmas Island being used to house Covid-19 patients and the failed hotel quarantine system. The cost is always borne by the Australian public, but all the profits are privatized into the pockets of the companies and government officials who make up the border-industrial complex. The techniques of repression have been perfected in Nauru and Manus Island, Christmas Island and in onshore facilities; the companies have built up corporate structures, physical facilities, worked out the logistics, and put in place the procedural foundation to be able to roll out this type of oppression for all ordinary Australian citizens when and if the government chooses or sees an opportunity to do so.

Immigration detention centres built by the border-industrial complex, are like weapons of war built by the military-industrial complex; once they are built, they will eventually be used by someone against someone else. The profit margins have been so high in the Australian border security industry that the policy has taken on an economic life of its own, creating its own parasitic financial ecosystem that feeds on its indifferent host, the Australian taxpayer. Unwittingly, casually and without debate, Australians have given their approval for this architecture of oppression, the immigration detention system both offshore and onshore. Of course, it is fine when the prisoners filling these jails are the brown and Black peoples, the Muslims, the bad people. But now that Scott Morrison has proclaimed his victory over 'the boats' and boat turn-backs have ended any new arrivals, how will the companies of the border-industrial complex feed the beast they have created? What will they do with the billions in prison infrastructure they have set-up? Inevitably it will be repurposed for the detention of other targets, other groups.

As we saw in 2020–1, Covid-19 positive Australian citizens were sent to Christmas Island during the pandemic, and Indigenous people were particularly targeted as part of lockdowns domestically.[7] While some might argue that there was a need for harsh measures to confront the pandemic, we must also recognize that there is always a compelling reason that governments will provide, always an emergency or crisis that needs immediate and drastic action against a target group. It is a slippery slope, if refugees could have their rights taken away and hidden away offshore, and if a citizen who has contracted a virus can be sent to a detention centre offshore, then the question must be asked what happens if there is a bigger crisis. What will be the price that Australians pay for normalizing this kind of response to crises?

The financial cost to Australia of maintaining its current bloated border regime has been a staggering cost; approximately 2 billion dollars every year since the start of the second phase of the offshore detention system in 2012, with little oversight and accountability over how contracts are awarded and the cost effectiveness of the operations. Indeed, the less cost effective the more profits are made by the private contractors and officials. Every worker and prisoner witnessed how this system failed over and over again, how it was designed to fail in its duty of care. When naked corruption is allowed to continue, when human rights and international obligations are not respected, when refugees are just a number and entire nations are exploited, and the facts about all this are simply explained away or ignored entirely by governments and the mainstream media, then we find ourselves on the precipice of a social, economic and political disaster for all involved.

This brings us to the border-industrial complex itself. Where did it come from? From where was it inspired? We believe we found our answers to these questions. It seems the forces that have created and operate the border-industrial complex are deeply intertwined with the global forces that have created and operate the military-industrial complex; they are supported by the same politicians, the same multinational corporations, and justified and sanitized by the same media outlets using the same false narratives and techniques to demonize the victims and obfuscate the truth – to turn the truth on its head – to divert public funds into the systems of oppression and exclusion.

The border-industrial complex expands and profits from new conflicts and tensions rising in the world, and the military-industrial complex's wars around the world keep a steady flow of refugees fleeing the instability and wars. It is a symbiotic yet parasitic relationship – while the two complexes keep each other alive in a symbiotic relationship, both of them parasitically feed off their hosts, the tax-paying citizens of their countries. Those refugees caught in the gears of the border-industrial complex, who are being slowly crushed, are expendable and only worth the dollars that they bring in. This was always apparent to anyone who has a lived experience of Nauru or Manus, that they were all just walking dollar signs. Nauru and Manus were used as an ATM; every week the Australians would come and fill it up with cash and then a host of companies, politicians and oligarchs would line up to withdraw their share and send it offshore again. That some refugees had to die to maintain this system was treated like an account keeping fee, a cost of doing business.

The border-industrial complex, and the new prototypes it has now field-tested in Nauru and Manus Island, and the horrors that have been committed in these places against the vulnerable and powerless is a danger not only to people fleeing wars and degradation, but to every peace-loving person in the world and to our planet itself.

On Mothers, Nature and the Body

Fatima Measham

Even when Behrouz Boochani was trapped on Manus Island, his mind in full flight could be perceived – a persistent subjectivity. I start here because the border-industrial complex makes objects of everyone, swapping names for numbers at the earliest instance. Names are embodied; numbers are not.

The point is to reduce people to components. As Boochani described for *The New York Times* in September 2020,[1] a system of torture and punishment let the Australian Government 'control our bodies through contractors and guards but not be held responsible for the horrors visited upon us'. It is a kind of engineering, one that maintains simultaneously the violence and the virtue of the settler-colony.

I grew up Catholic in a formerly colonized country. I tend to interpret politics in terms of their effect on bodies. That is where it ultimately manifests. The broken body is in fact a key image in my faith – the deterrent that had been raised (literally) through mechanics of power, the wounds and bruises an inscription for all to read. That a body could be made inarticulate and discursive at once is an ancient thing.

Another formative image: a former opposition senator lying face down on an airport tarmac in Manila, shot on arrival in 1983 after years of exile. In an interview with a journalist before disembarking the plane, Ninoy Aquino said, 'If it's my fate to die by an assassin's bullet, so be it.'[2] He was wearing a pale suit, as if offering a canvas for powerful forces.

His mother would go on to say, 'I want the people to see what they did to my son.' The body that came into view at the wake was encased in bloodied clothes, the face disfigured by a bullet. The things we record as history are made up of mothers who had fashioned another body from their own, only to see it desacralized.

In both ancient and contemporary practice, women play special roles in the preparation of the body for death rites and mourning ceremonies. In 2018,

Boochani marked the fourth anniversary of the death of Reza Barati with a poem called 'Our Mothers, a Poem for Reza'.[3] It references a Kurdish mourning hymn. The English translation reads:

> My heart is heavy because I am crying and listening to a Mour sung for my best friend, sung in a prison on the remotest island in the world.
> I never thought I would hear Mour sung for the bravest of Kurdish sons out on a remote island, out in the middle of a massive, silent ocean.
> I always think about the Mour my mother will chant for me when I die.

Ideas like freedom and dignity do not expire like bodies; they are by nature transcendent. But since ideas are materialized in the body – coursing through synapses in the brain, rendered as sound by vocal chords, fixed on a page by hand, propelled to the street on feet – then that is where attempts to crush them are made.

Governments and armed agencies, as well as other institutions, become didactic in the way of crude graffiti: 'We were here' written on bodies by means of torture, discrimination, impoverishment, displacement and murder. Sometimes there aren't even bodies left for mothers.

In Argentina in the late 1970s, the Madres de Plaza de Mayo were among the first to protest against US-sanctioned state terrorism, demanding the return of their children, the *desaparecidos*. 'I don't even have his bones to bury,' said one woman of her son.

It calls to mind other children who went missing. Like those in Canada and Australia who had been taken from Indigenous families – concurrent with and equivalent to the felling of trees and drying of rivers. First Nations peoples make no distinction between their bodies and the beneficent earth. Nor do colonizers in the erasing.

And what of the bodies that had once been cradled by Palestinian mothers, by Hazara, Rohingya, Tamil and Uighur mothers? By Black mothers in America?

> Who was there when their lives were taken?
> My mother, Reza's mother, and Fazel's mother,
> all together, all mourning, all chanting, the deepest Mour.

*

People seeking asylum in Australia were brought to offshore detention camps and stranded there so a single message could be amplified through their bodies: there is no sanctuary by sea. Bodies do not need to be dead to be made discursive.

But how to render such bodies otherwise unintelligible, so they do not broadcast unsanctioned messages, like the suffering of innocents?

One way is to control the amount, quality and delivery of food. Setting in motion conditions that lead to hunger – this does not leave bruises or open injuries like a fist or stick. You could lie about people being able to make a choice. Few people outside prison camps understand hunger as violent; it does not land a headline.

Yet a body in the grip of starvation experiences similar things to a beating: the acute sensation of being inescapably material, feeling winded and losing words, unable to focus, filled with dread it might never end, and fundamentally alone. Whether hungry or beaten, both fix you to an ever-present present.

That is how oppressive systems function. Taking the body out of the flow of time – the basis of imprisonment – reorganizes the central *here* or null-point according to the rules of the warden (to borrow from phenomenologist Edmund Husserl).

In one of his earliest correspondences for *The Guardian* in 2016,[4] Boochani mentions that 'during the first 20 months, nobody was permitted to take even a potato out of the canteen. This rule led asylum seekers to experience extreme hunger during the long nights of Manus.'

The following year, Boochani records the dispersal of refugees from the Manus prison camp to Lorengau. A *Guardian* editor prefaces a collection of diary entries, noting that Boochani has limited access to email and electricity, that sometimes 'he is simply too hungry to file'.[5]

> The agony of extreme hunger wakes me up early in the morning ... The quality of the food served to refugees has been so poor that it is practically inedible, and what food is provided is never enough; many refugees end up going without.[6]

> Last night the refugees were in a state of absolute exhaustion, starvation and thirst ... Hunger makes everyone angry, the atmosphere is full of tension, and there is struggle and tumult.[7]

> Starvation, thirst and terror slowly but surely dominate the prison ... Bodies are weak, muscles are fatigued, spirits are weary.[8]

> For two days I have not eaten a thing and gone without sleep ... I hope to find something to eat today.[9]

Bodies drained of energy and mass, dematerialized. The related risk for people in oppressive systems is that they learn a linguistic currency where bodies hold no substance, or hold only political meanings that others have defined, which also are hollow.

As many as twenty suicides have occurred in Australian immigration detention over two decades, with hundreds of incidents of self-harm recorded for men and women.[10] Children kept on Nauru have been known to show signs of resignation syndrome. They do not eat, move nor speak. Life receding from life: bodies made inarticulate to be discursive.

The paradox is that the disempowered body holds power. No human can ever be so dehumanized as to stop being human. I think that is how inhumane systems fail; they are built on a categorical error. I am not saying that they don't achieve murderous or traumatizing ends. The evidence is that they can be successful in that. But despite the absurdities manufactured to control bodies – the reduction from names to numbers, the regimentation around food and time, the absence of privacy, the farce of process under a policy of abandonment – something remains unassailable.

In the contest between absurdity and meaninglessness, Boochani relied in part on nature, an exercise of choice in a setting where the senses are otherwise held hostage by others. His attentiveness to the environment was of course first shaped by the landscapes of his birth, as evoked in the poem 'Our Mothers':

> I heard the Seymareh river crying with them . . .
> I heard all the beautiful mountains in Kurdistan are crying. All of Sirwan is crying. Mountain, rivers, wild flowers . . . all crying . . .
> When I was in Kurdistan, I climbed up the highest mountain on many occasions. The oldest chestnut oak trees reside up there. I hear the chestnut oaks crying too.

The attentiveness surfaces in *No Friend but the Mountains*, in an aesthetic contrast that testifies to forced exile: 'the sound of the jungle',[11] 'the haunting music of the waves',[12] 'the pungent smell of the ocean',[13] 'the tender sand'.[14]

'Nature is oblivious to our motive and history,' I wrote in another essay.[15] 'It asks nothing. It takes nothing. The forest receives us as we are; as do the rivers, the shores, the mountains and the plains. To be received as we are – the heart of a refugee.' The title of the essay: Love in a time of apocalypse.

To be a politicized body is to feel that you never belong entirely to yourself. But to catch the scent of blossoms – this can feel like your body being returned to you; the senses reinstating an organic nature in someone made an object, inert.

The central *here* disassembled by mechanics of control finds ways to click into place: at the sight of stars, under swaying leaves, in proximity to other animals. For those who have been alienated from their body or suffer in it, it can feel like reprieve. It offers insight into the most consistent approximation for our relationship with nature: 'Mother'. There is where we feel at home in our body.

For all the machinations involved in converting persons into objects, the body retains and signals unsanctioned meanings. I'm trying to figure out why this should be the case.

Perhaps it is because even the systems that oppress us do not have a monopoly on meaning. Our bodies mean something to us; immersed in nature we experience it in a way that denies – defies – objectification. Our bodies also mean something to our friends and children, and of course our mothers or those who have mothered us.

I think in particular about the way mothers re-sanctify what has been desecrated: their grief, memory and protest asserting the dignity and worth of the embodied person. In this light, mothering becomes a mode for dismantling oppressive systems, one that is open for everyone to enact.

Part Seven

2018 (August)–2019 (April) – Manus Prison Theory

Creating a Body of Knowledge

The Queensland Corner found that the death of Hamid Khazaei in Manus could have been prevented if he was transferred to Australia sooner for medical treatment. Behrouz Boochani won the 2018 Anna Politkovskaya award for journalism at the Internazionale a Ferrara Festival, Italy. *No Friend but the Mountains: Writing from Manus Prison* was published in Australia, on 31 July 2018. Boochani was appointed non-resident Visiting Scholar at the Sydney Asia Pacific Migration Centre (SAPMiC), University of Sydney. Médecins Sans Frontières (Doctors Without Borders) were forced to end their work and leave Nauru in October 2018. Boochani won the 2019 Victorian Prize for Literature in addition to the 2019 Victorian Premier's Prize for Nonfiction. Manusian man Poruan (Sam) Malai, who was featured in *Chauka, Please Tell Us the Time* and collaborated during filming, dies in Manus due to lack of medical treatment. All the children incarcerated in Nauru were evacuated to Australia with the last child leaving on 3 February 2019. The Medevac Bill passed, allowing refugees in urgent need of medical care to go to Australia for treatment. It became law on 1 March 2019. Scott Morrison reopened Christmas Island detention centre on 12 February 2019, only to close it again on 2 April the same year. Boochani won the Special Award at the 2019 New South Wales (NSW) Premier's Literary Awards and the 2019 Australian Book Industry Award for Nonfiction Book of the Year. Omid Tofighian received the award of Highly Commended for the Translation Prize at the 2019 NSW Premier's Literary Awards. Mahnaz Alimardanian collaborated with Boochani for her anthropology research and helped connect him with the anthropology community in Australia and internationally – the Australian Anthropological Society later established the

Behrouz Boochani Award. Tofighian was deported from PNG on his fourth attempt to visit Manus; Helen Davidson, a journalist for *The Guardian*, was travelling there at the same time and witnessed what happened. She later interviewed Boochani in Manus during her visit. In her role as journalist for *The Guardian*, she has been reporting on themes and topics pertaining to Australia's border regime, including the detention industry. Davidson was also part of *The Guardian* Nauru Files team.

Manus Prison Theory[1]

Behrouz Boochani

During these years I have witnessed the ways in which hundreds of imprisoned refugees have resisted the policy of exile and torture, how they have stood up against the political establishment from this forlorn island. However, I have also seen many people lose their lives fighting against the oppression and I have regularly encountered dozens of individuals suffering physical and psychological harm.

My book *No Friend but the Mountains* endeavours to describe life in Manus prison. Until now, nothing has been published that approaches the prison and the system that governs it in the same way – I have yet to use this approach in my journalism and other writings. Until now, I have not been successful in conveying to readers what life is like in this prison in exactly the way I want.

I do not wish here to analyse the book using principles from literary theory or aesthetics. Nor is my intention to interpret the book as a historical phenomenon or a political issue. What I wish to explore here is the extent to which the major theme of the book and its conceptual basis have an existence on the outside, in the world beyond this prison. I want to discuss the way in which Manus prison has its own life within Australia, the way in which it exists throughout Western society.

In fact, one of my main stylistic objectives in this book was to render Manus prison as a complex and twisted phenomenon and introduce a new discourse I call 'Manus Prison Theory'. In order to explain my analysis here I wish to refer to the film by renowned English director Ken Loach called *I, Daniel Blake* (2016), a remarkable film that tells the story of a 59-year-old English man who recently suffered a heart attack. From start to end, the film depicts Blake's struggle to obtain financial assistance from the government. Still recovering from his heart attack, he is deemed unfit to work and enters a twisted and complex bureaucratic system. The film ends tragically when Blake's heart stops and he dies in the bathroom of the office where he sought help.

What is extraordinary for me is that, in many ways, *I, Daniel Blake* can be interpreted as a meditation on Manus and Nauru. Blake dies in the grip of the system, exactly like the refugees on Manus and Nauru who have lost their lives under the watch of the nurses, doctors and immigration authorities.

Over the course of the film, Daniel's life becomes intertwined with that of a young woman and her two children. The family is also struggling to get financial assistance from the government. As a result of poverty and hunger, the young mother is driven to prostitution.

In *No Friend but the Mountains*, I frame events in Manus prison through the concept of the kyriarchal system – a web of intersecting oppressions (racism, sexism, colonialism, etc.) that maintains society's dominant hierarchies. This system has total control over the prison and was designed specifically with the purpose of torturing the incarcerated refugees. The twisted and extremely complex system of rules and regulations entangles the refugees – an absurd labyrinth that functions as its own cruel form of incarceration. Imprisoned refugees are absorbed into a highly mechanized system – the all-powerful kyriarchal system – and they begin to experience the deterioration of their human identities.

The process transforms prisoners' identities and reduces them to a basic numerical value. In most cases, the kyriarchal system governs the prison landscape using what I consider to be a form of implicit violence. What I mean by implicit violence here is that over time the rules and regulations wear down the prisoners' mental health – this form of violence is targeted and a form of psychological torture.

Although I describe many examples of physical violence, the most important aspect of the book is the deep examination of how one's mental health and sense of self are destroyed. In this respect, the shadow of death always hovers over our heads.

For years now the refugees suffering from different health problems have been captives of one extreme bureaucratic feature of the kyriarchal system – International Health and Medical Services (IHMS). The system has been designed to sustain itself for years so that a sick prisoner in need of health services must wait in excruciatingly long queues, he must fill out request forms every day, he must hang on to delusional hopes ... he must live in this prison with the absurdity of it all.

As a major element in the kyriarchal system, IHMS has entrapped refugees inside a maze of paperwork for years and subjected them to rules and regulations of micro-control and macro-control. Ultimately, a sick refugee can do nothing other than search for his name on waiting lists. But no one ever receives medical care. In fact, this is all very well planned and after persevering through countless troubles and stressful situations the refugee experiences the full force of this perverse form of torture.

In a scene from *I, Daniel Blake*, Blake's young friend responds to his efforts to seek assistance from the state by saying: 'Dan, they'll fuck you around – I'm warning you. Make it as miserable as possible. No accident, that's the plan.'

Blake answers: 'Well, they've picked the wrong one if they think I'm gonna give up. I'm like a dog with a bone me, son.'

This is exactly what has occurred on Manus and Nauru over the years. The system in these prisons has been created so that incarcerated refugees experience an unbearable amount of pressure, reach the point of hopelessness, and finally decide to return to their country of origin.

What is happening on Manus and Nauru – the reality I have tried to reveal in my work – is the exact same system that functions in hospitals, schools, universities and other institutional structures in the outside world.

What takes place in the prisons on Manus and Nauru is, in fact, the perfect manifestation of a system that strips human beings of their personhood and autonomy.

For years now, I have been gazing over at Australia from here on Manus Island and it is clear to me that, day by day, the vulnerable in society are being stripped of their identities by merciless structures, their humanity stolen by the kyriarchal system. I see the most vulnerable in society become invisible in this system. However, I must mention one crucial point here, and that is that these people are living, breathing human beings and are significant parts of society – it is impossible to completely erase them.

Both in the film *I, Daniel Blake* and in Manus prison, the system has been designed so that humans treat each other with enmity – without mercy – regardless of social status and cultural background. They become robots or machines and are trained to act as such at all times. They become indifferent to the pain of their fellow human beings.

When the protagonist of the film, Blake, dies he leaves behind a letter that his friend reads at his church service. The same friend, the woman with two small children, who has also been victim to this system. Blake writes:

> I am not a client, a customer, nor a service user. I am not a shirker, a scrounger, a beggar, nor a thief. I'm not a National Insurance Number or blip on a screen. I paid my dues, never a penny short, and proud to do so. I don't tug the forelock but look my neighbour in the eye and help him if I can. I don't accept or seek charity. My name is Daniel Blake. I am a man, not a dog. As such, I demand my rights. I demand you treat me with respect. I, Daniel Blake, am a citizen, nothing more and nothing less.

It is striking when you compare this tragic story with those who have lost their lives in the prisons on Manus and Nauru; the similarities are uncanny. Faysal Ishak Ahmed was a Sudanese refugee imprisoned on Manus Island who lost his life because of a heart problem. He left behind many letters indicating that, until his final moments, no one paid any attention to his pleas – none of the authorities cared enough about this human being, no one cared that he was a person deserving of respect.

In his letters we read that Faysal tried over and over again to persuade IHMS that he is 'a human being who is sick and not a number, a human being who really has a heart problem'. In his unanswered letters, he wrote in Arabic: 'I swear I'm sick and I need medical treatment.' Just like Daniel Blake, Faysal died within the grip of a system that ignored him and his humanity until his last moments. Like Hamid Khazaei, who died while the nurses looked over him. And Salim, a Rohingya refugee, and Fariborz, an Iranian refugee.

In all these cases, each person had their name on the waiting lists for years, constantly anticipating treatment. Each wrote letter after letter urging the kyriarchal system to process their requests.

The soul of Manus prison and the system that created and governs Manus prison is in the process of replicating itself throughout Australian society, reproducing itself in unlimited numbers. This is the merciless system that takes humans as captives and subjects them to rules and regulations of micro-control and macro-control, a system that takes their human identities. I wish to conclude on this last point and ask that you reflect on this reality.

Australia Needs a Moral Revolution[1]

Behrouz Boochani

Five years ago, on a boiling hot day, Australian Immigration Minister, Scott Morrison, entered Manus Prison. A number of refugees who represented various groups were invited to meet with him. In that meeting, the refugee representatives found themselves being threatened – Morrison pointed his finger at them and yelled: 'You have no chance of coming to Australia and you must return to your countries.' I depict this exact scene and its aftermath in my book *No Friend but the Mountains: Writing from Manus Prison*.

It was a time when few people had heard of the prisons on Manus Island and Nauru. The refugees felt isolated and forgotten, the refugees felt extreme pressure. It was in this context that the refugees were confronted with that single threatening line by Morrison. That sentence conjured up a wave of hopelessness, so much so that a few people attempted suicide.

His despicable behaviour was also subject to serious criticism from the prison authorities. For days the situation was out of control. Actually, the circumstances created by this event eventually led to a riot in February 2014 – it led to the killing of Reza Barati. It also resulted in hundreds of refugees suffering serious injuries.

In fact, Morrison has been accused of playing a crucial role in inciting this riot. Even the guards were critical of him in this respect. Then on the day that Reza Barati was killed Morrison appeared on TV and lied by saying that Reza was killed outside the prison. But after a few days he was forced to admit he was wrong. After Reza's death Hamid Khazaei lost his life due to a very basic infection. Just one month ago the Queensland coroner found that Hamid's death was totally preventable.

It is clear that Morrison – the man who is now prime minister of Australia – has been instrumental in establishing a system that is responsible for the deaths of 12 human beings. He is a merciless individual. During a week of chaos in the political sphere which resulted in a change of prime minister, many Australians who did not have a good impression of Peter Dutton breathed a sigh of relief when Morrison was chosen as leader. The general perception is that Morrison has a more moderate approach compared to Dutton.

We can learn a lot from this fundamental error; this error may also impact the upcoming elections. Morrison is in no way a moderate figure. The biggest difference between him and Dutton is that the latter is an example of a new kind of Western politician who has no fear of being seen as a bad person. However, Morrison is a demagogue who tries to present himself to society as a moderate politician.

During the past five years the refugees incarcerated on Manus Island and Nauru have witnessed many shifts in Australian politics. We have experienced four prime ministers and two federal elections. But, ultimately, our situation has remained unchanged. We have hit a dreadful dead end. What I mean is that both major political parties in Australia are in competition to see who will be successful in totally destroying us. Replacing one individual will never transform our situation; it makes no difference whether the prime minister is Peter Dutton or Scott Morrison – or anyone else for that matter. What is clear is that we continue to be trapped on these two islands and Australia does not have the moral courage or political will to make the necessary changes to its policy of exiling refugees.

A deep analysis of the policy used to exile refugees reveals how Australian's sociopolitical culture has led to the creation of these island detention centres. This pertains to every aspect of Australian political and social life; that is, the failures of its civil society. During these years many advocates in the media, politics, academia and Australian civil society have criticized the barbaric policies of the government – they have worked to combat the policy used to exile innocent refugees. However, history will remember the mainstream sociopolitical culture of Australia during this period as an embarrassing phase in Australia's history that will plague generations to come. The point I wish to make here is that the prisons on Manus Island and Nauru are the logical consequence of Australia's kyriarchal system.

These two prisons are an extension of Australia; they are an integral part of the state and this connection cannot be denied. One must investigate the origins of Australian society and politics in order to realize the extent to which Manus Prison is the logical consequence and product of Australia's education system, its cultural scene and political developments.

Australia needs to instil humanitarian principles within its centres of power.

Manus Prison is the creation of Australia; however, it has also impacted the nation by, in turn, recreating significant aspects of Australia. I refer to this critical analysis as the Manus Prison Theory. Perhaps Australian analysts do not pay sufficient attention to the situation on Manus Island and Nauru and do not consider it to be such a vital issue. But it is clear that the ideology that has given rise to the prison is profoundly rooted in Australia's political system. Regardless of whether one accepts this or not, Manus Prison is having a destructive effect on Australia's political culture.

No one can ignore the relevance of Manus Prison Theory. With the passing of time this theoretical approach will become increasingly more salient. Basically, how can a nation look to the future when its leaders cage little children for years, in a remote and forlorn prison? What future does a nation have when those same leaders take selfies with little children as part of their PR campaigns? Are these leaders not demagogues?

Australia needs a serious wake up call. Australia needs to instil humanitarian principles within its centres of power. Australia needs to think very seriously about the value of life and what constitutes a democratic and humane society. More than anything else, Australia needs a new ethical vision and love. Australia needs a moral revolution to escape this dead end.

Two thousand people have been incarcerated, but there are other things at stake here for Australia: human virtues, freedom, the sense of what it really means to be human . . . and love. These qualities have also been incarcerated. This is exactly what is absent today from Australia's political culture. How can one expect a nation that has suppressed these qualities to promote educated, wise and respectable people to leadership positions?

In this morally bankrupt political climate people who aim for the highest qualities of humanity find themselves in situations where they have to choose between either bad or worse. What we have here is not only a political quandary resulting from a discredited and scandalous political system, we also witness a profound moral quagmire.

Australia has to ask itself the difficult question about where it is heading, and reflect on this stage in its political and cultural history. It needs to question why it has a leader who is toying with far-right ideologies but who is interpreted by many as being a moderate politician.

What has happened to the nation? Why has it reached this point? Why must Australians feel that they have no choice but to choose between bad and worse? As someone who has been gazing over at the political landscape in Australia for more than five years from Manus Island, I ask myself sometimes: where is Australia heading?

Five Years in Manus Purgatory[1]

Behrouz Boochani

Two months ago, the refugees on Manus Island and Nauru experienced the fifth anniversary of exile and incarceration. It was like a sledgehammer, reminding them of the painfully long and tortuous period they have had to endure.

It seems this anniversary reminded everyone how many opportunities they have lost, the extent to which they have lost their freedom, how many dreams and hopes have been crushed. The people who have been separated from their children all these years suddenly realized how much their children must have grown. The milestone conjured up a profound longing that can tip anyone over the edge, and the younger people among us realized how far away they really were from their hopes and dreams.

It was for these reasons that during the past two months the mental health situation has become dire on Manus Island.

It is perhaps hard for people who have not spent time in prison to fathom how a prisoner's sense of time is different from other people's. Sometimes prisoners forget how long they have been locked up. The reality of being forced to live in a tightly confined space with a large number of humans for a long period of time, being forced to see the same people every day, every night . . . This harsh reality disrupts and distorts one's sense of time. This reality propels you into the realm of the surreal. It only takes one event to remind you how long you have been forced to live in purgatory.

It is not my intention to discuss the private lives of refugees here on Manus – it is enough to know that every single person's life here is a tragedy. But my aim in this article is to provide a report of the past two months, during which a number of terrible incidents have taken place on the island. This report only applies to Manus Island. The refugees on Nauru are experiencing a different humanitarian crisis, which involves more than 100 incarcerated children.

Shahed is a young man who fled Iraq to escape the dangers of war. I have known him for more than five years. He is a brave man who arrived on the same boat as me. The bond created by travelling together on that boat carries the same meaning as the connection some have with those from the same city or neighbourhood. You can empathize with one another's pain and trauma on a profound level.

The presence of strong individuals such as Shahed on Manus is always a source of solace for those around them. Engaging with people such as him evokes a feeling of strength regardless of the affliction and torment.

But the prison is ever so merciless.

On many occasions the prison debilitates people like Shahed, leaving them utterly hopeless. It crushes and drives them to collapse. He was pushed to this point all of a sudden; he did not leave his room for a month and suffered from severe depression. He did not eat for a 10-day period. It was not as if he was on a hunger strike. No. He could not bring himself to eat. At the end of August, he poured petrol over himself, so he could self-immolate. But the other refugees held him back. Shahed is a person who has been totally destroyed. He is totally depressed. He is not the same strong Shahed we once knew, the one who retained his hopes and dreams.

Rasil is an Iranian refugee who also suddenly experienced a rapid psychological decline. He harmed himself and for more than a month now he has not been able to move his arm properly. With the current situation the way it is he will be disabled from now on. The court ordered immigration to transfer him to Port Moresby, and he was there for a few weeks, but he was returned to Manus without receiving treatment. For the past week, he has been held in a tiny room in the police station for quarantine reasons. He is suffering alone.

At time of writing, another refugee from Hillside Camp who tried to take his own life was taken to a quarantine cell in the police station by the guards. Both he and Rasil are now held in isolation.

These problems came after yet another incident last week, which involved a young Iranian refugee named Ben. Early in the morning, as the refugees were getting up to have breakfast, they were confronted by a terrifying sight. A noose and rope were set up in the middle of West Haus Camp. The noose was around Ben's neck. The other refugees immediately brought him down. After being hospitalized for a few days, Ben was transferred to Port Moresby.

What is interesting here on Manus is that Immigration and others in charge of the system do not spend one second interacting with the patients. Some refugees end up becoming prisoners right there in the isolation cells, others are set free to leave on their own, others are transferred to Port Moresby. The system is always opaque, riddled with selective treatment and games for which no one can ever work out the rules.

Hussein is a 25-year-old refugee. He was exiled to Manus when he was just 19 years old. During all these years he has been grappling with mental health issues and trying to cope by taking all kinds of psychiatric pills. He says that from 2015, he has been using them every day in order to tolerate this situation in detention, and to get some sleep at night. In the first week of September, Hussein harmed himself. He was taken to hospital where he received some dressings for the wounds. The next day he wounded himself again, only deeper this time. He is just one example of a young guy here who is in the prime of his life but feels that he has lost everything.

Perhaps the most distressing incident in the past two months involved a man, about 45 years old, who swallowed material to injure himself. After a few hours, he swallowed more. The day after this incident he was in the bathroom of the hospital and cut his head in a number of places. For some hours he refused to allow the nurses to stitch up his wounds. I have known this man for years – he is a stateless Kurd, meaning that he is not recognized as a citizen of any nation. For years, he has been suffering from various physical ailments. For years he has been refused proper treatment and has been a captive of the tortuous bureaucratic systems designed by International Health and Medical Services, the Department of Home Affairs and PIH (the Pacific International Hospital in Port Moresby). He has two sons, aged 8 and 12.

In the second half of September, Dr Nilanthi Kanapathipillai from Central Gippsland Health in Victoria visited Manus for one week and met with many of the refugees. I asked her about the current situation and she explained:

> Mental health is a significant, if not the largest, health concern here amongst previously well men aged 22–54 … Problems range from major [reactive] depression, depression with psychotic features, significant and untreated PTSD [Post-Traumatic Stress Disorder] and outright psychosis … The escalation in the rates of self-harm and suicide attempts over the past few months is reflective of not only the desperate need for a voice, but the total inadequacy of psychiatric care provided to the vulnerable … It's disgraceful.

The situation for the refugees on Manus has become extremely dangerous. If this continues in the same way there is no doubt more people will die. Over the past years, four people have died from suicide alone – all clear examples of men who were isolated and left alone to deal with the pain and suffering of purgatory. Clearly, there are still men here with deteriorating mental health and on the verge of collapse, and they are affecting everyone else around them who are also battling to cope.

‘Sam could have been saved’

Where Does the Money for Healthcare go on Manus?[1]

Behrouz Boochani

Sam was a Baluan man of Manus province, living on Manus Island. He was thin and muscular with a warm smile and acute observations. I had known him for over a year. Like most Manusians he had a deep love for Manus, its islands, waters and its people. Sam was a man who objected to the way Australia treated refugees; he often expressed his solidarity with the refugees. He had special insight about the history of Manus, and if you ever had the opportunity to listen to him he would share his knowledge for hours about music, nature and culture.

A strong friendship developed between us and to be in his presence was always a pleasant experience. For this reason, when I wanted to make the film *Chauka, Please Tell Us the Time*, I sought his help. Sam had a significant role in the making of this film and we discussed for hours the history and culture of Manus. During the filming Sam criticized Australia from a Manusian perspective for its colonial politics and treatment of refugees. He also stood up for the dignity of his people.

One day, I made plans to see Sam at his place but when I arrived, I only saw his niece who was smoking outside. She said: ‘Sam had heart pains a few days ago and died.’ It was one of the most painful moments during my time on Manus Island. This feeling was the same as the pain I felt every time a refugee died on this island of medical neglect. His niece explained: ‘Sam could have been saved. The GP said that had he encountered this pain anywhere else other than Manus he could have been treated with ease.’ The problem was that he was extremely poor and it was not easy for him to travel to Port Moresby. Sam’s tragic death made me contemplate. I still think of his wonderful laugh and kindness, I think about his life, I think about his untimely death . . . these things will always remain with me.

Today, the hospital on Manus Island looks more like a ruin about to crumble.

Over and over again, incidents such as this one have occurred through the years we have been imprisoned here. The people on Manus have died even though hundreds of millions of dollars have been paid to companies who are assigned to run the prison camp. According to the agreement between PNG and Australia the main road of Manus must be repaired, a police station must be built and the hospital on the island must be adequately equipped. But after years the hospital has fallen into disrepair. A few months ago, the roof of the primary school was destroyed by a storm and the school requested assistance from the community. But no one had the capacity to help rebuild the school. For months the children had to attend their lessons within a hazardous zone and under the rain. The condition of the hospital is getting worse by the day.

Dr Nilanthi Kanapathipillai from Central Gippsland Health in Victoria recently inspected the island's medical facilities. She told me,

> The clinic is totally ill-equipped to deal with medical and surgical emergencies such as an acute myocardial infarction or diabetic ketoacidosis or severe sepsis warranting intravenous antibiotics. Emergency acute surgical procedures such as appendectomy cannot be reliably performed here. Radiology facilities are inadequate with no CT scanner. Sterility is questionable and hence local procedures such as simple lancing of abscesses are unable to be performed without risking further sepsis.

She went on to say,

> There are enormous delays to accessing appropriate medical care [for refugees] through this bizarre triage system involving application to the nurse first. Basic asthma medication and oral hypoglycaemics or even blood glucose strips to access glycaemic control is totally unavailable. I was shocked to see a 28-year-old with persistent untreated hypoglycaemia for weeks, no basic education of patients with chronic illness such as diabetes; orthopedic injuries were startling . . . left unreduced and untreated for years; ophthalmology reviews should be easily accessible but I have seen to date significant deterioration in at least two men who have been waiting for an ophthalmology review for at least three years. There is a specialist ophthalmologist on the island, and has been for years!

Kanapathipillai continues listing the conditions she observed, repeating, 'I am still shocked.'

Pacific International Hospital (PIH) in Port Moresby is the hospital that has been contracted to provide medical services to refugees on Manus Island. As Kanapathipillai noted: 'PIH is a huge tertiary referral centre with all the facilities available.' Yet, she continues: 'Late transfers and unequal access to the same gold standard medical and surgical care towards refugees even whilst in PIH was palpably noticeable even from an outside perspective'

In January, the Australian Federal Government refused an order from the Senate to release documents on the health, construction and security services for refugees on Manus Island. The Home Affairs Minister, Peter Dutton, refused the request, telling the Senate: 'I believe the disclosure of the requested material would, or could reasonably be expected to, cause damage to international relations: specifically, Australia's relations with Papua New Guinea.'

We know very little about the payments, obligations and terms of contracts signed by the Australian Government with companies such as Paladin, JDA Wokman, Toll Group, NKW and International Health and Medical Services (IHMS), all involved in the offshore immigration regime. In January, the *Guardian* pointed out that the security firm Paladin Solutions was being paid $72 million for providing security on Manus Island for four months with the contract extended an extra month even though a local security firm had kicked the Paladin workers off the island.

What is most interesting here is that Australia has signed a contract with PIH for them to provide medical services to refugees, yet their clinic is made up of just a few small rooms. They seem to do little but give sick refugees some paracetamol, afterward referring patients to the general hospital, which is unequipped and decrepit. But as the condition of the PIH clinic is even worse than the general hospital, the refugees are forced to go to the hospital. The contracts are probably worth hundreds of millions of dollars and are given to companies working on Manus Island. Where does all this money go? A fraction of it could have been spent and equipped the island's hospital or built a school for the children of Manus Island.

What seems clear is that the Australian Government does not care about what happens to the local people. Sam used to speak of how the lack of Australia's investment in schools and health was a part of the colonial project: 'If many of us get education, have a good hospital, then we will become bigger. Australia wants to control us.' Today, the hospital on Manus Island looks more like a ruin about to crumble. At the hospital the local workers are extremely kind and show empathy with the refugees. However, hierarchies of power make it impossible for Manusians or anyone else to provide adequate care. No matter how many deaths have occurred on Manus, Sam's death feels the most tragic to me. He did not receive the support he needed and lost his life from something so simple. The hospital is a wreck of a place where companies make hundreds of millions every year. This place embodies the essence of discrimination.

The Paladin Scandal is Only a Drop in the Ocean of Corruption on Manus and Nauru[1]

Behrouz Boochani

Recently, the Paladin controversy has dominated political discussions. The company was contracted to provide security for the refugees detained on Manus Island. The questions at the centre of this debate relate to the conditions under which this contract was made and the ways in which the agreed $423 million were spent.

However, all the focus of the media has been directed only at this one company, simply questioning the figure in the contract. For years I have been scrutinizing the security companies and medical service providers on Manus. I question why this critical approach to Paladin has only been taken up now and why it is exclusive to one company. The Paladin scandal is only one small part of this issue – hundreds of millions of dollars have been wasted in the detention centres on Manus and Nauru during these years.

There are many companies operating on Manus. Firstly, there is the security company G4S that worked on Manus for a six-month period and then left the island after the riot of February 2014 during which Reza Barati was killed. The Australian Senate inquiry concluded that the company could have managed the riot, and the death and injuries should not have occurred. In relation to Barati's death, there are two individuals who allegedly contributed to this crime – they were guards who are citizens of Australia and New Zealand. They have never faced trial. We need to seriously consider the role of this company in addition to that of the Salvation Army which had the responsibility of providing welfare services inside the prison camp.

After the departure of G4S and the Salvation Army a contract was made with Transfield to replace them. This company changed its name to Broadspectrum, obviously in order to save their reputation and avoid being seen as a company that once managed the Manus Island prison camp. Transfield (Broadspectrum) had the responsibility to provide food and other welfare services in the prison; however, they also operated in minor ways with the company Wilson.

Wilson took over the same responsibilities that were previously supposed to be carried out by G4S. The company had a major role in suppressing the hunger strike involving 800 refugees during January 2015. And Wilson guards allegedly drugged and raped a Papua New Guinean woman in the same year.

In November 2017, Broadspectrum and Wilson left Manus Island. Their departure was at the beginning of the 23-day siege which left refugees without water and food. The vacant contracts were practically all local. The largest contract was given to Paladin.

Paladin pocketed a handsome $423 million. But it has been claimed that they do not fulfil any duties other than employ 500 locals who assert to be underpaid, with no risk allowances added to the rates of $2–$3 an hour, or overtime paid for shifts of up to 12 hours. The locals either play cards under the tents inside the prison camp or sit in groups of 10 in front of the prison gates while checking the coming and going of refugees.

On Manus Island the police have a duty to ensure the safety of refugees when they are in Lorengau town – Paladin have nothing to do with that.

In recent days when the Paladin contract scandal broke, the locals became extremely angry. During the last year, the local staff wrote numerous letters to Paladin complaining about their low wages, and they also protested. They tried to pressure Paladin into increasing their salaries to a decent rate.

A series of smaller companies such as JDA, Kingfisher and KNW also work within the Manus Island detention industry. They only occupy very specific responsibilities such as transportation and providing food.

However, from all the companies working on Manus during these years it is International Health and Medical Services (IHMS) that has the worst record. This company played a central role in the death of Hamid Khazaei and a few others who were killed over the years. This medical services company has been operating on Manus for four and a half years – throughout this time a number of refugees have lost their lives due to medical neglect. They have a series of rooms at their disposal from which they issue painkillers to dozens of sick refugees, or their psychologists prescribe sleeping tablets and medicine for psychological conditions. IHMS still operates on Nauru.

PIH is a medical services company that took over from IHMS in November 2017. I have already detailed how they play with the health of refugees. They employ the same approach that IHMS had been implementing for years. Their strategy involves nothing more than issuing painkillers and referring refugees mainly to the public hospital in Lorengau – which is just a decrepit building with no real use.

The hospital is closed one day a week and during the days it is open it only operates until 4 p.m. and refuses emergency cases after this time. The PIH site does not have the most rudimentary of medical facilities, and they do not have the capability to perform the most basic surgery.

During these years the Australian Government has always used propaganda to influence public opinion and prove that they have been providing refugees with welfare and medical services. However, what they portray in the media is in stark contrast with the reality on Manus and Nauru. The most convincing evidence we can use to justify this accusation is the deaths of 12 individuals. The only things these companies have achieved during these years has been to assist immigration in torturing refugees psychologically and emotionally. They have not only withheld services from refugees but have in fact been a significant element in a system aimed at stripping people of their humanity and afflicting suffering.

The Paladin scandal is only a drop in the ocean of corruption. The bigger picture has yet to be exposed. If there is an independent and comprehensive investigation into these companies in future we may very well witness on of the greatest scandals in Australia's history.

Every company working on Manus and Nauru throughout these years have been instruments of oppression and subjugation for the Department of Immigration. What needs to be investigated is not only the financial agreements with companies and the manner of spending taxpayer's dollars, but also the many obvious human rights violations. What is clear is that when a political institution acts covertly on a remote island they create the conditions for corruption and human rights abuses.

The 'Papua New Guinea Solution' in Australian Public Discourse and Human Rights Activism

Mahnaz Alimardanian

In October 2017, weekly rallies were organized by independent Australian political and human rights activists in support of refugees on Manus Island. Rallies took place during 23 days of collective resistance by the refugees against being transported to three new camps after four years of imprisonment in Lombrum Naval Base, or 'Manus Prison'.[1] At one rally in Melbourne, the crowd marched along the streets of the central business district (CBD) when three young people from Papua New Guinea, who happened to be visiting the city, walked out of a shopping centre. I saw the unease in their eyes as they encountered colourful placards demanding the refugees' immediate evacuation from Manus Island, drawing me away from the crowd and towards their direction. Our brief chat – in the middle of the mayhem created by heavy police presence and a crowd of right-wing extremists that were attacking demonstrators – reminded me of the challenges the Manusian host community had faced since 2013. The re-activation of the Australian Government's so-called Pacific Solution (2001–8) and the Regional Resettlement Arrangement (RRA), colloquially known as the 'Papua New Guinea Solution' meant their homeland was being used as a site of refugee incarceration.

At the time, Australian public opinion was significantly influenced by the dominant political discourse which emphasized border security and regional cooperation to combat people smuggling. Absent from debate was the perspective of the local community, who in Melbourne now faced the realities of their country's participation in refugee resettlement and detainment. Occasionally, the Manusian community's perspective on resettlement was incorporated into critical legal and social analysis, with news media pointing out the problematic nature of the arrangement, referring to its colonial heritage, and the reality of hosting the carceral-industrial complex.[2] Yet, when the dominant theme of the public discussions in Australia was not swinging like a pendulum from pro- to anti-refugee debates, discussions focused on how the island was unsafe for refugees. Likewise, for human rights activists invested in the lived experience of detainment and the success of campaigns such as 'No Business in Abuse' (NBIA),[3] the focus was not on Manus Island but on mobilizing resources to discourage the involvement of industries in incarceration on Manus Island. Therefore, local perspectives did not find an adequate place in Australia's public discourse nor in activist dialogues, regardless of reports and analyses on the human impact of the arrangement on Manusian society. This includes taking into consideration the effects on the economy and governance, social order, wellbeing and equity.[4]

In this absence, Behrouz Boochani, as the only journalist witnessing and reporting directly from inside 'Manus Prison,' turned his journalistic gaze from inhumane living conditions and the resistance of refugees against misrepresentation and mistreatment toward the local community and the socio-political disadvantages they experience. In 'An Island off Manus', Boochani gives his readers a new account of Manus, visiting Mendirlin Island, one of the over two hundred islands in the province. Boochani is invited to the island by a family known to the refugees for their generosity and friendship. He writes about the family's empathy for the refugees alongside their aspirations for Manus Island and its tourism industry. In this and another article, 'Sam Could Have Been Saved' (2018), Boochani writes about local island life. Referring to the history of the colonial intervention and occupations of the island during two world wars, he points to a range of issues – from rising sea levels and environmental pollution to the absence of adequate infrastructure, roads, schools, and hospital medical equipment. He questions what the agreement between Australia and Papua New Guinea entailed, and what was provided to the Manusian people in return for hosting the carceral-industrial complex on their shores.

This question seems more critical considering the RRA was introduced to Manus Island in conjunction with Australian development aid to Papua New Guinea. The quality and rollout of the program and associated development projects were criticized over the years. The management of contracts and the allegations of corruption, particularly among transnational corporations charged with overseeing and servicing detention sites, were placed under heavy scrutiny ultimately affecting both refugees and local employees working there.[5] The type of development the agreement brought to Manus is what I name 'dark development'.[6] Dark development is a product of extrajudicial and extraterritorial arrangements creating concealed management 'bubbles' across and in between separate jurisdictions and state governance systems. Such arrangements free all involved parties, including financial investors and transnational corporations, from reasonable liabilities and proper accountability. In his article 'The Paladin scandal is only a drop in the ocean of corruption on Manus and Nauru' (2019), Boochani refers to alleged corruption in each of the companies involved in this arrangement, and he questions why this topic only receives limited attention from the Australian public and activists.

Clearly, at the time, Australians' attention was fixated on the life-and-death tragedies playing out at sea through people smuggling, and human rights activism was concentrated on resolving the ongoing humanitarian crisis on the island. Therefore, no one pieced together the fragmentary narratives of harm brought about by the carceral-industrial complex to present a full picture of the human impact of this arrangement. Consequently, the importance of bringing local voices and perspectives into media and human rights debates was overlooked. In the case of the 'Papua New Guinea Solution', the common opposition of both refugees and locals to the arrangement provided powerful ground for demanding systemic change and social justice. Their objections also embedded a shared experience of exclusion and exploitation, impacting mostly indigenous, marginalzed or disadvantaged groups.

These specific commonalities not only echoed a collective voice coming out of Manus but linked indigenous perspectives across the borders between Papua New Guinea and Australia, with people in both countries finding common ground in government-imposed displacement. Indeed, the struggle for self-determination and protection of communities' rights and interests, particularly in relation to development projects, land rights and the protection of cultural heritage, are familiar issues to First Nation Peoples of Australia.[7]

Surely human rights activists could have invested more energy into highlighting the call of these collective voices and connections by providing platforms for them in the demonstrations and protests they organized. If they had, rallies could have been more welcoming space for those three young people visiting from Papua New Guinea in October 2017 and many others by presenting a dynamic and richer picture of the situation on Manus Island. Finally, a focus on the collective voice of the refugees and the Manusian community in the context of the Papua New Guinea Solution and the RRA could have opened new horizons for dialogue and alliances, raised Australian public awareness further and mobilized people to political action more effectively than was achieved at the time.

Australian Corruption and the Pacific

Dollars, Displacement and Deaths

Helen Davidson

Five years into his detention, and three or four years into working together, Behrouz Boochani and I finally met in person in 2019 in Lorengau, the largest town of the Manus archipelago.

A few hours earlier I'd stepped off the plane at the tiny wire-fenced airstrip with a small party of Australians but without Omid Tofighian. It would have been his fourth trip to Manus but his activities on the third had led to his being blacklisted, and so he'd been pinged on arrival at immigration in Port Moresby and deported back to Brisbane. Arriving on Manus without Tofighian's experience and knowledge of the place was daunting. I was jumpy in the stifling humid air, especially when I saw a group of Mobile Brigade officers hanging by the 4WDs parked at the entrance. But it turned out they were just there to pick up a friend.

That night at Lorengau's Harbourside hotel – the go-to accommodation for journalists, lawyers, activists, and friends visiting the refugees in what used to be an undisturbed and traditional island community – we drank local SP beer and Boochani and I caught up as colleagues. It felt like we were making up for all the harried and impersonal WhatsApp messages about news, violence, commissions, life and death over the years. There were even jokes.

I'd planned to stay only a couple of days. My camera and I would stand out in Lorengau, and I had interviews scheduled in Port Moresby I couldn't miss. I didn't want to be picked up and sent off to follow Tofighian without getting to them. And so we rushed through what felt like a pantomime of clandestine reporting – interviewing officials in cars parked behind shipping containers, while the rain poured outside; sitting in hotel rooms with curtains drawn after arriving by different routes, or under timber huts hidden in the mosquito-filled jungle.

By mid-2019, there was no formal detention centre, at least not officially, and the refugees, long displaced from their old homes, were largely free to walk around their new one. Mostly they stayed inside the new accommodation blocks. Still heavily fenced off and guarded by paranoid security, surrounded by jungle, they were not so materially different from the previous centre, what Behrouz called the Manus Prison. An attempt by Boochani to blag our car past the gate failed.

As well as meeting the detainees I had gotten to know over the years, I also wanted to use the opportunity of being on the ground to report the impact Australia's policy had had on Manusians.

Walking around Lorengau the community appeared used to the new neighbours (and their frequent visitors) but many were clearly sick of the intrusion. As I wrote in one story[1] we eventually published from the trip, no one had asked them about what they called the 'Project'. The military and contractors just showed up one day, and the refugees soon after.[2] People were welcoming, but feared the impact on their tight-knit community, traditions and customs.

The Australian Government was paying corporations billions of dollars to establish and run its detention and 'processing' regime, but few locals felt they were benefitting. There were jobs, sure, but they were impermanent, low paid and run by sub-contractors with difficult-to-trace finance structures. I spoke to some who were happy for the work, even if it was temporary, but many others felt frustrated and powerless over what they saw as unfair, even exploitative, working conditions which mostly profited expats and corporations. In February we had reported Papua New Guinean employees at Paladin had walked off the job in protest over low pay of $2-3 an hour and poor working conditions, following sustained scrutiny of Paladin's $423 million contract with the federal government.[3]

Paladin had grabbed headlines with the cartoonish backstory of a headquarters in a shack on Kangaroo Island, contracted through a limited tender. The company was eventually paid more than $530 million to provide security for the refugees, hiring workers on wages which drew complaints and eventually protests. But as Boochani wrote for *The Guardian*, 'there were many companies operating on Manus'. JDA Wokman, G4S, Wilson Security, Toll Group, NKW, Kingfisher, International Health and Medical Services and its problematic successor Pacific International Hospital – awarded the contract through yet another limited tender[4] – contractors and subcontractors – it was a dizzying array of exorbitant government tenders, and while not all were embroiled in scandals, to the tiny town of Lorengau they were all parts of the same Project.

Tensions had boiled over into protests, land disputes, alleged arson, and violence. At least one local woman was allegedly sexually assaulted by fly-in expat workers[5] who were allowed to leave PNG before any charges could be laid. Thrown into the mix were allegations of local corruption between landowners and governments, and it left the community disenfranchized, and a little resentful.

Hopes that this genuinely beautiful place had a future in tourism had been dashed by their new, somewhat unfair, reputation as a prison island.

It was my third time in PNG, and my previous trips had mostly been investigating the country's failing health system. With the billions of dollars poured into the Manus Project, there had been expectation that the local hospital – and with it the community – would benefit. But as Boochani and I walked through the grounds, and then in and out of the open clinic rooms, it looked like any other PNG hospital I'd seen: utterly and inexcusably inadequate.

The facility was running on the memory of the smell of an oily rag. In November 2018 Boochani wrote about his Manusian friend, Poruan 'Sam' Malai, who had been an integral partner in creating the film, *Chauka, Please Tell Us the Time*. Sam had died needlessly because he could not access appropriate care. The circumstances were as common as they were tragic.

'Where does all this money go? A fraction of it could have been spent and equipped the island's hospital or built a school for the children of Manus Island.' Boochani wrote that Sam often spoke of Australia's lack of real investment in the community as an act of colonialism.[6]

'If many of us get education, have a good hospital, then we will become bigger. Australia wants to control us,' he quoted Sam saying.

Most of the infrastructure would leave Manus with the Australians, that had always been a given. But the failure to even leave behind a better health clinic was a stark reminder of who the Project benefited, and who it didn't. It was still many months before PNG would be devastated by the pandemic which Tofighian and Boochani later wrote put human beings "on a precipice", even those with good health clinics.[7]

At the end of my short trip as I sat at Lorengau airport waiting for a flight to Port Moresby, a dozen people dressed in black and religious white walked across the tarmac from an incoming plane, bringing the body of a relative home for burial. Others in the waiting room shook their heads in sadness. One man lamented: 'So many deaths here.' Another spoke of outer island communities where they were running out of space to bury people, forced to stack three bodies to a grave. Between the growing cemeteries, rising sea levels, and combined impact of the Project and government failures, I reflected that this Australian-made system had been built in response to displaced people from far away, but was now displacing Manusians.

Part Eight

2019 (May–October) – Writing to Keep Hope Alive / New Dimensions to Systematic Torture

Scott Morrison's Liberal–National Coalition government won the 2019 federal election (18 May). There was a massive increase in attempted suicide and self-harm in Manus Island after the results were announced. Behrouz Boochani was transferred to Port Moresby along with many other refugees in mid-2019. He won the 2019 National Biography Prize. Over fifty people were imprisoned in Bomana Prison in Port Moresby in August that year. The Peter McMullin Centre on Statelessness at the University of Melbourne partnered with the Australian Book Review to create the ABR Behrouz Boochani Fellowship – the first recipient was Hessom Razavi. Sayed Mirwais Rohani was driven to suicide after spending years in Manus and then transferred to the mainland for treatment on 17 October 2019. Medivac legislation was repealed on 4 December 2019 and hundreds were left stranded in hotel detention on the mainland without medical treatment. Boochani managed to escape PNG after being invited to a literary festival for his writing, especially *No Friend but the Mountains*, and he arrived in Aotearoa New Zealand from Port Moresby on 14 November 2019. He appeared at the WORD Christchurch Festival on 29 November 2019. Moones Mansoubi travelled to Christchurch to meet Boochani for the first time in person, attend his main event at the festival, and participate in a panel with him to discuss *No Friend but the Mountains*. Australian scholars of forced migration, such as Claudia Tazreiter, continued to collaborate with Boochani – she visited him in Manus before he was moved to Port Moresby. She also supported his appointment, through the Forced Migration Research Network, as Adjunct Associate Professor in Social Sciences at University of New South

Wales. Boochani was also appointed Visiting Professor at the School of Law, Birkbeck College, University of London. Upon arriving in Aotearoa New Zealand, Boochani began collaborating with New Zealand-based academics, including interdisciplinary scholars specializing on the Pacific and Indigenous knowledge such as Steven Ratuva at the University of Canterbury (where Boochani was Senior Adjunct Research Fellow – Ngāi Tahu Research Centre).

This Election is an Opportunity to Vote for Humanity and Freedom[1]

Behrouz Boochani

Christina Coombe campaigned for change until her last breath. I'm telling her story to inspire all Australians to fight against indifference.

Christina Coombe was a 56-year-old Australian woman who died last week after a long battle with cancer. Before she left this world, she attended a pro-refugee rally calling for the release of those on Manus and Nauru. She also visited an art exhibition in Melbourne which showcased the work of Farhad Bandesh, an artist still on Manus. Also, just a few days before she passed away she cast her vote for the federal election and supported a candidate who opposes the policy of exiling and imprisoning refugees.

Christina was a woman who for years resisted the inhumane and merciless political program of consecutive governments; she actively resisted the policy that exiles and imprisons refugees on Manus and Nauru. Her political participation was not limited to fighting for refugees; she also tried to play a significant role in important social campaigns such as climate change action.

I have known Christina since 2017 when the Australian Government withheld food and water from us for 23 days before transferring us to new camps in Lorengau town. During those days, many refugees were extremely traumatized because the local police beat most of us. One of the people they physically attacked was a young musician named Moz. I remember he suffered intense mental anguish and his hands would not stop trembling. During that crisis it was Christina who communicated with him to offer support. Every day she would talk to him for hours by phone and comfort him; she treated him as a human being, a friend, a family member . . . an equal.

Christina Coombe at a rally.

Christina committed herself wholeheartedly to the resistance of the refugees stuck in Manus, the resistance of forgotten people. Now she has departed from this life but Moz is still suffering from the same political strategy.

I asked Moz about Christina and he said: 'The main thing I can say about this woman is that she helped empower me to continue resisting. She was like a fighting spirit who suddenly came into my life and stood by me as I tried to pull myself out of the depths of darkness . . . Christina reassured me there was hope.' However, Moz also indicated something else: Christina's greatest wish throughout all these years was that one day Moz and the other refugees experience freedom. During this whole time, she was fully aware of the violence directed at the people held on Manus and Nauru. It was as though she lived and suffered with us throughout this time.

Christina could be seen as someone who represents an emancipatory consciousness – she is a symbol for a significant group within Australian society – those who have never been indifferent to the humanitarian crisis and tragedy unfolding on these two islands. She was someone who remained active in this cause until her dying days. She never stopped fighting for change.

This policy of exile and incarceration of refugees has also injured the Australian people.

Throughout these years many Australians have tried to support the forgotten human beings on these islands using many approaches. They have tried to assist people whose bodies and souls have been used as instruments for politics and power. They have tried to help human beings incarcerated without charge; human beings who have been ignored by the mainstream media; human beings who at the same time struggle to expose the violent face of the Australian Government for all to see; unique human beings whose faces are unknown; human beings who are an important part of the refugee resistance; human beings who have no choice but to resist; human beings who have no way of turning back to the countries from which they fled.

This is the reality – during these six years the refugees have endured unrelenting affliction. However, a large part of Australian society have also been traumatized by this political programme, and they continue to suffer in different ways. There are many untold stories about the relationships between Australian citizens and refugees in Manus and Nauru. Christina's life is inspirational, but she is only one example. A lot can be learned from this one person and others like her.

This is the reality: Manus and Nauru are a part of Australia. These prisons have had a profound effect on Australia's political culture and society. It is true that the current generation is not fully aware of this reality but, undoubtedly, in the future Australia will come to fully understand the consequences of this political strategy and its violent impact on the nation.

Just imagine the hundreds of Australian citizens who have worked in the prisons on Manus and Nauru throughout these years. The difference between this group of people and people like Christina is significant. Christina resisted the policy of exile and hostage taking of refugees and the others facilitate it. The group of people who have worked there have had a role in our torture and have been affected enormously as a result. They have inflicted all this violence, and in turn all this violence has been ingrained in them. By extension, they have imported all this violence back into Australian society. They exist within Australian society, I know that many of them suffer from mental health problems. Because of this, a significant number of them have made claims against the government or against the companies contracted to run these prisons and have in some cases taken them to court.

A massive part of Australian society has been worn down by this ruthless political strategy. This policy of exile and incarceration of refugees has also injured the Australian people, and this is exemplified by those who have worked for this prison industry.

Many Australians want a change to this situation; clearly, this is a demand made by the wider society. I'm telling Christina's story because I think that it is vital for Australians – and of course for refugees on Manus and Nauru – that everyone fights against indifference. Christina went out to vote for change even as she was breathing her last breath.

This election is an opportunity for the Australian people to impact a central political issue and restore Australia's broken political landscape, they have the chance to move society towards a brighter future … to instil justice … freedom … humanity … a cleaner environment.

Christina's message for us is that the main pillar of any democratic system is a commitment to humanity, justice, freedom, love and compassion. Australians must vote for those politicians who want to work for a future that embodies these values. Christina had this vision for Australia's future. She voted with her heart.

'The Boats are Coming' is One of The Greatest Lies Told to the Australian People[1]

Behrouz Boochani

In less than a month, the political strategy of exiling and incarcerating refugees on Manus Island and Nauru will hit the six-year mark – we enter the seventh year of illegal imprisonment. If we pay attention to the discourse and propaganda techniques of consecutive governments over these years, we notice that essentially the same language and rhetoric has been maintained without the slightest change. Every government has imposed the same logic on society: the policies have been designed and implemented to 'stop the boats'. As a result of this simplistic reasoning, they have justified an inhumane political programme.

The most prominent slogan for groups opposing this policy over all these years has been 'Bring Them Here'. This slogan has been the basis for many pro-refugee activist groups and featured in so many campaigns to free the refugees from offshore prisons. Unfortunately, this slogan and these campaigns have been unsuccessful in achieving their objectives.

The greatest error that many have committed is accepting the government's reasoning which is based on the simple formula: 'We have incarcerated these people on Manus and Nauru to "stop the boats".' If one analyses the different dimensions of this particular exile policy it becomes obvious that the government is lying.

The policy of exiling refugees to offshore prisons is in no way a deterrent. Even if we just entertained the idea that the policy of exile really worked then it would have been relevant to roughly the first six months to a year of its implementation. There is no reasoning that justifies over six years of incarceration of innocent people – an imprisonment that continues to this day. This is a lie that the Australian Liberal Party has ingrained in the minds of the public and the media for years. However, it is very likely that at some point they actually started to believe their own lie.

A simple question needs to be discussed in detail regarding the refugees in Indonesia, those people who the Australian Government has always considered a danger to national security and Australian values: why haven't refugees in Indonesia been coming to Australia by boat over recent years?

The Australian media have continuously validated and promoted the announcements of the Home Affairs Minister, Peter Dutton. But have any mainstream media organizations investigated the situation and experiences in Indonesia? How many of them have considered the details and dynamics from the place where they fear the boats might embark? The truth is that refugees stuck in Indonesia will never risk losing their money to people smugglers, risk their lives battling the dangers of the ocean, and risk being pushed back to Indonesia in the end.

Why has the Liberal Party failed to resolve this issue after all these years and after spending billions of dollars?

The reality is that no one is observing the situation in Manus and Nauru, no one considers our fate, no one is waiting to see when we are freed, no one is looking to see where we will be settled.

Many Australians liken the policy of exiling people to Manus and Nauru to a brick constituting a structure constructed by the government. According to this view, if one brick is removed from this building the whole edifice will suddenly collapse. I argue that this view is completely wrong. Over six years, the Australian Government has transferred about 1,000 people from these two islands to Australia. In contrast to the government logic, not one boat has come into Australian waters. In addition to this, since 2013 the government has transferred to Australia hundreds of refugees who had been incarcerated on Christmas Island. These refugees were always told they would never make it to Australia and would be eventually exiled to Manus and Nauru. Again, no boats made it into Australian waters. According to official statistics, the government sent more than another 700 people to the USA. Again, no boats came in. The group of refugees in Manus decreased from 900 in 2016 to 450 in 2019. In Nauru, the numbers decreased from 1,200 to 250 in the same period, respectively.

One conclusion can be reasonably arrived at. Obviously, the government's intention has never been to close these prisons. Dutton says he would like to free everyone overnight if he could but cannot because the boats would start coming again. This is an outright lie.

The question remains, however, if this policy has no relationship with boats arriving in Australia then why does the government insist on keeping people imprisoned on these islands over these years?

The exile and incarceration of refugees on Manus and Nauru is based on three fundamental pillars. (1) Political profit for both major parties; (2) Economic gain; (3) An ideological basis which is associated with the individual psychology of people such as Dutton.

First, this policy guarantees the accumulation of political capital for the Liberal Party. In the 2016 elections they made very good use of the issue of 'border protection' for gaining votes, putting the Labor Party on the defensive. During the last elections two months ago the Liberal Party again tried to make use of this approach as part of the campaign of fear they were planning – the most prominent example of this intention was manifested in Scott Morrison's visit to Christmas Island as a campaign tool. However, the Christchurch terrorist attack in New Zealand influenced the government's decision not to use the 'refugee card' for the first time since the Howard era.

The existence of these two-island prisons has always been a justification for the political profit-making of the Liberal Party. By making these sites the highlight of their campaign they were sending a message to voters that they were prioritizing national security. They were creating the impression that they were strong and the Labor Party weak.

For years the Labor Party sought to resist the political attack by adamantly supporting the same political project, especially before the last election. For years, the two parties have been in competition over who could better sustain the cruel and inhumane policy. Over the years, the government has been open about the fact that they do not want to do away with this political tool; a policy that has been instrumental in keeping the Labor Party on the defensive.

The second pillar of this political project is the economic gain involving these two island prisons. According to the architects of this very political strategy there has always been the need for secrecy around the contracts given to operate the prisons. There has been a lack of transparency on how the Manus and Nauru contracts are run.

Exact figures are difficult to establish but more than $9bn has been spent on this state-sanctioned hostage taking and boat turnbacks. At least ten large companies have signed multimillion-dollar contracts with the government over these years.

The healthcare company IHMS has been working in these island prisons for six years – why hasn't any other company been able to take their place? There is also the contract scandal involving security company Paladin, an agreement worth $423 million. How is this money being spent? Where is the money going?

What is clear is this: There are strong lobbies that see it in their best commercial interests to maintain this political strategy. Through this whole process millions of dollars have exchanged hands. Financial profit is one of the main pillars of this political programme.

But the third fundamental pillar pertains to individual gain and can be understood by a psychological examination of Dutton and the Home Affairs Department Secretary, Mike Pezzullo. The roots of this pillar are ideological.

Dutton has become the most influential minister in the country's history by abusing the concept of national security. Over recent years he has increased his power, step by step, and at one time was vying for the post of prime minister. His political success has come from maintaining this political project at any cost.

Dutton uses every opportunity available to attack the character of refugees. In one recent example, he targeted women who have been victims of rape and other kinds of sexual abuse and were transferred to Australia for treatment. He accused them of lying.[2] On many occasions he has labelled refugees as criminals, rapists and murderers. Without a doubt, this political strategy has ideological foundations based on racism.

In the beginning, the policy of exiling refugees to Manus and Nauru might have been a simple policy; it was supposed to be in place for less than one year. However, with the passing of time and the influence of historical, ideological and sadistic dimensions the policy mutated. Now, after six years, we must pose some fundamental questions. Why has the Liberal party failed to resolve this issue after all these years and after spending billions of dollars? Why are they still exploiting the public and lying to them using the fabricated notion of national security? Why are they still terrifying the public regarding boats? Why are they exploiting Manus and Nauru and justifying their actions using the rhetoric of stopping the boats?

A general look at this situation reveals that the Australian Government never had the intention of resolving this issue.

If the government had intended to gradually remove one person from this island every three days then all the refugees would be freed by now. By accepting the New Zealand offer to take 150 people a year the government would have ended this situation. Right now they could use the medevac law to evacuate all the sick refugees from the island over a period of two to three months. Over these years, the government could have easily emptied these prison camps, but the reality is that they earn political profit for their parties; there are people who benefit financially; and there are also the individual ideological gains. For these reasons they have never intended on solving this issue. 'The boats are coming' is one of the greatest lies told to the Australian people in decades. History will reveal all.

The Truth About Self-harm in Offshore Detention[1]

Behrouz Boochani

In recent weeks, political debate over the medevac legislation has re-emerged in the Australian media. The Liberal Party pushes its view that the legislation needs to change. In order to achieve its objectives, the party has continued its chaotic programme of propaganda and hate – a tactic Peter Dutton and his fellow ministers have used for years to maintain the policy of exiling refugees to Manus and Nauru.

Dutton made scathing accusations against refugees, saying they self-harm only so they can come to Australia using the medevac laws. He claims advocates push them to engage in these acts.

Dutton has always attacked the victims, rather than provide explanations for their actions. But his rhetoric is damaging for many reasons, not least because it denies refugees agency. He assumes advocates are influencing their decisions. He thinks of refugees as people empty of political will.

In truth, this is a system so cruel and inhumane that it forces the imprisoned refugees to hurt themselves. These forms of violence are in their very essence the consequences of this violent system. Fundamentally, it is a system that has for years exploited the bodies and souls of human beings and absorbed them into its own ruthless logic. These examples of violence within the system represent the spirit of the oppressive overlord – self-harm is a product of the system.

This violence produced by the system spreads through every part of the prison and, ultimately, is reproduced by the imprisoned refugees. If anyone should be forced to offer an explanation for this situation, it is Peter Dutton and the Department of Home Affairs.

Dutton's thinking is based on an equation that positions knowledgeable Australians on one side and ignorant refugees on the other. This equation is oppressive. It figures refugees as nothing but children waiting for others to tell them what to do. But these latest comments are not the first time he has made this kind of gross reduction without providing any evidence.

In November 2017, the refugees on Manus resisted the extreme violence of the prison system for 23 days. On a number of occasions, the Home Affairs Minister explicitly accused certain politicians and advocates of guiding the collective resistance, that the mastermind behind it resided outside the island. In reality, it was the refugees who rallied together and made decisions as a group about how to proceed. They were the ones who understood exactly how best to challenge the system.

Dutton's attempts to frame refugees as passive and incapable victims, devoid of any decision-making ability, is nothing but another dehumanization. This system has never acknowledged refugees as human beings. It has tried to erase our existence in almost every instance; and whenever there was some reference to our existence we were always stripped of agency. The system depends on this perspective, and it has tried its best to justify and consolidate the perspective at the same time. Therefore, from this point of view, the following statement becomes a logical interpretation: 'Other people are ordering you to self-harm.'

Self-harm and suicide in Australia's detention industry is an extremely complex issue; it has resulted in death on many occasions. But it is impossible to reduce it to a simple general insult, as Dutton has tried to do.

For years our bodies have been made the subjects of politics and power. As such, they have become the last thing we have left with which to make a statement regarding the abuse of our human rights. Just imagine a young man battling many illnesses for six years only to be ignored by the system and refused treatment. What other option does he have?

A week has never gone by when we have not experienced an instance of self-harm on Manus. And when someone self-harms here they do not only harm themselves – in fact, they perpetuate stress and a particular form of violence throughout the community around them. This is the cause of great suffering. It is extremely difficult to see a young man in agony. You soon realize both of you are suffering the same pain. Many people who have not self-harmed are still traumatized to a large extent by witnessing many self-harm incidents. When someone attempts suicide or self-harm, everyone is absorbed in the pain.

For many, the 2019 federal election was a great shock. 'I always believed in miracles,' the prime minister responded. But on Manus, after the results were announced, we experienced a massive increase in self-harm. On some days, there were as many as 10 incidents. The situation was out of control. Within three months more than 100 incidents were recorded. Many ended up in the local hospital on Manus, a filthy place with very poor conditions. It does not have facilities for psychological care. It does not even have the most basic equipment necessary to provide medical treatment to sick refugees. And yet, in the months after the election, at least three or four beds in the hospital were always occupied by injured refugees. This situation certainly has a direct relationship with the outcome of the Australian election.

And we were not alone. During the campaign, and in its wake, I participated in dozens of events for my book, *No Friend but the Mountains*. Although I am only able to communicate with the Australian people using my mobile phone, the difference in mood before and after the election among Australian civil society was clear to me. Pre-election, the atmosphere was full of hope for change. Then came a climate of defeat and hopelessness.

Australians who are experiencing this sense of hopelessness and defeat are living a free life and have opportunities to be active in society. But for the imprisoned refugees on Manus and Nauru, the election results had an immediate impact on our fate. This election could have resulted in our freedom from these islands and settlement in New Zealand. This was the plan announced by the Labor Party and it was likely they would have accepted the New Zealand offer if they had been successful at the federal election.

Instead, the Morrison government remains in power. And the weary human beings locked up on these islands, who have already lost years of their lives, experience an even more extreme psychological shock. It is hard to convey the intensity of the hopelessness and fear the election evoked on Manus and Nauru. For us, it was like a sledgehammer crushing our heads. Many fear we will never get off this island, that we will be forgotten.

Now just imagine that during this tragic period someone like Peter Dutton makes an insulting and completely baseless statement about refugees exploiting the medevac legislation. The minister showed no concern whatsoever for the wellbeing of these damaged and weary souls. He blamed advocates for coaching people to self-harm.

For years the Australian Government has been lying to the nation. They always say refugees receive proper medical services on these islands. This is certainly not the case. If it were true then the medevac legislation would never have passed. If Dutton were telling the truth, no refugee would have been transferred to Australia through this process. It is a massive lie – and Dutton knows better than anyone else that, in this system, illness is weaponized against refugees.

The fact is that dozens of sick people have been denied treatment for years on Manus and Nauru. But the Department of Home Affairs is terrified of the medevac law being recognized as appropriate. And so Peter Dutton levels his baseless and demonizing insult against refugees. Self-harm and attempted suicide are part of the reality of incarceration on Manus Island and Nauru. This is exactly what the Australian people and the politicians who represent them need to acknowledge.

The imprisoned refugees here on these islands always feel the shadow of death hovering overhead. Death is as close as it possibly can be. The truth is that 12 people have lost their lives here in the past six years and hundreds of others have injured themselves.

But the truth is not what Dutton tells us. This man and his department are responsible for this situation, and one day they must answer for what they have done. This is the truth.

Purification by Love[1]

Behrouz Boochani

You kissed me
Thousands of times, you kissed me
With anxious lips – those lips reveal the mysteries in your eyes
Those lips – I had to traverse thousands of oceans to arrive at those lips
You kissed me deep within a jungle
Among a carnival of crickets
In amongst the friction between the light upon the leaves
You kissed me, I sensed your lips like salt . . . or possibly they were sweet

You embraced me
Thousands of times, you kissed me
. . . upon a bed that played host to our sweat
. . . on a balcony facing the rain
. . . beside the innocent gaze of a cat while it nourished kittens with milk
. . . in the middle of an island, looking up at the flight of an eagle with crown of white
You embraced me
In that moment of wonder you devoured me
You enveloped me, up alongside the course veneer of a branch
That branch epitomizes the land

You cried my name
Thousands of times, you cried my name
. . . among the sound of waves
. . . facing the moon and clouds
. . . under a starless night
Penetrating
Sitting on a tree trunk that lays there on the sand

You called my name
. . . through the choir of song that surrounded us

You beheld my face
Thousands of times, you beheld my face . . .
in the sunlight, your eyes concealing tears of the past
In the middle of gentle rainfall, moistening your cheeks
Flowing with dew
Beside a seaside abundant with identical boats
Boats carrying stocks of bananas . . . possibly coconuts
Within a cottage . . .
this could be a dream
You beheld my face beyond the hundreds of eyes gazing at you
Through the smoke that evokes the memory of a clan

You smiled at me
Thousands of times, you smiled at me
Beside an indigenous woman who embodies the smell of fish
Beside a man whose skin embodies the bitterest bitterness
. . . he feels like the coarseness of a branch
. . . his arms resemble bloodied axes
He was gentle, but full of desire
You smiled at me
With lips the scent of wine

But . . .
But this is a confession

However . . .
However, none of these draws me in like the depths of your eyes
I am a man purified by your love

Emotion, Responsibility and Hope for Different Futures

Claudia Tazreiter

The journalism of Behrouz Boochani in this section is remarkable and hopeful in many respects. The three articles collected in this section were published toward the end of the six-year long incarceration of refugees on Manus Island, Papua New Guinea. This is, of course, retrospective knowledge. At the time of writing these articles, Boochani, along with the other refugees on Manus Island for years of indeterminate incarceration by the Australian Government, had no knowledge of when their circumstances might change and when resettlement in a third country might be possible. This is what is so remarkable, indeed, quite unimaginable for average Australians, who continued with their everyday lives during the long years of ongoing and indeterminate incarceration of refugees on Manus Island, Nauru as well as other sites of 'off-shore' disappearance of persons.[1] Along with many Australian academics, activists and human rights practitioners, I have written, taught, protested and agonized over the Australian Government's cruel and inhumane policies toward refugees, particularly those arriving by boat.[2] On a visit to Manus island in 2019, the realities of Australia's carceral archipelago were tangible not only in the men I met who had lost years of their young lives in remote detention, but also in the faces of the local people, the Manusians, implicated in this horrific geopolitical stalemate.

What shapes human hope in the face of inhumanity and state-sanctioned horror? How is it that people persist with energy, with advocacy not only for themselves, but on behalf of others in the face of personal annihilation and death? In turn, what responsibility do average citizens bear for the policies and laws of their governments? These questions strike me as fundamental and also critical in the face of the truth telling of Boochani's journalism. His journalism is so much more than the witnessing and testimony that journalists impose on themselves as key to their trade in holding those in power to account for their actions on behalf of those they represent. For Boochani, reporting is also personal testimony, the lived experience of horror, deprivation and as he characterizes it, of torture.

In the article, 'This Election is an Opportunity to Vote for Humanity and Freedom', the selfless resistance of Christina Coombe is described. In the face of spirit-breaking ill treatment such as the withholding of food and water in 2017, Christina offered daily support to one refugee, Moz, with long calls to comfort him and remind him of the care that did exist for him and other refugees. This article, along with the articles on self-harm and death in indefinite detention and the fiction of the narrative of 'the boats are coming', question the validity of core principles of democracy and human rights values in the Australian public sphere.

Responsibility is a key concept in social and political theory, exploring the relation between members of a political community, those that are in leadership positions and the various hierarchies, networks and systems created to manage complex societies and to monitor actions, policies and laws. Membership of a political community is commonly understood through the identifier and category, *citizenship*, denoting both formal membership as well as the sociocultural aspects of belonging. Ideally, responsibility ought to be a shared duty, rather than the more common contemporary manifestation of expecting the governing class (the state), to always act on behalf of the people. Indeed, a foundational concept predating the birth of the nation-state is that of active citizenship, where each person is expected to participate in public debates and express their voice. In this way, decisions, policies and laws are an expression of common sentiment and a shared vision of the future, rather than an imposition from above. Needless to say, this typification is an ideal, but nevertheless an important one for societies to acknowledge and strive toward if democratic and human rights values are held as important. And in this regard, many refugees are active participants with Australians in collective action in forms of resistance that articulate new possibilities for shared futures that centre on care, on love, on common humanity.

It is impossible to read the article 'The Truth about Self-Harm in Offshore Detention' without a deep feeling of shame. The previous Australian Home Affairs Minister, Peter Dutton, characterized refugees that self-harm as holding the Australian Government hostage in allegedly forcing it to bring them to Australia for medical treatment.[3] Such deeply twisted and inhumane logic underscores the systematized violence guiding Australian Government decisions on asylum seeker arrivals for almost three decades. Similarly, the rhetoric of 'stopping the boats' that began during the prime ministership of John Howard, is explored in another article.[4] Of course, what Boochani identifies as key to a more balanced understanding and approach, is a view from the international system rather than a view only from within one state. Moreover, the political economy of immigration borders and the systems that incarcerate, push-back and forcibly return refugee populations require more scrutiny.

The harm of the systematic torture Boochani describes and has lived, has many dimensions. The harms done to the bodies and minds of those subjected to the systematic torture such as on Manus and Nauru are, needless to say, perhaps the most important dimensions to scrutinize, and dimensions that also need redress. Australian citizens and residents are also implicated in this harm, and this is another key dimension of these harms. Australians are also liable to suffer harms from these policies, though in symbolic forms. Arguably, the very fabric of the democratic values undergirding Australia are left exposed and fragile without a clear-eyed view of the responsibility all Australians have to take action and express their voices about the policies carried out in their name.

Prison Notebooks and the Oceanic–Kurdish Connection

Boochani's Political Reflectivity

Steven Ratuva

'For 20 years we must stop this brain from functioning,' uttered the prosecutor at the 1926 trial of Antonio Gramsci, the iconic Italian socialist thinker and one of the most influential social scientists of the twentieth century.[1] Despite the Fascist government's attempt to silence the scholar, Gramsci defied all odds by producing the fabled *Prison Notebooks* from behind the prison walls.[2] Many decades later in the South Pacific, in almost similar circumstances, a Kurdish writer and journalist named Behrouz Boochani, while trapped behind the Australian barbed wire refugee camp in Manus Island (Papua New Guinea), wrote some of the most brilliant narratives about his reflections of despair and hope, barbarity and humanity that reflected his personal journey as a journalist, human rights defender and human being.[3]

Imprisonment is often a tool of psychological control, political subjugation, coercive intimidation and a statement of ultimate superiority by the oppressor. A number of Kurdish freedom fighters have met the fate of being arrested, imprisoned and tortured and these may have kept alive the flame of defiance in Boochani's struggle to connect with the world behind the barbed wire of Manus Island. One of the leading Kurdish freedom fighters and revolutionary intellectuals, Abdullah Öcalan, wrote more than forty books, four of which were written in prison.[4] One of the founders of the Kurdish Workers Party (PKK), Sakine Cansiz, was arrested, tortured and killed in 2013.[5] In relation to Boochani's own country of Iran, where Kurds are suppressed as a minority group, scholars and freedom fighters such as Shahla Talebi, in her work, 'Bahareh: Singing without Words in an Iranian Prison Camp,' provides a narrative of the trauma of those imprisoned through the power of memory and words.[6] Such traumatic moments are also captured in the prison memoirs (*Tilapia Sucks the Blood of Hur al-Azim*) by Sepideh Gholian, a citizen journalist and freedom fighter, who was arrested and brutally tortured.[7]

Boochani's writings, widely published digitally by the media around the world, were reflections of the subdued voices of hundreds of asylum seekers languishing behind the prison fences of the hot tropical climate of Manus Island.[8] They were voices of anguish seeking a human audience, they were sentiments of desperation seeking humanity, they were echoes of hope seeking light in a world where self-gratifying politics, racism, oppression and self-interest have come to define contested modernity and contemporary ethics.[9] A world where humanity is a mere blip in a swirling vortex of racism, sexism, predatory neoliberalism and cultural imperialism,[10] yet a world where 'hope is our secret weapon'.[11] Despite the solitary confinement[12] and 'appalling health care record',[13] Boochani, like Gramsci, saw his writings as part of his 'duty to history'.[14]

Although caged, Boochani's thoughts roamed freely and soared high like frigate birds which flew past Manus Island on a daily basis as they criss-cross the vast Pacific Ocean in search of food. The Pacific, as Epeli Ha'auofa, the Fijian/Tongan sulu-clad philosopher, once said, is a 'Sea of islands,' where the sea is the centripetal cosmological force that connects rather than seperates people.[15] Boochani has become part of this vast oceanic continent and his daily tears have permanently deposited his DNA in a part of the world which by some twist of horror, has become his home, a Pacific home away from his Kurdish birthplace. A strand of this connection is his consciousness of and sympathy with the people of West Papua, next door to Manus Island, where the indigenous population still live under the brutal and genocidal colonial rule of Indonesia.

Boochani's stories are more than just personal reflections; they are primary sources of historical realities – the history that Australia, with its sub-imperial ambitions and power, has been trying to suppress and possibly erase from memory. They manifest the deeper and darker layers of contradictions which has characterized the Australian state since the early settlement by Europeans in the 1700s. At one level it projects itself as a liberal, humanity-oriented, modern multicultural state, while at another level, it behaves in a different way – a country whose racist policies towards people seeking asylum is part of a well-documented history of discrimination against immigrants of colour and the despicable record of ill treatment of its indigenous people. Boochani's voice speaks not just on behalf of asylum seekers, but also resonates far and wide and echoes deep sentiments against the racist ideologies of a country founded on imperial land-grab and near-genocide of what they believed were subhumans who were barriers to the divine destiny of European civilization.

When Boochani was finally 'freed' he was still faced with the psychological dilemma of what his future holds as the prison prism has changed his life, his hopes, his dreams and his identity. The pen (or rather keyboard) has become his weapon of choice, words his means of intellectual self-realization and weaponization against his tormentors and human relationship his mode of moral reaffirmation in a world where hostile forces are still bent on silencing the voices of the subaltern, including his.

Reading through Boochani's writings is like making a journey through the crucible of time and infinity of space. One feels a sense of semi-guilt and semi-disgust about how humans can oppress other humans. The universality of the message and transcultural inspiration of the narratives speak so strongly, affirmatively and directly to the hearts of people everywhere. His words are powerful ambassadors of the powerless asylum seekers escaping the oppression in their own countries, only to become entrapped in a wired cage like animals in a zoo in another country.

Epistemic reflectivity and the Oceania–Kurdish connection

The confinements of prison can be a nurturing space for a groundswell of creativity as we saw in the case of Gramsci. Likewise, Boochani's writings show that the barbed wire fences did not limit the boundaries of his thought processes but rather inspired him to connect the outside world with his inner reflections, a mode of intellectual analysis I would refer to as epistemic reflexivity.

In the process of connecting intellectually with himself, his fellow prisoners and the outside world, he had to overcome a series of deeply frustrating obstacles ranging from the psychologically repressive and physically overpowering atmosphere of Manus Prison to the right-wing and racist policies of the Australian Government. By writing, he was able to transcend these barriers in a creative and liberating way, while engaging in a knowledge creation process which traversed the boundaries of culture and politics. The writings provide not just his voice but the collective experience and knowledge formation of his fellow prisoners. This is where the cry of anguish of the prisoners become the discourse of resistance of the subaltern. Where personal reflexivity is magnified into a political narrative for humanity.

These experiences created the circumstances for discovery of new liberating knowledge. Boochani's prison notebooks have provided a new meaning for knowledge creation through the prison prism. The mind can be free and fertile even behind the physical, political and mental barbed wires. This is a major inspiration for all those faced with the misfortune of imprisonment, oppression, human rights abuse and humiliation. As Gramsci demonstrated in his famous prison notebooks, confinement can ferment creativity, intellectual innovation and even revolutionary thoughts which have the capacity to inspire, transform and regenerate knowledge, social consciousness and human desire to live.

Boochani's ideas have become a meeting place for Kurdistan and Oceania, a new intersection of cultural, historical and political experiences and representations. They are geographically far apart, yet they share common historical experiences. These experiences are in the form of colonial powers carving out their spheres of interests and imposing borders which terminated centuries old cultural connections and created new artificially constructed identities as subservient entities. Manus Island, despite its horrendous reputation, has become the heartland and symbol of this pan-Pacific–Kurdish connection. In an unintended and rather ironic way, Australia has played a critical role in this new dimension of knowledge connectivity.

The Kurdish–Pacific knowledge connection has been forged and will blossom in time. Boochani has made this connection a reality. A connection borne of languishing misery and inhumanity in an Australian prison, an institution that symbolizes so much that is wrong with humanity.

Part Nine

2020 (May–June) – New Narratives and Knowledge

New Writing and Collaboration

No Friend but the Mountains was awarded Audiobook of the Year at the 2020 Australian Book Industry Awards. Calls to evacuate all refugees still held on Manus and Nauru as the World Health Organization declared Covid-19 a pandemic – after seven years, nearly four-hundred remained captive in the Pacific islands and over two-hundred were detained after being transferred to Australia, all without any clarity about their future. Behrouz Boochani was granted asylum in Aotearoa New Zealand on his birthday – exactly seven years after originally seeking asylum in Australia and the beginning of his incarceration. Boochani's writing is increasingly studied in universities around the world, including by long-time collaborator Anne Surma in Australia – who specializes in literature, creative writing and writing studies – and scholars in the UK and Europe such as Lida Amiri who approaches displacement, exile, migration and diaspora studies through the lens of literature and translation.

As I Learn to Live in Freedom, Australia is Still Tormenting Refugees[1]

Behrouz Boochani

It has been more than five months since I began living in New Zealand. After the first month – during which I was travelling to participate in panels and events – I spent my time trying to comprehend freedom.

For someone who has been immersed in a tragedy and humanitarian crisis for years, living in a quiet and calm city like Christchurch represents a profound transformation. I have been able to contemplate my life on Manus. Not a day has passed that I have not thought about the refugees in Port Moresby, Nauru or Australia.

My experience on Manus is like an ongoing nightmare – what felt like years of struggling to crawl out of a pit. It gives me pleasure that after years I can be by myself; I can listen to music by myself; walk to the city centre; go to the cinema on the weekends; sit in the corner of a cafe and drink coffee while watching people walk by; make new friends and talk to them about the city and its history; and immerse myself in the stories of people who have lived their entire lives in freedom.

Recently I bought a bicycle and every afternoon I ride along the river that runs through the middle of the city until I reach the sea. I watch the birds as I sit beside the lagoon next to the ocean, or I traverse the hills surrounding the city and enter the beautiful town of Lyttelton.

In the place where I live alone, I make myself coffee and read books. I remain in touch with many refugees who are in Port Moresby or locked up in Australia. I am always afraid to tell them about my life in New Zealand; what could I possibly tell them? Each and every little thing I do is something they dream of: walking down a street; talking to a new friend; sleeping in a room that is yours and no one else's.

Like other countries, life in New Zealand has entered a new stage: quarantine. For someone who lived in a prison camp for six years, it is extremely surreal; it is as if I have carried Manus prison with me as I entered freedom, as if I spread that place all over the world.

I have been receiving many messages from friends regarding Australians being confined to their homes and how they might begin to understand the years of offshore and onshore incarceration experienced by refugees. Many became hopeful that with the current situation the government could no longer indefinitely detain people who have not committed a crime.

The Portuguese Government granted full residency rights (temporarily) to all immigrants and people seeking asylum. The British government released hundreds of refugees from detention centres.

But in Australia, hundreds of innocent refugees have been standing on hotel balconies just staring at a city and hoping that eventually they will be spared this life-threatening situation; the refugees remain imprisoned in hotel rooms. There are some activists who have travelled to the hotels to protest and show support. The police have tried to stop them with bullying tactics and fines.

The refugees look over at the city, thinking the majority of people will hear their voices. I must admit I am horrified when I think of this image. I lived with each and every one of these people. I cannot understand how it is that Australians who have been isolated for over a month – even though they are next to their families – can allow this situation. How can they put up with people living away from their families for seven years?

What the people of Australia and the rest of the world are undergoing now is not in the same category as that torture which the incarcerated refugees experience. The psychological dimensions of many people's current isolation, which are the subject of many daily media reports, pale in comparison with what the refugees have been enduring – there are some refugees whose incarceration has lasted ten years.

They have been crushed, never given access to legal avenues to appeal and never provided with acceptable justification for their imprisonment.

Australia is a country where the government spends millions of dollars imprisoning a mother, father and their vulnerable children alone on Christmas Island; a country where there is no legal rhyme or reason that can oblige a person like Peter Dutton to respect human rights; a country where many innocent people have been killed on Nauru and Manus with no independent investigations into their deaths.

I am horrified by the image of incarcerated human beings standing innocently on a balcony looking over at a city they cannot touch. What does humanity mean in Australia?

'A Human Being Feels They Are on a Precipice'

Covid-19's Threshold Moment[1]

By Behrouz Boochani and Omid Tofighian

Many people around the world have been in isolation for months and in many places people continue to die from Covid-19; the suffering of Black people in the USA is increasing under the pandemic, and the video of 2020 of a police officer murdering George Floyd became the tipping point which led to protests and uprisings. These protests have spread around the world and taken on a particular kind of power in Australia due to systemic violence against Indigenous peoples, particularly in relation to policing and deaths in custody. These events are examples of how security, military and prison systems are connected, and how real change needs to address them together.

The lives and dreams of human beings imprisoned in Australia's offshore and onshore immigration detention centres – which contract for-profit businesses for management, maintenance and security – have been totally destroyed, with no end in sight. Prisoners were killed and others injured in very brutal ways under the supervision of companies such as G4S, Transfield/Broadspectrum, Wilson Security, IHMS, Paladin and many more. Refugees have been crushed, never given access to legal avenues to appeal and never provided with an acceptable justification for their imprisonment. Protests and campaigns in support of the refugees have not been successful in changing the system – a new strategy and better tactics are necessary.

What Australia has been doing represents a perverse kind of obstinacy. It is an unjustifiable political programme feeding a border-industrial complex that ensures the continued incarceration of human beings. Australia is a country where politicians and the public are privy to so much damning evidence of violence in these camps, including rape, and nothing has been done to end the abuse and change the situation for the people within them. In light of recent events, serious questions need to be asked about the relationship between the detention industry and the systems and institutions in Australia. A new worrying development is the growth of the surveillance industry which will affect displaced and marginalized people in even more destructive ways. There is a close relationship between the way imprisoned refugees are treated and the technologies of control designed and implemented for citizens. The relationship between the border and the nation shifts regularly and without logic; sometimes the prison camp is active and functions as a laboratory for testing technologies of control, and sometimes it is passive so that government policy dominates life in the prison. This critical analysis is part of what we refer to as Manus Prison Theory.

Technologies of border security, like all technologies, are products of society, but in many discourses – especially legal and governmental discourses – there is a tendency to speak of them as neutral. The argument that it is the fair or unjust use of those technologies that require scrutiny ignores the fact that the very design and purpose of those technologies already embody social hierarchies and inequities. Technologies of border security are racialized instruments that disproportionately impact certain groups of people and exist as forms of discrimination and exclusion, at the same time feeding into narratives of privilege and power. The interconnection between the corporate and government sectors is disturbing when one considers the fact that profit is such a dominant factor when producing, implementing and maintaining technologies and infrastructure of border security (not to reduce the significance of deeply imbedded ideologies, norms and systems of oppression). We are also witnessing how the coronavirus pandemic has created opportunities for institutions of power to manipulate technologies of border security for the purposes of controlling citizens – in these cases, human rights violations and the perpetuation of inequalities is concealed and normalized among dominant groups in society. Therefore, protection of refugee rights and pushing back against border violence is in fact a way of protecting everyone's rights and promoting humanity.

There are many examples one could use as case studies of the border-nation dynamic: the raids on the ABC (Australian Broadcasting Corporation); the consistently passive role of the Labor Party in the face of the Liberal Party's border regime; the quarantining of Australian citizens in the Christmas Island detention centre; new examples of deportation and stripping of citizen rights; the terrorist attack in Christchurch, New Zealand, by an Australian white supremacist; and many new extreme laws to stop protests.

The systems used to govern the prisons on Manus, Nauru and onshore share aspects and conditions similar to the current Covid-19 situation. First, the shadow of death weighs heavily on the imprisoned refugees for the entire time they are held in these prison camps – from the moment they wake up in the morning until the moment they fall asleep, and even when they are asleep and caught deep within their nightmares. The omnipresence of death is an inseparable part of life under these detention systems. Every prisoner senses death in a different way; no doubt, the one who has to deal with a pre-existing illness experiences a more destructive form of death. These circumstances represent a threshold, a situation where a human being feels they are on a precipice. The situation with Covid-19 is exactly like this. Now we all listen to the news every day, news about the impending death of humans; we hear of their deaths within our very own cities or countries, we realize the pandemic's magnitude. Certainly for the elderly, the ill and people in developing nations now living with quarantine laws, acquiring enough food is an ordeal – this is similar to the life of those on Manus. Now compare this with the feelings of people who know that they can overcome the virus if they are ever infected. A young, healthy and wealthy person living in a developed country has less to be afraid of in comparison with people who are living in more vulnerable circumstances.

Another point to consider is that the Manus Prison system was founded based on competition and hate. In this system, humans have to compete even just to get something to eat and have other basic needs met, otherwise they will deteriorate or perish. In such circumstances, people are positioned between human and animal. Principles of morality and human values begin to collapse. While there was competition and loathing, the culture of brotherhood always prevailed in Manus Prison. This culture helped refugees support each other during periods of collective hunger strikes and other protests, and it helped them unite against the system. This culture of brotherhood ultimately enabled collective resistance. It is a contradiction, but refugees were living in this space with these two cultures: hate and competition on the one hand, and collective resistance on the other. If we compare this situation with the current struggle with Covid-19 all over the world, it seems that societies like Australia are at the height of competition; it is worth considering how citizens began to swarm on supermarkets in vulgar and distasteful ways to fight for toilet paper. Actually, in these situations human beings have deteriorated – it is difficult to speak of humanity in these contexts. Now imagine what would happen if society continues to be affected by Covid-19, if society lacks food and basic goods and is plagued by famine.

What is clear about the fight against the border-industrial complex and the struggle to hold governments accountable for protecting all citizens during the pandemic is that both highlight the need to engage seriously with abolition movements, on a philosophical and practical level. This urgency for dismantling ideologies and technologies of securitization, militarization and incarceration, and investing in community well-being and empowerment, has become even more prevalent since the protests and uprisings in response to recent murders of Black people around the globe. Refugees held in Papua New Guinea, Nauru, Christmas Island and in onshore detention are at serious risk of contracting the virus and the Australian Government has not taken steps to release them. There is a high possibility that staff in these facilities will infect each other – and by extension their family and friends – and the imprisoned refugees. Covid-19 presents a mortal danger to refugees around the world, including those held by the Australian Government in offshore and onshore detention, and those stranded in places like Indonesia whom Australia will not resettle. The coronavirus pandemic has made it clear how interrelated we are as communities of human beings. When underprivileged groups suffer, there is a good chance it will impact others as well.

There are calls for broad systemic change. We must fight for a society in which racism, violence and marginalization are no longer profitable, where refugees and asylum seekers are treated with dignity, and where there are no more black deaths in custody. Governments must no longer be able to exploit bodies for power, and the private sector must no longer be allowed to profit from abuse.

Boochani's 'Political Poetics'

Subverting and Reimagining the Fiction of Real Politics

Anne Surma

Philosopher Jacques Rancière asserts that today 'real politics appears to be the implementation of a fiction: the fiction that decides who is legal and who illegal on a territory and the thresholds of tolerance that ensure security and harmony in a country'.[1] Through his 'political poetics',[2] Behrouz Boochani's own distinctive use of language also expressly challenges this fiction, as well as the competitive (neoliberal) register of present-day politics. Alert to historical injustice, contemporary political struggle, and the uncertain future of humanity, Boochani rebuts the claim that some lives matter less than others, or that some lives do not matter at all. His writing ruptures the seeming coherence of dominant truths, producing alternative narratives – structures of fiction – to inform the possibility of critical social change.

In his artistic practice, Boochani puts into question the logic of narratives that construct as both real and necessary the detention of refugees in offshore and onshore locations, as dictated by powerful coalitions. These include, on a national level, the Australian Government and its colonialist legacy; and, on a global level, the behemoth that is the border-industrial complex, 'the intersection of border policing, militarization and financial interest'.[3] For example, Boochani exposes the lie touted by successive Australian governments adopting 'the same logic': that the incarceration of refugees offshore is designed to 'stop the boats'. Such logic is mobilized to justify an 'inhumane political program'.[4] It is in this sense that Boochani's writing brings into view what Rancière identifies as the specific 'structure[s] of rationality',[5] which are variously used to constitute not only the worlds depicted in fiction but those of contemporary politics, power, and competition as well.[6]

Thus, for Boochani, language and art have the critical potential to open up alternative ways of mediating, shaping, and making sense of experience. When he declares the detention of refugees as both brutal *reality* and cruel *fabrication*, each based on a seemingly implacable narrative, his stance echoes Rancière's assertion that fiction is 'not the invention of imaginary worlds in contrast to solid reality. It is first and foremost a structure of rationality'.[7] Rancière goes on to explain that:

> politicians, social scientists, or journalists must use fiction just as novelists whenever they name subjects, identify situations, link events, and deduce from all this the possible or the impossible. But they readily forget it and claim they deal only with solid realities.[8]

Boochani responds to what Rancière calls real politics[9] by attending to the fictiveness of its exclusionary practices, which (typically) produce refugees and people seeking asylum as dupes, aggressors, or criminals. While such dominant accounts claim to be 'the mere expression of reality',[10] Boochani's writing – the writing of 'history from down below'[11] – remains alert to the forms and styles in which those discourses are shaped; to their incongruity with the world(s) they claim to reflect; and to how and why they gain traction in the world. Boochani thus provokes the reader to consider that the interpretable real is *never* simply given but is shaped (fictionalized, as Rancière would have it) through dominant discursive practices, systems and institutions, which accord significance to certain lives and ways of living while denying such recognition to others.

Moreover, through his commitment to a distinctively relational and imaginative use of language, Boochani recasts dominant narratives in the form of a political poetics, thereby making the very constructedness of texts visible through combining (and often bringing into dissonant contact) genres, voices, discourses, vocabularies and styles. This motivates a process of both distancing readers from, and bringing them close to, the precise ambivalence of poetic meaning. The distancing provides readers with critical space to work out how language does its work; the bringing close enacts the relational potential of language, as readers actively (emotionally and intellectually) engage in making alternative meanings.[12] In other words, Boochani's texts thus de-naturalize the fiction of real politics, making visible its constituent elements through a poetic re-patterning. Indeed, as he says, poetry – 'a form of expression that dismantles all these structures'[13] – is the mode of writing that best expresses refugees' resistance of their treatment by a kyriarchal system.

It is the refugee produced as deviant that looms ever larger in the contemporary kyriarchal system. Under an instrumentalist and financially competitive global order, governed by a structure of rationality in which human beings are accorded worth merely according to their ascribed market (dollar) value, the refugee, along with other marginalized groups, is increasingly narrated as criminal threat, or looming burden of debt, or both. Political theorist Jodi Dean suggests how criminal figures 'embody and occlude' the inability of neoliberal ideology to account or allow for 'loss and losers'.[14] The criminal (and here, by extension, the refugee) thus becomes 'a strange attractor for displaced anxieties around the brutality of the neoliberal economy'.[15]

In their piece 'A Human Being Feels They are on a Precipice: Covid-19's Threshold Moment',[16] examining how the inequities and injustices rife in the contemporary historical moment are thrown into cruel relief by Covid-19, Boochani and Omid Tofighian interrogate the national and global contexts in which anxieties, such as Dean describes, intensify the oppression of both refugees and other vulnerable groups. Switching between a third- and first-person voice, Boochani and Tofighian highlight the resonances between myriad contemporary stories in circulation at the time of writing: the deeply uneven and devastating impacts of Covid-19 around the world;[17] in the USA, George Floyd's murder by a police officer, prompting nationwide protests; and the global Black Lives Matter movement, having particular resonance in Australia given the colonial legacy of 'systemic violence against Indigenous peoples'.[18]

The text explores how these manifestations of social, political, and economic inequity – which disproportionately, and sometimes fatally, affect people living 'on the precipice' – are interconnected via 'security, military and prison systems . . . and how real change needs to address them together'.[19] In this context, Boochani and Tofighian identify Australia's policy of incarceration of refugees as perhaps the most disturbing example of control by such systems:

> The lives and dreams of human beings imprisoned in Australia's offshore and onshore immigration detention centres—*which contract for-profit businesses for management, maintenance and security*—have been totally destroyed, with no end in sight. Prisoners were killed and others injured in very brutal ways under the supervision of companies such as G4S, Transfield / Broadspectrum, Wilson Security, IHMS, Paladin and many more. Refugees have been crushed, never given access to legal avenues to appeal and never provided with an acceptable justification for their imprisonment.[20]
>
> [italics added]

The success of Australia's refugee detention regime is reliant on these highly profitable private commercial entities.[21] The excerpt above parodies the depersonalizing, distancing effects that abstract, ostensibly neutral, language typically favoured by such organizations produces through its use of nominalized forms to describe the benign-sounding 'management, maintenance and security' they provide. The parody is heightened to the point of satire by the nestling of these nominalized forms within the sentence's larger main clause: 'The lives and dreams of human beings imprisoned in Australia's offshore and onshore immigration detention centres . . . have been totally destroyed, with no end in sight'. There is no equivocating here. In reading the authors' damning assessment of corporate and state systems, their hierarchical structures and their bureaucratic bulwarks, readers attune to the human breath infusing the writing. Even in the 'crush[ing]', the 'brutal[izing]' of its myriad 'lives and dreams', this breath blows open the stubbornly persistent hegemonic stories, which speak of security and protection, but which actually translate as violence against vulnerable human beings.

The border-industrial complex[22] mobilizes technologies of surveillance and control, which, in turn, serve a culture of (neoliberal) competition and profit-seeking by discriminating against marginalized peoples: the losers – refugees, racialized others, the poor, the sick. Just as the Manus Prison system imposed an environment of 'competition and hate' between the prisoners on Manus, and just as it threatened (though could not quash) their capacity for 'collective resistance'[23] so, the authors argue, does a competitive response to the pandemic threaten to undermine a recognition of our shared humanity.

In this piece, Boochani and Tofighian do not simply expose how structures of rationality shape how things have been, the way they are, or how they will inevitably turn out. They also imagine the possible real – making visible what could be, what might be. And this approach infuses the work with hope, by superimposing the privileged real, the world as given, with an alternative vision:

> There are calls for broad systemic change. We must fight for a society in which racism, violence and marginalisation are no longer profitable, where refugees and asylum seekers are treated with dignity, and where there are no more Black deaths in custody. Governments must no longer be able to exploit bodies for power, and the private sector must no longer be allowed to profit from abuse.[24]

However, such is the grip of the fiction constituting contemporary real politics on an impoverished social imaginary that readers may find this vision of a different future impossible. Yet Boochani's distinction as a writer, artist and activist is *always* to resist: to reconfigure the temporal and cultural horizon of solid political realities, thereby provoking readers to critique the rationality of entrenched narratives. In other words, Boochani's political poetics challenges readers to imagine the realm of what is, and what is possible, otherwise.

Journalism as Dialogue

Creating Collective Activism Through the Prison Writings of Behrouz Boochani

Lida Amiri

What crime have we committed
to deserve detention and torture?
It is an anguished question with no answer.[1]

The politicization of border crossing around the world has become increasingly extreme and more damaging in recent decades with the mainstream media functioning as an organ of nation-state border regimes. In the Australian context, media coverage of people seeking asylum by boat has been indispensable to the dominant border control narratives perpetuated by both major political parties.[2] The mainstream media has played a crucial role in demonizing people arriving by boat with some of the most intense anti-refugee rhetoric and propaganda occurring during John Howard's time as prime minister (1996–2007), a disastrous and ruthless legacy that continues today. The mainstream media was influential in helping to solidify and disseminate the dangerous narrative about the influx of 'boat people' taking advantage of Australia's 'weak borders'. Leading up to, and during, the time when the 'Pacific Solution' was first introduced in 2001 – offshore (and indefinite) immigration detention in the Pacific islands, Manus Island in Papua New Guinea and the Republic of Nauru – Howard's Liberal–National Coalition government managed to influence the mainstream media and manipulate their perspectives. Together, government and media stoked racist and xenophobic sentiment within the electorate in support of Howard's draconian border control measures, which included opening Australia's first privately run offshore immigration detention centres in 2001.[3]

Due to severe restrictions on all media from entering detention centres (both offshore and onshore), journalists have not been able to report on cases of human rights abuses, and at one period detention centre staff were threatened with imprisonment for speaking up.[4] Some critical journalism prevailed, but lack of access was always going to function as a silencing mechanism. After more than two decades of suppressing accounts of life inside onshore and offshore detention centres by the detainees themselves, Behrouz Boochani's voice as a journalist broke the silence. Importantly, Boochani's writings represented an image of the detained refugee that most Australians from across the political spectrum had never encountered through the media, nor even within most activist spaces. Fundamental to his position as a reporter, and as first-hand witness of crimes at the Manus Island detention centre, was claiming agency by 'resist[ing] media representations of him as a victim'.[5] And Boochani's literary style and rhetorical devices decentred numbers and data by foregrounding the narratives of the incarcerated individuals and the lived realities in the prison. His reporting avoids passive and pejorative refugee stereotypes associated with weakness and need; instead, he represents detainees as people actively involved in protest, leaders of a resistance, people fighting and finding creative ways to survive – human beings with agency demanding to be free. The Australian mainstream media uses language created and employed by the government such as 'processing centre', 'processing and 'transfer' (of people seeking asylum), 'unauthorized maritime arrival', and, in many cases, 'illegal'. Mainstream journalists seek out the perspectives of officials and those entangled in the detention industry and give those voices priority in their writing. Moreover, their reporting centres data and statistics pertaining to individual people; that is, the complex and disastrous plight of human beings. In contrast, Boochani's journalism employs a special interactive approach: in his writing he demands interlocutors, not just readers; his reporting methods are aimed at opening frank dialogues with readers. Therefore, his articles create possibilities for cross-border interaction and collective activism.

Another key aspect of Boochani's writing pertains to the means of production; the processes of writing, networking, translation and distribution of his work all involve complex interactions and developments that represent unconventional forms of collaboration and action. Engaging with issues such as the politics and art of translation is pertinent for interpreting Boochani's writing since the practice is indispensable to making the work available to diverse global audiences. His published contributions, many of them translated from Farsi into English and then other languages, arise from contemporary translation practices, as examples of cultural and linguistic exchange in the twenty-first century. In his study of journalistic poetry on refugee routes, Pietro Deandrea claims that 'translation cannot but be seen as part and parcel of this artistic endeavour'.[6] In significant ways, then, Boochani's literary style of journalism can be considered dialogic, characterized by an interactive, inquisitive, and conversational style, which distinguishes it from conventional journalistic modes. In particular, his articles can be interpreted as a shared process of meaning-making with his readership, as well as with collaborators, such as translators.

Boochani's lyrical account of the refugees' lived experience and psychological trauma in the Manus Island detention centre,[7] overcomes spatial constraints and challenges mainstream media coverage of refugees that aims to reduce them to mere statistics and limits their identities to one-dimensional victims or supplicants. Frustrated with even some of the more progressive reporting on the topic, Boochani claims that such media narratives 'cannot penetrate the depth of the issue'.[8] In order to raise political awareness and encourage activism in his readership, Boochani's journalism incorporates literary and dialogic techniques. Boochani invites the reader to question governmental regulations and reject degrading stereotypes by asking philosophical questions: 'What has happened to the nation?'.[9] Expressing the voice of someone resisting torture in an offshore immigration prison, Boochani asserts himself within the Australian mediascape, demands accountability from Australian authorities and citizens, and encourages discussion on key socio-political matters. He steps into Australia's political discourse not simply as a detained refugee but as an intellectual, a creative, a respected journalist. His stance and style both invite the Australian public to participate in a meaningful and transformative debate. Gillian Whitlock accepts the invitation to engage; she defines her role as an Australian reader of Boochani's writing and holds Australian society accountable as 'suffering [was] imposed in our name and in our presence'.[10] By resisting neutral language to detail human rights abuses, Boochani's literary style is designed to provoke the reader's self-reflection, demand an immediate response, and stimulate collective action. Boochani appeals to the mutual interests he shares with his Australian readership by warning them about strategic and intrusive policies: "His [Peter Dutton's] decisions not only impact the destiny of refugees, but moreover, his footprint can be seen in the everyday life of Australians, in the private sphere, and even throughout airports".[11] It is rhetorical techniques such as these that encourage readers to question the veracity of narratives about refugees that pervade mainstream media and political propaganda; Boochani's journalism interrogates the integrity of the Australian systems and institutions that produce hateful and divisive opinions about people seeking asylum. In fact, his powerful and provocative stylistic choices, in particular his dialogic technique function by challenging the current mode of engagement related to discourses of Australian border politics and history of migration: 'We are confined to the task of writing, we are confined to the practice of creativity so that generations to come have resources at hand'.[12]

Boochani's journalism was the first personal account of imprisoned asylum seekers in Australian onshore and offshore detention centres, first translated by Moones Mansoubi.[13] Boochani's collaboration with his translators, Mansoubi and Omid Tofighian, evolved into a special literary style of journalism in English. Intellectual discussions about issues such as terminology and tone, and creative exchanges during the translation process, all contributed to shaping meaning, form and reception. *No Friend but the Mountains* contains many examples that indicate how the collaboration between author and translator created a new language in English for critically analysing the realities of border violence. Key terminology used in the autobiographical novel also plays an important role in Boochani's journalism. For example, Boochani and Tofighian created a neologism, the 'Kyriarchal System', to capture the multi-layered and interlocking systematic terror in Manus Prison:

> [E]ssentially the term that Behrouz uses in Farsi for what we call the Kyriarchal system in English ... I say we because we came to that conclusion together ... *system-e hākem* ... can be translated in numerous ways ... sovereign system, controlling system, ruling system, governmental system, dominating system, oppressive system, subjugating system, ruling system ... but none of these actually capture the essence of what Behrouz is saying when he talks about *system-e hākem* ...[14]

Lyndsey Stonebridge encapsulates the urgency of Boochani's literary style, asserting that he 'consciously pushes against a language that might naturalize the political and historical conditions of its telling'.[15] And she recognises the role of collaborative translation and a shared political and philosophical vision as integral to this process. Clearly, a translator's commitment to activism is key when engaging with writing produced under extreme conditions.[16] In order for the translations of Boochani's work to be effective, a shared critical outlook is vital; committed political and philosophical discussions between author and translator enhance the potential for exposing the depth of the human rights catastrophe across detention centres.[17] Boochani's literary style engages his audience in dialogue, but the process of translation is itself reflective of another dialogic encounter which enriches the work: the collaborative effort involved in producing the journalism; the investigation into meaning and interpretation when selecting appropriate words in translation; discussions about cross-cultural nuances and necessary changes to communicate writerly intent; clarifying information; and networking and interacting with publishers. All these features contributed to the unique conditions of writing, as well as to the circulation and impact of Boochani's completed work.

Translations of Boochani's work were a means by which to communicate the traumatic experiences in Manus Prison to an audience that had been subjected to decades of anti-refugee journalism and political manipulation. His writing has clearly reshaped discussions about Australian (and global) border politics and, in less than a decade, a significant number of journalists, scholars, artists and activists around the world have begun to engage with his work in productive and complex ways.[18] Boochani's unconventional approach to writing is designed to generate political and social transformation. His journalism invites dialogue, a frank and provocative conversation fostered by his literary style and the collaborative political and philosophical work necessary for successful translation.

Part Ten

2020 (September) – Neocolonial Experiments / Creative Resistance

Behrouz Boochani's work continues to be the subject of many publications, teaching and research projects, including studies by long-time collaborator Arianna Grasso in Italy who specializes in language, linguistics and literature, particularly in the context of social media content produced in Australian immigration detention. Others such as Helena Zeweri in the USA has been researching and teaching the work of people involved in creative resistance from Australia's carceral-border archipelago (Manus, Nauru, Christmas Island and the mainland, and Indonesia); her work situates Australian border violence and racist migration policies within the history of colonial violence. Abdirahman Ahmed Mohammed died of a heart attack after spending years on Manus and then transferred to Nauru and the mainland on 15 February 2021. Peter Dutton became minister of defence in March 2021 and then leader of the Liberal Party after Labor won the 2022 federal election under Anthony Albanese. Hundreds remain in Papua New Guinea, Nauru and in onshore hotel detention centres or on temporary visas (there are an additional 30,000 asylum seekers in Australia on temporary visas who arrived by boat between 2012 and 2014, referred to as the 'legacy caseload'; and nearly 14,000 refugees remain stranded in Indonesia without a pathway to resettlement.). The literary journal *Southerly* published a special issue in 2021 dedicated to the writing of people who have experienced indefinite detention in Australia's carceral-border system (in Papua New Guinea, Nauru, Indonesia, Christmas Island and the Australian mainland); 'Writing Through Fences: Archipelago of Letters' is edited by Janet Galbraith, Hani Abdile, Omid Tofighian and Behrouz Boochani.

For the Refugees Australia Imprisons, Music is Liberation, Life and Defiance[1]

Behrouz Boochani

Years ago, during one of those hot Manus Island days, a few Australian guards entered the refugee prison camp. They snatched a broken guitar from the hands of a young musician and exited with an air of invincibility and sense of victory. The young man followed them for a whole 100 metres stretch in the prison and begged them to return his guitar. But every time he asked one of the officers they replied in absolute terms that he should forget about his guitar. In response to the question of why the guard was taking his guitar, he received the reply: 'Having a musical instrument in prison is prohibited because you might hang yourself by using the strings.'

That refugee is Farhad Bandesh, a Kurdish refugee who, after over seven years, still does not know what crime he has committed and is currently imprisoned in a detention centre in Australia. Struggling to hold on to an instrument has been a part of life over the last seven years for Farhad and other musicians in the Australian-run detention centres. However, after the Papua New Guinea Supreme Court ruled that it was illegal to imprison refugees, possibilities opened up so that Farhad and other musicians could get some instruments into the prison. In those days they formed a band and would practise under the large tent called 'Charlie Compound', which was in the corner of the prison. This band performed a number of concerts for the refugees, they were able to evoke some sense of living life, although for a short period of time and in a violent prison.

Farhad is also an artist and has had a number of exhibitions in Australia up until now, although getting hold of art materials and then getting artworks out of the detention centre was a difficult process. For a long time he was denied access to art materials – for some time he was only allowed to produce art on his own bedsheets. During these years, Jenell Quinsee – an Australian activist – supported Farhad in organising exhibitions and recoding his songs. 'Don't Forget

Me', 'Flee from War' and 'Cruel Policy' are among his musical works. In July of 2019, after six years, Farhad was transferred to Australia for medical treatment under the Medevac law together with many other refugees. Until now he is still in indefinite detention and does not know what his future holds.

Another musician is Mostafa 'Moz' Azimitabar. He is a young man who plays the guitar and has recorded a number of songs during these years. In 2017 he recorded the rap song called 'All the Same' which is a protest song that challenges Australia's detention regime.

After that he made 'The Birds 'in 2018 and finally 'Love' – all these songs were recorded on his mobile phone. Moz also lost his musical instrument a number of times. In his most recent struggle with immigration he requested that they allow him to leave the detention centre for a few hours to record the two new songs that he had written in a studio. He even had a letter from the mayor of Preston in Melbourne; he attached the letter to his request but it was rejected on every attempt. Moz says:

> Music is a tool for preserving my sense of personhood, it is so I don't forget that I am a human being. Music is the language with which I can communication with the Australian people in a deep and meaningful way. My message is nothing more than the fact that we should love each other.

Another musician is Kazem Kazemi. This Kurdish musician plays metal on his electric guitar. Kazem fled Iran precisely because of his music. Up to now he has written six pop songs and one rock song, and he hopes he will have the opportunity to record them one day. When I ask him about his life in Iran and why he fled, he replies:

> I love metal. My whole life can be summed up this way – this style of music catapulted me to the other side of the globe. Metal is banned in Iran and has been pushed underground. I would always play music with stress and fear, I was socially ostracised because according to Iran's religious government metal is Satan worship. This music is a form of protest and because of the emotion involved it has the potential to defy all forms of authority. It stands against racism or political structures; for this reason the government is terrified of it.

Before Kazem was transferred to Australia, he was denied access to an electric guitar because of its metal strings. At the moment he is detained indefinitely in a hotel in Brisbane.

When I think of the stories of Farhad, Mostafa and Kazem, what comes to mind is tragedy, but it is also important to acknowledge that for them playing music is possibly the most radical act against the violence of the prison and the system as a whole, a resistance that manifests itself in different forms. They are not passive human beings, the themes they express are forms of defiance. They are not merely playing their guitars, their music is essentially a political act. For them, music is the language with which they can fight for their human rights – human rights that have been violated. Music is the language with which they can determine their personhood in the face of a system that aims to control them. Their works are ways of asserting their identity and existence; they are expressing their independence and individuality. Through this form of musical resistance they are able to survive.

The image I described at the beginning of this piece – the confiscation of Farhad's guitar by the guards – is surreal; the system that governs the prison camp is the source of much mental and physical violence and the system thinks of music and art as instruments with which the prisoners can enact violence. But, in fact, for the refugees, music is liberation and life. This detention system is against any form of life; during these years it has clearly tried to confiscate or restrict, for whatever reason, their possessions – in this case a guitar.

I will never forget that final moment – it played out like the scene of a drama. The day that Moz was transferred to Australia he embraced me in his arms. He took a few steps, danced for a moment, opened his arms and recited a poem by Ahmad Shamlou . . . then he left.

> 'Someday we will find our doves once again . . . and Compassion will take Beauty by the hand . . . and I yearn for that day. . . even if I do not survive to see that day.'

'White Australia' Policy Lives on in Immigration Detention[1]

Behrouz Boochani

Christchurch, New Zealand – Growing up in a Kurdish family in the Ilam Province of Iran, I never expected my life to be affected by Australia's history of white supremacy and settler colonialism. I had little awareness of Australia, a faraway country founded as a penal colony, and built on the massacres of its Indigenous people and on European migration. It was to be decades before I would hear about the White Australia policy, an official state immigration policy, in effect between 1901 and 1973, barring non-white people from immigrating to the country and intent on making Australia a white nation.

Yet, the xenophobic legacy of the White Australia policy had a significant impact on the trajectory of my life and choked the lives of thousands of asylum seekers and migrants who were held by Australia in offshore detention centers in its former colony Papua New Guinea and on the island of Nauru, a former protectorate.

After graduating from a public university, I wrote a bit for a Kurdish magazine in Ilam but mostly contributed to Kurdish publications outside Iran and advocated the preservation of Kurdish culture, which was seen as a threat by Iranian hard-liners. In 2013, the Iranian Revolutionary Guards Corps arrested some of my journalist colleagues. I was being followed and surveilled, and I went into hiding. The pressure was relentless; I had no choice but to flee Iran.

I flew to Indonesia and from there travelled with 60 other people by boat to Australia. We were intercepted and taken by the Australian Navy to Christmas Island, an Australian territory in the Indian Ocean. Subsequently, in a shocking move by the Australian Government, I, along with hundreds of other people seeking asylum, was banished from there to a remote prison in the middle of a silent ocean in Manus Province on Papua New Guinea.

I arrived there during the same week that Kevin Rudd, then the prime minister of Australia, brought in a horrific immigration policy. On 19 July 2013, he announced that asylum seekers arriving on the Australian shores on a boat would never be allowed to settle in Australia and would be forcibly taken to Papua New Guinea and Nauru. Australia paid the government of Papua New Guinea to keep hundreds of asylum seekers like me imprisoned in a disused naval base on Manus Island.

When I set foot on the island I was confronted with a decrepit and filthy prison, and saw a group of refugees – men, women and children – who had been imprisoned there before us. They told us they had been there since 2012. A few days after we arrived, they were transferred to Australia. We were their replacements.

I had no pre-existing knowledge of this prison and thought it was extraordinary after I found out that hundreds of people had been held there in 2001. The Australian Government led by Julia Gillard, the prime minister between 2010 and 2013, had reopened it in 2012.

In 2013, we were forced to be the new subjects of this system of torture and banishment; a system by which the Australian Government could control our bodies through contractors and guards but not be held responsible for the horrors that were visited upon us.

From the very beginning I realized that I was submerged in a tragedy, and that I had been thrown into an important chapter of Australia's modern history. After struggling for six years to expose Australia's detention system through writing hundreds of articles and a book and making a film – every paragraph, every image – created and transmitted text message by text message, shot by shot, on a smuggled mobile phone, I was eventually invited to participate in the 2019 WORD Christchurch Festival in New Zealand.

After a 36-hour flight, a remarkable journey, I arrived in Christchurch in beautiful New Zealand. During that first week in the country, I spoke at the Gus Fisher Gallery in Auckland. After my talk someone told me that his father wanted to see me. He insisted I visit their family. I went to their home and spoke to a 60-year-old man who said to me, 'I also came here from Manus Island.'

It was unbelievable. He was an Iranian asylum-seeker who had been imprisoned on Manus Island in 2001. I was face to face with someone who was imprisoned there in 2001. It was as if two parts of Australia's forgotten history were meeting in another land after two decades.

When I was on Manus Island, I saw small strips of fabric tied to the fences of our remote prison. The prisoners from 2001 had tied them there to symbolize the days of their captivity. There were also drawings and poetry written on the walls of the rooms. Those material remnants represented the human beings who had been there a decade before us.

Looking at those signs, I would try to imagine who those people were and wonder where they were. Now I was sitting across the table from one of them, hearing the accounts of the torture he and hundreds of others had to endure.

I met a man at a winery who told me he was among the 438 refugees who were rescued in 2001 from an Indonesian fishing boat stranded in the Indian Ocean by a Norwegian freighter, MV Tampa. The Australian Government blocked the captain of the freighter from bringing the refugees onshore, sending troops onboard the ship.

What became known as 'The Tampa Affair' intensified the brutal anti-immigrant policies that culminated in the offshore incarceration of people like me at Manus Island and Nauru. The people on MV Tampa were rejected by Australia and accepted by New Zealand. Two decades later, one of them was there opposite me. It seemed it was another part of the puzzle of Australian history.

Australia presents a beautiful and attractive image of itself to the world but the modern history of Australia is full of puzzles. The more you investigate the more absorbed you become in its history. My journey educated me in its hidden, darker history of prejudice and xenophobia. It is a history written in places like Manus Island and Nauru, and has its roots in its settler colonial origins.

The Stolen Generation is another chapter in this story; for many decades, thousands of Indigenous children were separated from their parents by the state and forced to assimilate into settler colonial society.

Twelve years have passed since 2008 when Mr Rudd, during his first term as prime minister, apologized for Australia's violent mistreatment of its Indigenous people, for stealing their children. Still a disproportionate number of children and youth incarcerated in the Northern Territory, in Queensland and elsewhere in Australia, are Indigenous.

Five years after apologizing to the Indigenous people, the same Mr Rudd forcibly sent me and thousands like me to imprisonment at Manus Island. His government's policies, hardened further by the three prime ministers who came after him – Tony Abbott, Malcolm Turnbull and now Scott Morrison – have resulted in many children being separated from their families for years.

The White Australia policy, which officially ended in 1973, continued under another guise. The colonial habit continues in Australia, with the government using Nauru and Papua New Guinea for exiling undesirable people. Australia's presence on Manus and Nauru seems like a thread that leads you further into a dark cave with no end.

Australia is a beautiful country with great artists and writers but it is also a country where brutality and suffering are interwoven into the sociocultural fabric, ingrained in the soul of the nation. People like me represent a part of its unofficial history, a history that is full of trauma and violence.

On Documentation, Language and Social Media

Arianna Grasso

Reading through Behrouz Boochani's writings from Manus Prison is an unsettling experience that can never fully represent the brutality of the detention system to the reader. Similarly, comprehending freedom after years of unjust incarceration produces an existential vacuum that not many of us are able to make sense of. However, through Boochani's poignant documentation style, we are thrown in the visceral reality of the prison where we encounter the excruciating struggle for survival of a human being and his companions. Learning about this struggle educates us on how we should restrain from talking *about* or *for* refugees, and instead speak *with* them and finding creative and practical ways to support them. On this premise, I want to reflect upon the pivotal role social media played *in* detention and shed light on the digitally mediated language(s) used by refugees to articulate their own resistance practices *from* detention.

When, in April 2016, the PNG court ruled that Manus Prison was unconstitutional,[1] mobile phones were first allowed in the prison, and served a vital communicative bridge between refugees and people on the outside world, most of whom were unaware of the appalling conditions under which refugees were forced to live. Until that point, the geographical remoteness, fragile digital infrastructure of the detention facility, expensive phone cards sold to refugees to connect with their loved ones, as well as media embargos imposed by the PNG government to prevent journalists and humanitarian organizations from reaching the island, had all contributed to exacerbating the sense of isolation and abandonment felt by the refugees.[2] In this situation, digital technologies entering the prison space marked a turning point. As the systematic violence experienced by refugees began to be exposed to the world from a remote island in the Pacific Ocean, refugee advocates, activists and international organizations mobilized to oppose the Australian Government and their neocolonial agenda, which operated through the displacement, dispossession and erasure of the refugee subjects.

In response, refugees engaged in decolonial forms of resistance, by harnessing social media to counteract the government's punitive practices and to dismantle the structural violence of the prison system. According to former detainees on Manus and Nauru, including Boochani, social media were powerful modern tools which were used in a range of ways, including as historical archives, where the history of the Manus and Nauru facilities were recorded as integral parts of the colonial history of Australia; as ideological battlefields, where conflicting and often irreconcilable perspectives emerged; as digital pathways towards advocates, human rights defenders, Australian citizens, the international community, government, politicians, and even white supremacists; as mediums that provided temporary healing and respite or, conversely, addiction and further isolation; as a springboard for visibility and media attention for the most active users; as surveillance tools used to control and monitor refugees; and as a vehicle for xenophobic propaganda against the detainees.[3]

For his part, Boochani inaugurated a complex and articulate mode of resisting the annihilating dynamics of detention precisely through the use of his mobile phone. In the face of the possible repercussions of his dogged documenting of events, experiences and personal, political, philosophical and artistic reflections, Boochani's capacities for reporting on social media were extraordinary and crucial for providing an insight into the oppressive and subjugating logic of Manus Prison's Kyriarchal System.[4] Even though, at one point, Boochani critiqued the language of journalism for being ineffective and inadequate for creating change,[5] it was precisely through his unique inflection of this mode of communication that the urgency of the disaster unfolding while he was writing was digitally expressed. For example, the daily report of the 'Manus Siege' (see Part Five of this book)[6] is a petrifyingly vivid description of the limbo experienced by Boochani and the refugees during their last days inside the original detention facility before its closure: a recurring nightmare whose end is both coveted and dreaded. More often than not, the immediacy of the digital medium through which this experience was rendered allowed Boochani and his fellow refugees to inform the wider international community of the impending humanitarian catastrophe sanctioned by the government of Australia. The refugees' technological devices were effectively the window onto their world, which catapulted the digital audience into the gruelling reality of detention.

Through social media, the spectacle of suffering staged in Manus Prison took place in real time and before the eyes of a disconcerted public standing on the other side of the screen. By sharing his first-hand accounts digitally, in his own voice and words, Boochani, as narrator, aimed to rebuild their individual and collective sense of identity, by claiming that refugees *are* subjects for themselves and for nobody else.[7] In this light, his narrated lived experiences can be understood as the outcome of reactive reportage, whereby documenting becomes a form of dissent against the deliberate oppression of refugees, and its concealment, orchestrated by the Australian border regime. The subjective voice of the reporter is present in the reality described, 'both as an eyewitness and as a participant in the depicted events',[8] revealing the significant potential of bottom-up information counter-practices produced from marginalized places within the digital realm. In fact, the posts published from within the camp eventually succeeded in focusing public attention on Manus, igniting strong condemnation of the Australian Government.

Moreover, the communicative infrastructure of social media allowed the refugees to attach photos, videos, links and other content as evidence of that human tragedy. This material was widely circulated across a variety of online platforms and news media organizations, and was further remediated via online and offline contexts, such as street protests, awareness-raising campaigns and refugee-led events. By extension, Boochani's book, *No Friend but the Mountains* (2018) and his docufilm *Chauka, Please Tell Us the Time* (2017, co-directed with Arash Kamali Sarvestani), are outstanding and unprecedented examples of how content produced on social media can travel from one medium to another, crossing countries and prison fences, transcending established literary and cinematographic genres, and engendering concerned and outraged but also enthralled and captivated responses in publics across the world.

If journalistic language appeared to Boochani as an ephemeral instrument for conveying meaning, he defined the language of art as an everlasting and timeless language, able to surpass temporal, spatial (one could also add digital) limits.[9] From his perspective, the forgetfulness of journalism and the transitoriness of its language can be supplanted by the permanence of the artistic, which takes the shape of poetry, music, painting, acting, filming and so forth. The personal life stories of Mansour, Kazem, Farhad, Moz, Hamed, Mehdi and others discussed in Boochani's prison writings well exemplify the meaning of art in the trajectory of imprisoned human beings towards freedom.[10] Conveyed by the digital to the outer world, a variety of artistic languages coexisted and intersected in and outside the prison context, ultimately converging into a single language, that of resistance. In a space where dehumanizing practices were systemically perpetrated against refugees, affirming one's political existence seeped, in fact, into every minuscule act. A tweet, a song, a poem, a performance, a caress to a stray dog, all counted as acts of hope, 'a secret code enabling refugees to be resilient', a way ahead towards the future.[11]

In conclusion, given that access to institutionalized media was repeatedly restricted on Manus Island, both the language of journalism *and* the language of arts synergically attempted to restore to refugees their subjectivity. While, on the one hand, social media provided an avenue where the human rights violations perpetrated within the Australian detention system could be historically recorded, witnessed and hopefully one day accounted for;[12] on the other, the resources offered by digital platforms were employed to articulate the refugees' emancipatory and aesthetic perspectives in and from detention. These digital devices were ultimately crucial to 'make the invisible visible', the unseen seen, allowing refugees to gain a space of visibility, self-legitimation, and unmediated expression.[13] Refugees thus managed to successfully 'reshape the understanding of [them] as politically inept' and 'projecting an image of who they [were]' against those who sought to suppress their individual and collective voices.[14]

. . . A question echoes throughout the pages of *Freedom, Only Freedom* and beyond, 'what does humanity mean in Australia?'.[15] The question is still left unanswered. And yet, while refugees continue to be hostage to the brutal juridical apparatus of the Australian Government, there is a new definition of hope in the vocabulary of resistance.

Carceral Coloniality as a History of the Present

Helena Zeweri

What does it mean to call something a crisis? According to anthropologist Janet Roitman in her book *Anti-Crisis*,[1] crisis is a historiographic move – it is a way to mark time. More specifically, according to Roitman, it denotes what makes a particular moment different from other moments that preceded it. How far back the storyteller goes is often at their own discretion. In that way, crisis is a particular frame through which one diagnoses the present through curating which historical formations are relevant to understanding our present condition. As historian Michel de Certeau has written, history is not an innocent way of accounting for the past, but also fulfils the ideological and political needs of the present.[2]

Critiques of crisis as an organizing diagnostic logic argue that it can limit the horizon of events that come to matter in accounts of the present. While crisis is an ethical and political anchor of humanitarian and liberal discourses of care, it can prevent us from doing a full inventory of the conditions of possibility for some of today's gravest forms of injustice. In erasing those conditions, it demands an exclusive focus on victim testimonials of suffering and pain, while omitting the complex histories, subjectivities, desires and aspirations that shape experiences of systemic injustice.

Behrouz Boochani sheds light on the importance of historicizing systems of oppression and repression, and the rich, complex narratives of the people who have been thrust into such systems by the Australian border control regime. In doing so, Boochani's writings use his experience of offshore detention as a point of departure for articulating relational histories of violence. In this way, he deftly brings together the history of settler colonialism with the history of border control in Australia. At the same time, he also makes clear that people seeking asylum are not simply passive victims of systems of domination – but rather, that joy and the preservation of one's multidimensional identity is how human beings navigate global structures of penal power. In doing so, these pieces are the ingredients for a critical historiography of the crisis of offshore border control regimes. They help us to see that if there is in fact a crisis in Australia, it did not begin with offshore detention.

Boochani reminds us that offshore detention does not mark a turning point in Australian cruelty – but in fact is an extension of multiple and interconnected systems of cruelty that have been in existence since the founding of this British penal colony. He begins from his individual experience, and ties it to broader structures of repression in Iran; seeing his fellow Kurdish journalist colleagues being silenced by the Iranian Revolutionary Guards Corps is the impetus to live a life of integrity and authentic personhood – for Boochani, the act of escape is not only an act of desperation, but also an act of self-love and the desire to live an authentic life.[3] He details his journey to Christmas Island and being transported to an offshore prison in Manus Island. We might expect that Boochani's analysis would situate offshore detention as part of a more recent history of Australian border control policies that we might trace to the 2001 Tampa Affair. However, while Boochani does address this, his analysis does something unexpected – it goes back much further. He forces the reader to engage seriously with the conditions of possibility for his more than six-year imprisonment. He writes, 'Yet the xenophobic legacy of the White Australia Policy had a significant impact on the trajectory of my life and choked the lives of thousands of asylum-seekers and migrants who were held by Australia in offshore detention centres in its former colony Papua New Guinea and on the island of Nauru, a former protectorate'.[4]

Here, Boochani situates not only the MV Tampa Affair, or the policies of the Howard, Rudd, Gillard, Abbott, Turnbull or Morrison administrations, as the historical precedents for offshore detention. Instead, he goes back further and identifies the White Australia Policy as a key condition of possibility for the imprisonment of him and thousands of others seeking asylum. The White Australia Policy of 1901 essentially barred non-white people from immigration to Australia through a cluster of laws and eligibility criteria that made it virtually impossible for non-white immigrants to be allowed entry. Having only been nullified in 1973, the racist ethos and principles of the White Australia Policy live on today in the offshore detention policies – what political geographer Allison Mountz has called a neocolonial enforcement archipelago that seeks to contain migrant mobility.[5] Today's Australian immigration policies operate with a carceral logic that values white immigrants from the developed world and actively seeks to deter and punish non-white immigrants from the Global South.

But as Boochani tells us, the engineering of a White Nation, while flouting a commitment to welcoming cultural difference,[6] is a fundamental premise of

Australian nationhood. Boochani writes, 'The White Australia policy . . . continued under another guise. The colonial habit continues in Australia, with the government using Nauru and Papua New Guinea for exiling undesirable people. Australia's presence on Manus and Nauru seems like a threat that leads you further into a dark cave with no end.' In revealing Manus Prison's colonial genealogy, Boochani continues the project of decolonizing knowledge. As Omid Tofighian has written in his translator's note in *No Friend but the Mountains*, Boochani's writings represent a 'decolonial way of thinking and doing'.[7] Boochani's conceptualization of the coloniality of carcerality reappears in his mobilization of the term 'kyriarchy'. Inspired by radical feminist theologian Elisabeth Schüssler Fiorenza, kyriarchy refers to interlocking systems of oppression, and is the entry point into understanding relational formations of race, class, Indigeneity, citizenship, and gender. As Tofighian writes, the use of this term allows Boochani to encompass 'multiple, interlocking kinds of stigmatization and oppression, including racism, heteronormativity, economic discrimination, class-based violence, faith-based discrimination, colonialty, Indigenous genocide, anti-Blackness, militarism, and xenophobia'.[8] This rendering of kyriarchy, Tofighian tells us, is a way to connect the prison with Australian colonial history.[9]

What is this dark cave with no end that Boochani refers to? In my view, Boochani speaks about this in two senses: (1) it is the depths of violence that the state will go to to prevent undesirable people reaching its shores and (2) it is the darkness of Australia's settler colonial history – its elimination of Indigenous peoples and their ways of living and being that marks the foundational mode of violence that infects every social and political institution in Australia. The darkness of settler colonialism pervades all modes of governance that are generated by the nation state, including offshore prisons. Boochani's writing situates those seeking asylum as embodiments of multiple iterations of the coloniality of incarceration. He writes, '[Australia's history of prejudice and xenophobia] is a history written in places like Manus Island and Nauru, and has its roots in its settler colonial origins.' He goes on to mention the Stolen Generations, another chapter in settler colonialism's ugly violences. that represents a part of this unofficial history, 'A history that is full of trauma and violence.' The crisis is not simply the offshore imprisonment of migrants–it is the ongoing incarceration and governance of one group of people to facilitate the state's own nationalist imaginaries and its ongoing erasure of Indigenous life.

While Boochani represents this history of violence and trauma, he also shows the multi-dimensional and complex life narratives that people seeking asylum have led even prior to being taken to Manus Island. Boochani writes about

Mostafa 'Moz' Azimitabar. He plays the guitar and in 2017, recorded the rap song called 'All the Same', which protests the detention regime. Boochani shows that migrants are not engaging in creative practices as part of some larger project on resilience or heroism; rather, he argues that they are actively working to preserve their humanity and sense of personhood. Boochani tells us that in trying to preserve their sense of personhood, migrants resist a regime that seeks to constantly dehumanize and strip people of their identities whether it be through assigning them numbers as identities or refusing to allow them to play music. Moz tells Boochani, 'Music is a tool for preserving my sense of personhood, it is so I don't forget that I am a human being. Music is the language with which I can communicate with the Australian people in a deep and meaningful way. My message is nothing more than the fact that we should love each other.'

Systems of power are not abstract; they are made up of real human beings, infrastructures, environments, landscapes, and the interactions therein. They do not simply appear as a result of a series of causal events situated in the recent past. They have deep histories. A film Boochani clandestinely shot in 2017, *Chauka, Please Tell Us the Time*, explores life in detention through the symbolism of the Chauka bird native to Manus Island. Chauka is important to Manusians because its singing alerts Manusians to what time of day it is. And yet for those detained on Manus, Chauka was the name of a solitary confinement unit – a prison within the prison. As the film tragically captures, there are multiple layers of crisis at work in offshore detention. In conditions where the erasure of personhood is part of the quotidian logics of confinement, crisis becomes a futile way to describe sustained dehumanization; where one crisis ends and another begins does not tell us much about the necropolitical and biopolitical foundations of Australia as a project in which the imprisonment of migrants (both the governance of how they live and die) becomes key to the sustained elimination of Indigenous worlds, ways of being, and lives and by extension, the reinvigoration of settler modes of living.

By turning to the deeper past, Boochani shows that offshore detention is the expression of foundational and dark truths about the enduring Australian settler colonial project. I am deeply affected by these pieces because they force us to move beyond the language of humanitarianism and crisis and in doing so, allow us to make settler colonialism a thinkable part of the history of migrant incarceration. What would it mean to think about the landing on Botany Bay as the first crisis that was never addressed? The crisis is ongoing, it began hundreds of years ago, and it continues to play out on the bodies and souls of migrants who, despite this, will never stop recovering their humanity.

Map and Plates

Map

Plates

Notes

Writing in Languages of Freedom

1 It must be noted that Indonesia is not a signatory to the Refugee Convention or Protocol and is unsafe for people seeking asylum. At the time of writing, there are nearly 14,000 people living in limbo in Indonesia who have been left stranded after Australia implemented extreme and violent measures to stop people seeking asylum by boat.

2 See B. Boochani, 'Mountains and Waves/Chestnuts and Death/That River . . . This Sea', in *No Friend but the Mountains: Writing from Manus Prison*, translated by O. Tofighian, with translator's note and essay (Sydney: Picador, 2018), chapter 2.

3 B. Boochani, chapter 3, 'The Raft of Purgatory/Moons Will Tell Terrible Truths', and chapter 4, 'The Warship Meditations/Our Golshifteh is Truly Beatuiful' in *No Friend but the Mountains: Writing from Manus Prison*, translated by O. Tofighian, with translator's note and essay (Sydney: Picador, 2018).

4 B. Boochani, chapter 5, 'A Christmas (Island) Tale/A Stateless Rohingya Boy Sent Away to Follow the Star of Exile' in *No Friend but the Mountains: Writing from Manus Prison*, translated by O. Tofighian, with translator's note and essay (Sydney: Picador, 2018).

5 B. Boochani, chapter 5, 'A Christmas (Island) Tale/A Stateless Rohingya Boy Sent Away to Follow the Star of Exile' in *No Friend but the Mountains: Writing from Manus Prison*, translated by O. Tofighian, with translator's note and essay (Sydney: Picador, 2018).

6 Although Manus Island was used in the 1960s to hold West Irians, or West Papuans (detained in what was known as the Salasia Camp), who were fleeing Indonesian invasion of their land and had crossed into Australia's former colony – what is now known as Papua New Guinea.

7 B. Boochani, *No Friend but the Mountains: Writing from Manus Prison*, translated by O. Tofighian, with translator's note and essay (Sydney: Picador, 2018).

8 O. Tofighian, 'Translator's Tale: A Window to the Mountains', in B. Boochani, *No Friend but the Mountains: Writing from Manus Prison*, translated by O. Tofighian, with translator's note and essay (Sydney: Picador, 2018), xi–xxxiv.

9 S. Bennett and O. Tofighian, 'Translation as Freedom, Experimentation and Sharing: Omid Tofighian on Translating *No Friend but the Mountains*', *Biography*, 43, 4 (2020): 748–54.

10 For detailed study of this phenomenon from a Manusian perspective see N. Rooney, 'As Basket and Papu: Making Manus Social Fabric', *Oceania*, 91, 1 (2021): 86–105, DOI: https://doi.org/10.1002/ocea.5289; and M. N. Rooney, 'The Chauka Bird and Morality on Our Manus Island Home', *The Conversation*, 2 February 2018.

11 2019 WORD Christchurch Festival.

12 Mandatory detention of people seeking asylum was first introduced by the Labor government in 1992.

13 O. Tofighian, 'Behrouz Boochani and the Manus Prison Narratives: Merging Translation with Philosophical Reading', *Continuum: Journal of Media and Cultural Studies*, 32, 3 (2018): 532–40.

14 See B. Boochani, 'Manus Prison Theory', *The Saturday Paper*, translated by O. Tofighian, 11 August 2018, available online: https://www.thesaturdaypaper.com.au/opinion/topic/2018/08/11/manus-prison-theory/15339096006690 (accessed 30 April 2022); B. Boochani and O. Tofighian, '*No Friend but the Mountains* and Manus Prison Theory: In Conversation', *Borderlands Journal*, 19, 1 (April 2020): 8–26; O. Tofighian, 'Introducing Manus Prison Theory: Knowing Border Violence', *Globalizations: Law, Love and Decolonization; Reclaiming Democracy from Below*, 17, 7 (2020): 1138–56; B. Boochani and O. Tofighian, 'In Conversation: Manus Prison Theory: Borders, Incarceration and Collective Agency', *Griffith Review, Crimes and Punishments*, 65 (August 2019): 275–88; O. Tofighian, with B. Boochani, 'Narrative, Resistance and Manus Prison Theory', *Review of Middle East Studies*, Special Focus: Pluralism in Emergencies, 54, 2 (2020): 174–95; O. Tofighian, 'Manus Island and Manus Prison Theory', in R. Braidotti, E. Jones and G. Klumbytė (eds), *More Posthuman Glossary* (London: Bloomsbury, forthcoming, 2023): 77–80.

15 See the article by Roza Germian in this collection. There are also the many references by Boochani and other contributors to Kurdish culture, writers, thinkers, creatives and detainees such as Reza Barati, Fazel Chegeni, Behnam Satah, Farhad Bandesh, Mostafa 'Moz' Azimitabar, Kazem Kazemi and Fariborz Karami. In particular, *No Friend but the Mountains* and *Chauka, Please Tell Us the Time* (2017, co-directed with Arash Kamali Sarvestani) represent strong Kurdish themes, symbols, narratives and ideas. *No Friend but the Mountains* was translated into Kurdish (from English) by Iranian Kurdish scholar Hashem Ahmadzadeh. Also, see Ö. Belçim Galip, 'From Mountains to Oceans: The Prison Narratives of Behrouz Boochani', *Biography*, 43, 4 (2020): 724–35, *Project MUSE*, DOI: doi:10.1353/bio.2020.0103; and O. Tofighian, 'Behrouz Boochani and the Manus Prison Narratives: Merging Translation with Philosophical Reading', *Continuum: Journal of Media and Cultural Studies*, 32, 3 (2018), 532–40.

16 I address this issue in a thought experiment at the beginning of my supplementary essay in Boochani's book, O. Tofighian, 'No Friend but the Mountains: Translator's Reflections', B. Boochani, *No Friend but the Mountains: Writing from Manus Prison*,

translated by O. Tofighian (Sydney: Picador, 2018), 359–74. I explore the details of the thought experiment in O. Tofighian, 'Behrouz Boochani and the Manus Prison Narratives: Merging Translation with Philosophical Reading', *Continuum: Journal of Media and Cultural Studies*, 32, 3 (2018): 532–40.

17 Tofighian, 'No Friend but the Mountains: Translator's Reflections', 365.

18 Tofighian, 'Manus Island and Manus Prison Theory'.

19 E. Schüssler Fiorenza, *But She Said: Feminist Practices of Biblical Interpretation* (Boston, MA: Beacon Press, 1992); E. Schussler Fiorenza, 'Glossary', in *Wisdom Ways: Introducing Feminist Biblical Interpretation* (New York: Orbis Books, 2001), 207–16; and E. Schussler Fiorenza, 'Biblical Interpretation and Kyriachal Globalization', in Susanne Scholz (ed.), *The Oxford Handbook of Feminist Approaches to the Hebrew Bible* (Oxford: Oxford University Press, 2020), 3–20.

20 I have used the term 'horrific surrealism' as an interpretive schema for describing and examining the kyriarchal system, and for exploring other details of Manus Prison Theory, see O. Tofighian, 'Horrific Surrealism: New Storytelling for Australia's Carceral-Border Archipelago', in H. Gilbert, D. Pigram and R. Swain (eds), *Marrugeku: Telling that Story – 25 Years of Trans-Indigenous and Intercultural Performance* (Aberystwyth: Performance Research Books, 2021), 306–19.

21 O. Tofighian and B. Boochani, 'The Weaponisation of Time: Indefinite Detention as Torture', in M. Bhatia and V. Canning (eds), *Stealing Time: Miigration, Temporalities and State Violence* (Cham: Palgrave Macmillan, 2021), 65–82.

22 Also see B. Boochani and O. Tofighian, 'The Last Days in Manus Prison', *Meanji*, Summer (Melbourne: Melbourne University Press, 2018), available online: https://meanjin.com.au/essays/the-last-days-in-manus-prison/ (accessed 30 April 2022).

23 B. Boochani, 'I Write from Manus as a Duty to History', *The Guardian*, translated by O. Tofighian, 6 December 2017, available online: https://www.theguardian.com/commentisfree/2017/dec/06/i-write-from-manus-island-as-a-duty-to-history (accessed 30 April 2022); A. N. Paik, '"Create a Different Language": Behrouz Boochani & Omid Tofighian', *Public Books*, 1 April 2021, available online: https://www.publicbooks.org/create-a-different-language-behrouz-boochani-omid-tofighian/ (accessed 30 April 2022).

24 B. Boochani, 'Writing is an Act of Resistance', TEDxSydney 2019, video, 24 May 2019, available online: https://tedxsydney.com/talk/writing-is-an-act-of-resistance-behrouz-boochani/ (accessed 30 April 2022).

25 Paik, 'Create a Different Language'.

26 A saying that is also inspiration for Kurdish Canadian writer Ava Homa, author of the novel *Daughters of Smoke and Fire* (New York: The Overlook Press, 2020). See A. Homa, 'Resistance is Life: On Writing and Resiliency', Women Writers, Women['s] Books, 13 June 2020, available online: http://booksbywomen.org/resistance-is-life-on-writing-and-resiliency/ (accessed 30 April 2022).

27 Tofighian, 'Translator's Tale', xiv–xvi, xxxii–xxxiv.

Part One

Unpublished Reports: Untitled

1 Translated by Moones Mansoubi, 17 November 2015.

Unpublished Reports: One Soul, Two Bodies

1 Translated by Moones Mansoubi, 16 July 2015.

Translating Manus and Nauru: Refugee Writing

1 *Arts Everywhere*, 7 September 2020.
2 Amnesty International, *Island of Despair: Australia's 'Processing' of Refugees on Nauru*, 17 October 2016, available online: https://www.amnesty.org.au/wp-content/uploads/2016/10/ISLAND-OF-DESPAIR-FINAL.pdf (accessed 2 June 2020).
3 B. Boochani, 'Becoming MEG45', *Mascara Literary Magazine*, translated by Moones Mansoubi, 20 October 2015, available online: http://mascarareview.com/behrouz-boochani/ (accessed 30 April 2022).
4 Paula Abood and Moones Mansoubi, 'On Being', paper presented at the University of New South Wales conference on New Australian Modernities: Antigone Kefala and Australian Migrant Aesthetics, Association for the Study of Australian Literature (ASAL), Sydney, 2019.

Collaborating with Behrouz Boochani: Journalists Against a System

1 B. Boochani, 'Australia, Exceptional in Its Brutality', *Overland*, 25 April 2016, available online: https://overland.org.au/2016/04/australia-exceptional-in-its-brutality/ (accessed October 2021).
2 B. Boochani, 'Malcolm Turnbull, Why Didn't You Answer My Question on Q&A', *The Guardian*, 21 June 2016, available online: https://www.theguardian.com/commentisfree/2016/jun/21/malcolm-turnbull-why-didnt-you-answer-my-question-on-qa-about-manus-island (accessed October 2021).
3 B. Boochani, 'This is Manus Island. My Prison. My Torture. My Humiliation', *The Guardian*, 19 February 2016, available online: https://www.theguardian.com/commentisfree/2016/feb/19/this-is-manus-island-my-prison-my-torture-my-humiliation (accessed October 2021).
4 B. Boochani, 'I Write from Manus Island as a Duty to History', *The Guardian*, 6 December 2017, available online: https://www.theguardian.com/commentisfree/2017/dec/06/i-write-from-manus-island-as-a-duty-to-history (accessed October 2021).

5 B. Doherty, 'Decay, Defiance and Despair: Inside the Manus Island Refugee Camp', *The Guardian*, 16 November 2017, available online: https://www.theguardian.com/australia-news/2017/nov/16/decay-despair-defiance-inside-the-manus-island-refugee-camp (accessed October 2021).

6 B. Doherty, 'Behrouz Boochani, Voice of Manus Island Refugees, is Free in New Zealand', *The Guardian*, 14 November 2019, available online: https://www.theguardian.com/australia-news/2019/nov/14/behrouz-boochani-free-voice-manus-island-refugees-new-zealand-australia (accessed October 2021).

Part Two

This is Manus Island: My Prison. My Torture. My Humiliation

1 Published with permission of Guardian News & Media, translated by Moones Mansoubi, 19 February 2016.

Life on Manus: Island of the Damned

1 *The Saturday Paper*, translated by Moones Mansoubi, 27 February 2016.

Australia, Exceptional in Its Brutality

1 *Overland*, translated by Moones Mansoubi, 25 April 2016.

Testifying to History

1 H. White, 'Historical Truth, Estrangement, and Disbelief', in C. Fogu, W. Kansteiner and T. Presner (eds), *Probing the Ethics of Holocaust Culture* (Cambridge, MA: Harvard University Press, 2016), 71.

2 D. Laub, 'Bearing Witness or the Vicissitudes of Listening,' in S. Felman and D. Laub, *Testimony: Crises of Witnessing in Literature, Psychoanalysis and Histor* (New York: Routledge, 1991), 60.

3 See, for instance, C. Caruth, *Unclaimed Experience: Trauma, Narrative and History* (Baltimore, MD: Johns Hopkins University Press, 2007); S. Felman and D. Laub, *Testimony: Crises of Witnessing in Literature, Psychoanalysis and History* (New York: Routledge, 1991).

4 See, for instance, M. de Certeau, *The Practice of Everyday Life* (Berkeley, CA: University of California Press, 1984), 122–5.

5 S. Felman, 'Camus' *The Plague*, or a Monument to Witnessing', in S. Felman and D. Laub, *Testimony: Crises of Witnessing in Literature, Psychoanalysis and History* (New York: Routledge, 1991), 93.

6 J. E. Young, 'Toward a Received History of the Holocaust', *History and Theory*, 36, 4 (1997): 34.

7 P. Levi, *Survival in Auschwitz: The Nazi Assault on Humanity*, trans. Stuart Woolf (New York: Touchstone, 1996), 123.

8 This is an instance of what Michael Rothberg has termed 'multidirectional memory'. See M. Rothberg, *Multidirectional Memory: Remembering the Holocaust in the Age of Decolonization* (Stanford, CA: Stanford University Press, 2009).

9 B. Boochani, 'This is Manus Island. My prison. My torture. My humiliation' *The Guardian*, 19 February 2016, available online: https://www.theguardian.com/commentisfree/2016/feb/19/this-is-manus-island-my-prison-my-torture-my-humiliation (accessed 8 November 2021).

10 B. Boochani, 'Four Years after Reza Barati's Death, We Still have No Justice,' *The Guardian*, 17 February 2018, available online: https://www.theguardian.com/commentisfree/2018/feb/17/four-years-after-reza-baratis-death-we-still-have-no-justice (accessed 8 November 2021).

11 On the impossibility of justice through the Australian colonial state see for instance M. Giannacopoulos, 'Debtscape: Australia's Constitutional Nomopoly', *Borderlands*, 18, 2 (2020): 116–36, available online: https://www.exeley.com/borderlands/doi/10.21307/borderlands-2019-013 (accessed 8 November 2021); A. Whittaker, '"Dragged Like a Dead Kangaroo": Why Language Matters for Deaths in Custody', *The Guardian*, 8 September 2018, available online: https://www.theguardian.com/commentisfree/2018/sep/07/dragged-like-a-dead-kangaroo-why-language-matters-for-deaths-in-custody (accessed 27 August 2020); Human Rights Law Centre, 'Police Officers Involved in Tanya Day's Death Avoid Prosecution', 26 August 2020, available online: https://www.hrlc.org.au/news/2020/8/26/police-officers-involved-in-tanya-days-death-avoid-prosecution (accessed 27 August 2020); C. McKinnon, 'Enduring Indigeneity and Solidarity in Response to Australia's Carceral Colonialism', *Biography*, 43, 4 (2020): 691–704.

12 S. Perera, 'What is a Camp . . .?' *borderlands ejournal*, 1, 1 (2002): para. 19, available online: http://www.borderlands.net.au/vol1no1_2002/perera_camp.html (accessed 8 November 2021). See also A. Nethery, '"A Modern-Day Concentration Camp": Using History to Make Sense of Australian Immigration Detention Centres', in K. Neumann and G. Tavan (eds), *Does History Matter? Making and Debating Citizenship, Immigration and Refugee Policy in Australia and New Zealand* (Canberra: ANU Press, 2009), 65–80.

13 Perera, 'What is a Camp?', para. 5.

14 See also, for instance, the collected documentation at *Deathscapes: Mapping Race and Violence in Settler States*, available online: https://www.deathscapes.org/ (accessed 27 August 2020).

15 P. Wolfe, 'Settler Colonialism and the Elimination of the Native', *Journal of Genocide Research*, 8, 4 (2006): 388. See also J. Kēhaulani Kauanui, '"A Structure, Not an Event":

Settler Colonialism and Enduring Indigeneity', *Lateral*, 5, 1 (2016), DOI: https://doi.org/10.25158/L5.1.7, available online: https://csalateral.org/issue/5-1/forum-alt-humanities-settler-colonialism-enduring-indigeneity-kauanui/ (accessed 8 November 2021).

16 B. Boochani, 'Australia Needs a Moral Revolution', *The Guardian*, 31 August 2018, available online: https://www.theguardian.com/commentisfree/2018/aug/31/australia-needs-a-moral-revolution (accessed 8 November 2021).

17 See, for example, B. Boochani, 'Faysal Ishak Ahmed's Life was Full of Pain. Australia had a Duty to Protect Him', *The Guardian*, 30 December 2016, available online: https://www.theguardian.com/commentisfree/2016/dec/30/faysal-ishak-ahmeds-life-was-full-of-pain-australia-had-a-duty-to-protect-him (accessed 8 November 2021); B. Boochani, 'Mohamed's Life Story is a Tragedy. But It's Typical for Fathers Held on Manus', 27 March 2018, available online: https://www.theguardian.com/commentisfree/2018/mar/27/mohameds-life-story-is-a-tragedy-but-its-typical-for-fathers-held-on-manus (accessed 8 November 2021).

18 B. Boochani, 'Mohamed's Life Story is a Tragedy. But It's Typical for Fathers Held on Manus', 27 March 2018, available online: https://www.theguardian.com/commentisfree/2018/mar/27/mohameds-life-story-is-a-tragedy-but-its-typical-for-fathers-held-onmanus (accessed 8 November 2021).

19 B. Boochani, 'I Write from Manus Island as a Duty to History', *The Guardian*, 6 December 2017, available online; https://www.theguardian.com/commentisfree/2017/dec/06/i-write-from-manus-island-as-a-duty-to-history (accessed 8 November 2021).

Part Three

What It's Like in Solitary Confinement on Manus Island

1 *The Huffington Post*, translated by Moones Mansoubi, 23 August 2016.

For Refugees Kidnapped and Exiled to the Manus Prison, Hope is Our Secret Weapon

1 Published with permission of Guardian News & Media, translated by Moones Mansoubi, 3 October 2016.

Untitled

1 *Cordite Poetry Review*, translated by Moones Mansoubi, 1 November 2016.

The Day My Friend Hamid Khazaei Died

1 Published with permission of Guardian News & Media, translated by Moones Mansoubi, 28 November 2016.

Faysal Ishak Ahmed's Life Was Full of Pain. Australia Had a Duty to Protect him

1 Published with permission of Guardian News & Media, translated by Omid Tofighian, 30 December 2016.

Time and Borders, Policy and Lived Experience: A Posthumanist Critique

1 N. Castree (2009), 'The Spatio-Temporality of Capitalism', *Time & Society*, 18 (1): 26–61.

2 D. Innerarity (2012), *The Future and Its Enemies*, Stanford, CA: Stanford University Press.

3 B. Boochani, and A. Kamali Sarvestani (directors) (2018), *Chauka, Please Tell Us the Time*, Sarvin Productions.

4 J. Galbraith (2019), 'A Reflection on Chauka, Please Tell Us the Time', *Alphaville: Journal of Film and Screen Media*, (18): 193–8.

5 B. Boochani (2018), *No Friend but the Mountains: Writing from Manus Prison*, Sydney: Picador Australia.

6 O. Tofighian (2020), 'Introducing Manus Prison Theory: Knowing Border Violence', *Globalizations*, 17 (7): 1138–56.

7 B. Boochani (2016), 'Faysal Ishak Ahmed's Life was Full of Pain. Australia had a duty to protect him', *The Guardian*, translated by Omid Tofighian, 30 December. Available online: https://www.theguardian.com/commentisfree/2016/dec/30/faysal-ishakahmeds-life-was-full-of-pain-australia-had-a-duty-to-protect-him?CMP=share_btn_fb (accessed 19 April 2022).

8 B. Boochani (2017a), 'A Kyriarchal System: New Colonial Experiments/New Decolonial Resistance', *9th Annual Maroon Conference Magazine*, translated by Omid Tofighian, Charles Town, Jamaica: Charles Town Maroon Council, 20–1. Available online: https://ctmcweb2020.maroons-jamaica.com/magazine-2017/ (accessed 19 April 2022).

9 B. Boochani (2017b), 'Manus is a Landscape of Surreal Horror', *The Guardian*, translated by Omid Tofighian, 2 November. Available online: https://www.theguardian.com/commentisfree/2017/nov/02/manus-is-a-landscape-of-surreal-horror (accessed 19 April 2022).

Kurdish Identity and Journalism: Reporting to Record History

1 B. Boochani (2016), 'Faysal Ishak Ahmed's Life was Full of Pain. Australia had a Duty to Protect Him', *The Guardian*, translated by Omid Tofighian, 30 December, available online: https://www.theguardian.com/commentisfree/2016/dec/30/faysal-ishakahmeds-life-was-full-of-pain-australia-had-a-duty-to-protect-him?CMP=share_btn_fb (accessed 3 March 2022).

2 B. Boochani (2018), 'Four Years after Reza Barati's Death, We Still have No Justice', *The Guardian*, translated by Omid Tofighian, 16 February.

3 S. Bekas ([1970] 1990), 'Diwani Şerko Bekes, Qesidey Koc' (1970) in *Collection of Poems*, vol. I, Stockholm: Sara Publishers, 1990.

Part Four

A Kyriarchal System: New Colonial Experiments / New Decolonial Resistance

1 *9th Annual Maroon Conference Magazine,* translated by Omid Tofighian, Charles Town, Jamaica, Charles Town Maroon Council, 2017, 20–1.

Unpublished Report: Untitled

1 Translated by Moones Mansoubi, March 2017

An Island off Manus

1 *The Saturday Paper*, translated by Moones Mansoubi, 6 May 2017.

The Tortuous Demise of Hamed Shamshiripour, Who Didn't Deserve to Die on Manus Island

1 *The Huffington Post*, translated by Omid Tofighian, 14 August 2017.

'The Man Who Loves Ducks': The Refugee Saving Animals on Manus

1 Published with permission of Guardian News & Media, translated by Omid Tofighian, 13 September 2017.

Epistemic Violence and the Man Who Loves Ducks

1 M. Fricker (2007), *Epistemic Injustice: Power and the Ethics of Knowing*. Oxford: Oxford University Press.; I. J. Kidd, J. Medina and G. Pohlhaus (eds) (2017), *The Routledge Handbook of Epistemic Injustice*, London and New York: Routledge.

2 C. Wahlquist and B. Doherty (2016), 'Manus Detainee Climbs Tree in Rejection of PNG Refugee Status', *The Guardian*, 24 April. Available online: https://www.theguardian.com/australia-news/2016/apr/24/manus-asylum-seeker-deemed-refugee-climbstree-to-protest-settlement-in-png (accessed 26 July 2019).

3 B. Boochani (2017), 'For Six Months I was Jesus', in M. Green and A. Dao (eds), *They Cannot Take the Sky: Stories from Detention*, 18–19, Sydney: Allen & Unwin.

4 A. Kamali Sarvestani (dir.) (2021), *Tall Fences, Taller Trees*, Sarvin Productions.

5 B. Boochani (2017), 'For Six Months I was Jesus', in M. Green and A. Dao (eds), *They Cannot Take the Sky: Stories from Detention*, 18–19, Sydney: Allen & Unwin.

6 B. Boochani (2017), 'The Man Who Loves Ducks: The Refugee Saving Animals on Manus', *The Guardian*, 13 September.

7 B. Boochani (2017), 'The Man Who Loves Ducks: The Refugee Saving Animals on Manus', *The Guardian*, 13 September.

8 J. Ranciere (2004), *The Politics of Aesthetics: The Distribution of the Sensible*, translated by G. Rockhill, London: Continuum: 38.

9 B. Boochani (2017), 'The Man Who Loves Ducks: The Refugee Saving Animals on Manus', *The Guardian*, 13 September.

10 D. Woodly (2021), *Reckoning: Black Lives Matter and the Democratic Necessity of Social Movements*, New York: Oxford University Press.

11 B. Boochani (2017), 'I Write from Manus Island as a Duty to History', *The Guardian*, 5 December. Available online: https://www.theguardian.com/commentisfree/2017/dec/06/i-write-from-manus-island-as-a-duty-to-history (accessed 26 July 2019).

12 B. Boochani (2017), 'A Letter from Manus Island', *The Saturday Paper*, 9 December. Available online: https://www.thesaturdaypaper.com.au/a-letter-from-manus-island (accessed 26 July 2019).

13 B. Boochani (2017), 'A Letter from Manus Island', *The Saturday Paper*, 9 December. Available online: https://www.thesaturdaypaper.com.au/a-letter-from-manus-island (accessed 26 July 2019).

14 E. Levinas (1990), 'The Name of a Dog, or Natural Rights', in *Difficult Freedom: Essays on Judaism*, 151–3, Baltimore, MD: Johns Hopkins University Press. Thanks to Claire Loughnan for drawing my attention to this comparison.

15 B. Boochani (2017), '"The Man Who Loves Ducks": The Refugee Saving Animals on Manus', *The Guardian*, 13 September.

Exposing 'Incalculable Cruelty': Writings on Border Harms and Atrocity as Resistance

1 Amnesty International (2019), 'Award-Winning Journalist Behrouz Boochani Freed from Manus Island'. Available online: Award-winning journalist Behrouz Boochani freed from Manus Island | Amnesty International UK (accessed 10 November 2021).

2 B. Boochani (2016), 'The Day My Friend Hamid Khazaei Died', *The Guardian*, translated by Moones Mansoubi, 28 November. Available online: https://www.theguardian.com/australia-news/2016/nov/28/the-day-my-friend-hamid-kehazaeidied (accessed 10 November 2021).

3 B. Boochani (2016), 'Faysal Ishak Ahmed's Life was Full of Pain. Australia had a Duty to Protect Him', *The Guardian*, translated by Omid Tofighian, 30 December. Available online: https://www.theguardian.com/commentisfree/2016/dec/30/faysal-ishakahmeds-life-was-full-of-pain-australia-had-a-duty-to-protect-him?CMP=share_btn_fb (accessed 10 November 2021).

4 B. Boochani (2018), *No Friend but the Mountains: Writing from Manus Prison*, Sydney: Picador.

5 B. Boochani (2016), 'Life on Manus: Island of Damned', *The Saturday Paper*, translated by Moones Mansoubi, 27 February. Available online: https://www.thesaturdaypaper.com.au/opinion/topic/2016/02/27/life-manus-island-thedamned/14564916002937#hrd (accessed 10 November 2021).

6 B. Boochani (2016), 'What It's Like in Solitary Confinement on Manus Island', *The Huffington Post*, translated by Moones Mansoubi, 23 August. Available online: https://www.huffingtonpost.com.au/behrouz-boochani/what-its-like-in-solitaryconfinement-on-manus-island_a_21456114/ (accessed 10 November 2021).

7 M. Bhatia and V. Canning (eds) (2021), *Stealing Time: Migration, Temporalites and State Violence*, Cham: Palgrave Macmillan see also O. Tofighian and B. Boochani (2021), 'The Weaponisation of Time: Indefinite Detention as Torture', in M. Bhatia and V. Canning (eds), *Stealing Time: Migration, Temporalities and State Violence*, 65–82, Cham: Palgrave Macmillan.

8 A. Mountz (2020), *The Death of Asylum: Hidden Geographies of the Enforcement Archipelago*, Minneapolis, MN: University of Minnesota Press.

9 B. Boochani (2017), '"The Man Who Loves Ducks": The Refugee Saving Animals on Manus', *The Guardian*, translated by Omid Tofighian, 13 September. Available online: https://www.theguardian.com/australia-news/2017/sep/14/the-man-who-lovesducks-the-refugee-saving-animals-on-manus (accessed 10 November 2021).

10 B. Agozino (2020), 'Fuck the Law: Decolonizing Nomophilitis with the Discourse of Love', *Globalizations*, 17 (7): 1091–103.

11 B. Boochani (2017), 'Manus is a Landscape of Surreal Horror', *The Guardian*, translated by Omid Tofighian, 2 November. Available online: https://www.theguardian.com/commentisfree/2017/nov/02/manus-is-a-landscape-of-surreal-horror (accessed 10 November 2021).

Part Five

Days Before the Forced Closure of Manus, We Have No Safe Place to Go

1 Published with permission of Guardian News & Media, translated by Omid Tofighian, 27 October 2017.

Diary of Disaster: The Last Days Inside Manus Island Detention Centre

1 Published with permission of Guardian News & Media, translated by Omid Tofighian, 30 October 2017.

The Refugees Are in a State of Terror on Manus

1 Published with permission of Guardian News & Media, translated by Omid Tofighian, 31 October 2017.

A Merciless Fear Provoked by Last Night's Events Has Gripped the Manus Island Camp

1 Published with permission of Guardian News & Media, translated by Omid Tofighian, 1 Novermber 2017.

Manus is a Landscape of Surreal Horror

1 Published with permission of Guardian News & Media, translated by Omid Tofighian, 2 November 2017.

The Breath of Death on Manus Island: Starvation and Sickness

1 Published with permission of Guardian News & Media, translated by Omid Tofighian, 3 November 2017.

All We Want is Freedom, Not Another Prison Camp

1 Published with permission of Guardian News & Media translated by Omid Tofighian, 13 November 2017.

I Write from Manus as a Duty to History

1 Published with permission of Guardian News & Media, translated by Omid Tofighian, 6 December 2017.

A Letter from Manus

1 *The Saturday Paper*, translated by Omid Tofighian, 9 December 2017.

23 Days of Resistance Alongside Behrouz

1 For examples of publications and social media postings, see S. Kanapahti, 'As a Refugee Detained Indefinitely by Australia, I wish You a Happy New Year', *The Guardian*, 31 December 2019, available online: https://www.theguardian.com/commentisfree/2020/jan/01/as-a-refugee-detained-indefinitely-by-australia-i-wish-you-a-happy-new-year (accessed 21 October 2021); S. Kanapahti, 'After Six Years We Leave Manus Island to Go to "Nowhere": An Asylum Seeker's Story', *Sydney Morning Herald*, 5 September 2019, available online: www.smh.com.au/national/after-six-years-we-leave-manus-island-to-go-to-nowhere-an-asylum-seeker-s-story-20190905-p52o9t.html (accessed 21 October 2021); S. Kanapahti, 'From Manus Island to Port Moresby', *The Saturday Paper*, 14 September 2019; S. Kanapahti, twitter post @Shamindan1, 18 December 2019, available online: https://twitter.com/Shamindan1/status/1207106981892214784; S. Kanapahti, twitter post @Shamindan1, 7 July 2019, available online: https://twitter.com/Shamindan1/status/1147640595201978368.

2 B.Boochani, 'As I Learn to Live in Freedom, Australia is Still Tormenting Refugees', *The Age and Sydney Morning Herald*, translated by Omid Tofighian, 17 May 2020 https://www.smh.com.au/national/as-i-learn-to-live-in-freedom-australia-is-still-tormenting-refugees-20200513-p54smg.html. (accessed 21 October 2021).

Words That Escaped from Prison

1 M. L. King, Jr, 'Letter from Birmingham Jail', *The Atlantic*, August 1963, available online: https://www.theatlantic.com/magazine/archive/2018/02/letter-from-a-birmingham-jail/552461/ (accessed October 2021).

2 B. Boochani, 'Island of the Damned', *The Saturday Paper*, 27 February 2016, available online: https://www.thesaturdaypaper.com.au/opinion/topic/2016/02/27/life-manus-island-the-damned/14564916002937 (accessed October 2021).

3 B. Boochani, 'A Letter from Manus Island', *The Saturday Paper*, 9 December 2017, available online: https://www.thesaturdaypaper.com.au/news/politics/2017/12/09/letter-manus-island/15127380005617 (accessed October 2021).
4 B. Boochani, 'The Torturous Demise of Hamed Shamshiripour, Who Didn't Deserve to Die on Manus Island', *The Huffington Post*, 13 August 2017, available online: https://www.huffpost.com/archive/au/entry/the-tortuous-demise-of-hamed-shamshiripour-who-didnt-deserve-t_a_23076393 (accessed October 2021).
5 B. Boochani, 'The Torturous Demise of Hamed Shamshiripour, Who Didn't Deserve to Die on Manus Island', *The Huffington Post*, 13 August 2017, available online:https://www.huffpost.com/archive/au/entry/the-tortuous-demise-of-hamedshamshiripour-who-didnt-deserve-t_a_23076393 (accessed October 2021).
6 B. Boochani, `The Torturous Demise of Hamed Shamshiripour, Who Didn't Deserve to Die on Manus Island', *The Huffington Post*, 13 August 2017, available online: https://www.huffpost.com/archive/au/entry/the-tortuous-demise-of-hamedshamshiripour-who-didnt-deserve-t_a_23076393 (accessed October 2021).
7 B. Boochani, 'Paladin Scandal is Only a Drop in the Ocean of Corruption on Manus and Nauru', *The Guardian Australia*, 27 February 2019, available online: https://www.theguardian.com/commentisfree/2019/feb/27/the-paladin-scandal-is-only-a-drop-in-the-ocean-of-corruption-on-manus-and-nauru (accessed December 2021).
8 I. Mohammad, 'Four Years on Manus Island', *The Saturday Paper*, 15 July 2017, available online: https://www.thesaturdaypaper.com.au/2017/07/18/four-years-manus-island/15003000004932 (accessed October 2021).

Part Six

Four Years After Reza Barati's Death, We Still Have No Justice

1 Published with permission of Guardian News & Media, translated by Omid Tofighian, 16 February 2018.
2 Only the two PNG guards faced court. They were sentenced and have now been released from prison.

Policy of Exile

1 *The Saturday Paper*, translated by Moones Mansoubi, 3 March 2018.

Mohamed's Life Story is a Tragedy. But it's Typical for Fathers Held on Manus

1 Published with permission of Guardian News & Media, translated by Omid Tofighian, 27 March 2018.

The Gay, Transgender and Bisexual Men on Manus Are Forced into Silence

1 Published with permission of Guardian News & Media, translated by Moones Mansoubi, 16 May 2018.

Salim Fled Genocide to Find Safety. He Lost His Life in the Most Tragic Way

1 Published with permission of Guardian News & Media, translated by Omid Tofighian, 25 May 2018.

Manus Island Poem

1 *The Saturday Paper* translated by Moones Mansoubi, 16 June 2018.

Journalism, Borders and Oppression: The Nauru Context

1 This was the same tactic employed by Australia in Manus Island, as reported by Behrouz Boochani in his piece 'Four Years after Reza Barati's Death, We Still have No Justice', reproduced above as the first chapter in this part of the book, B. Boochani (2018a), 'Four Years after Reza Barati's Death, We Still have No Justice', *The Guardian*, translated by Omid Tofighian, 16 February. Available online: https://www.theguardian.com/commentisfree/2018/feb/17/four-years-after-rezabaratis-death-we-still-have-no-justice (accessed 31 October 2021). He describes how 'immigration had fomented hate against the refugees among the locals', which directly resulted in the killing of Reza Barati.

2 Some of the photos and videos taken while inside detention can be viewed on my website here: www.ellieshakiba.com.

3 The issues of over-mining, over-fishing, environmental destruction, official corruption and Australia's role in Nauru are well summarized in the article by Anne Davies and Ben Doherty (2018), 'Corruption, Incompetence and a Musical: Nauru's Cursed History', *The Guardian*, 3 September. Available online: https://www.theguardian.com/world/2018/sep/04/corruption-incompetence-and-a-musicalnaurus-riches-to-rags-tale (accessed 31 October 2021).

4 Compare with Behrouz Boochani's chapter in this part of the book, 'The Gay, Transgender and Bisexual Men on Manus are forced into Silence', where he writes: 'Covering up rapes and sexual harassments has been the policy of the Australian government during these years.' B. Boochani (2018), 'The Gay, Transgender and Bisexual Men on Manus are Forced into Silence', *The Guardian*, translated by Moones Mansoubi, 16 May. Available online: https://www.theguardian.com/commentisfree/2018/may/16/the-gaytransgender-andbisexual-men-on-manus-are-forced-into-silence (accessed 31 October 2021).

5 Even a former president who later opposed the detention of refugees was blacklisted and denied medical treatment, as outlined in Davidson's article (2019), 'Sprent Dabwido: Former Nauru President and Leader of Nauru 19 Dies, Aged 46', *The Guardian*, 8 May. Available online: https://www.theguardian.com/world/2019/may/08/sprent-dabwido-former-nauru-presidentand-leader-of-nauru-19-dies-aged-46 (accessed 31 October 2021).

6 The denial of medical treatment was a major tactic used by Australian immigration authorities against refugees in both Manus and Nauru, as described in detail by Boochani in his chapter in this part of the book, B. Behrouz (2018), 'Salim Fled Genocide to Find Safety. He Lost His Life in the Most Tragic Way', *The Guardian*, translated by Omid Tofighian, 25 May. Available online: https://www.theguardian.com/commentisfree/2018/may/25/salim-fledgenocide-to-find-safety-he-lost-his-life-in-the-most-tragic-way (accessed 31 October 2021), where he wrote about a 'predetermined political strategy which smothers sick refugees and tosses them into a horrific bureaucratic maze. They not only leave refugees untreated, but they also aggravate the minor pains of healthy refugees and force them to return to the countries they fled.'

7 As detailed in L. Allam (2020), 'Aboriginal People in Prison and Out-of-Home Care Suffering under "Punitive" Covid-19 Restrictions', *The Guardian*, 26 May. Available online: https://www.theguardian.com/australia-news/2020/may/27/aboriginal-people-in-prison-and-outof-home-care-suffering-under-punitive-covid-19-restrictions (accessed 31 October 2021).

On Mothers, Nature and the Body

1 B. Boochani, '"White Australia" Policy Lives on in Immigrant Detention', *New York Times*, 20 September 2020, available online: https://www.nytimes.com/2020/09/20/opinion/australia-white-supremacy-refugees.html (accessed May 2021).

2 J. Laurie, 'Full Airplane Interview from August 21, 1983 with Ninoy Aquino', 2014, available online: https://youtu.be/eBD4vJS0dPk?t=360 (accessed July 2021).

3 B. Boochani, 'Four Years after Reza Barati's Death, We Still have No Justice', *The Guardian*, 17 February 2018, available online: https://www.theguardian.com/

commentisfree/2018/feb/17/four-years-after-reza-baratis-death-we-still-have-no-justice (accessed June 2021).

4 B. Boochani, 'This is Manus Island. My Prison. My Torture. My Humiliation', *The Guardian*, 19 February 2016, available online: https://www.theguardian.com/commentisfree/2016/feb/19/this-is-manus-island-my-prison-my-torture-my-humiliation (accessed June 2021).

5 B. Boochani, '"This is Hell out Here": How Behrouz Boochani's Diaries Expose Australia's Refugee Shame', *The Guardian*, 4 December 2017, available online: https://www.theguardian.com/world/2017/dec/04/this-is-hell-behrouz-boochani-diaries-expose-australia-refugee-shame (accessed May 2021).

6 B. Boochani (2017), 'Diary of Disaster: The Last Days Inside Manus Island Detention Centre', *The Guardian*, translated by Omid Tofighian, 30 October. Available online: https://www.theguardian.com/commentisfree/2017/oct/30/diary-of-disaster-the-last-days-inside-manus-island-detention-centre (accessed 28 September 2021).

7 B.Boochani (2017), 'A Merciless Fear Provoked by Last Night's Events Has Gripped the Manus Island Camp,' translated by Omid Tofighian, *The Guardian*, 1 November, Available online: https://www.theguardian.com/commentisfree/2017/nov/01/a-merciless-fear-provoked-by-the-events-last-night-has-gripped-the-camp (accessed 28 September 2021).

8 B. Boochani (2017), 'Manus is a Landscape of Surreal Horror', *The Guardian*, translated by Omid Tofighian, 2 November. Available online: https://www.theguardian.com/commentisfree/2017/nov/02/manus-is-a-landscape-of-surreal-horror (accessed 28 September 2021).

9 B. Boochani, 1 December 2017, 'There was our silence and their violence as Manus camp was evacuated', available online: https://www.theguardian.com/commentisfree/2017/dec/01/there-was-our-silence-and-their-violence-as-manus-camp-was-evacuated (accessed 28 September 2021).

10 M. Walden, 'Asylum Seekers in Detention 200 Times more Likely to Commit Self-Harm than Australians, Research Finds', ABC News, 14 October 2019, available online: https://www.abc.net.au/news/2019-10-14/asylum-seekers-in-detention-200-more-likely-to-commit-self-harm/11600148 (accessed July 2021).

11 B. Boochani, *No Friend but the Mountains: Writing from Manus Prison*, translated by O. Tofighian, with translator's note and essay (Sydney: Picador, 2018), 300.

12 B. Boochani, *No Friend but the Mountains: Writing from Manus Prison*, translated by O. Tofighian, with translator's note and essay (Sydney: Picador, 2018), 300.

13 B. Boochani, *No Friend but the Mountains: Writing from Manus Prison*, translated by O. Tofighian, with translator's note and essay (Sydney: Picador, 2018), 300.

14 B. Boochani, *No Friend but the Mountains: Writing from Manus Prison*, translated by O. Tofighian, with translator's note and essay (Sydney: Picador, 2018), 302.

15 F. Measham, 'Love in a Time of Apocalypse', *Meanjin*, 78, 3 (2019): 1–5, available online: https://meanjin.com.au/essays/love-in-a-time-of-apocalypse/ (accessed September 2021).

Part Seven

Manus Prison Theory

1 *The Saturday Paper*, translated by Omid Tofighian, 11 August 2018.

Australia Needs a Moral Revolution

1 Published with permission of Guardian News & Media, translated by Omid Tofighian, 31 August 2018.

Five Years in Manus Purgatory

1 *The Saturday Paper*, translated by Omid Tofighian, 29 September 2018.

'Sam could have been Saved': Where Does the Money for Healthcare go on Manus?

1 Published with permission of Guardian News & Media, translated by Omid Tofighian, 28 November 2018.

The Paladin Scandal is Only a Drop in the Ocean of Corruption on Manus and Nauru

1 Published with permission of Guardian News & Media, translated by Omid Tofighian, 27 February 2019.

The 'Papua New Guinea Solution' in Australian Public Discourse and Human Rights Activism

1 See B. Boochani, 'Days before the Forced Closure of Manus, We Have No Safe Place to Go', *The Guardian*, 27 October 2017 (accessed 1 November 2021); B. Boochani, 'All We Want is Freedom – Not Another Prison Camp', *The Guardian*, 13 November 2017 (accessed 1 November 2021).

2 For example, see J. Chandler, 'Welcome to Manus, the Island that has Been Changed Forever by Australian Asylum-Seeker Policy', *The Guardian*, 15 December 2014 (accessed 1 November 2021); J. Chandler, 'Manus in Balance', *The Monthly*, 1 February 2015 (accessed 1 November 2021); H. Davidson, 'Manus Island Residents

Air Grievances about Hosting Australian Detention Centre', *The Guardian*, 22 January 2016 (accessed 1 November 2021).

3 See Business & Human Rights Resource Centre, 'No Business in Abuse Website', 12 October 2015, available online: https://www.business-humanrights.org/en/latest-news/no-business-in-abuse-website/ (accessed 1 November 2021). Also, see B. O'Brien, 'Extraterritorial Detention Contracting in Australia and the UN Guiding Principles on Business and Human Rights', Business and Human Rights Journal, 1, 2 (2016): 333–40.

4 See M. N. Rooney, 'Reflections on How the Manus Island Detention Centre Promotes Gender-Based Violence', Dev Policy Blog, 9 May (2014) (accessed 1 November 2021); M. N. Rooney, 'Friday Essay: The Chauka Bird and Morality on Our Manus Island Home', *The Conversation*, 2 February 2018 (accessed 1 November 2021); M. N. Rooney, 'Manus Island: How a Small Community Agreed to Host an Australian Detention Centre in Return for Economic Benefits', *The Independent*, 9 February 2018 (accessed 1 November 2021); J. Wallis and S. Dalsgaard, 'Money, Manipulation and Misunderstanding', *Journal of Pacific History*, 51, 3 (2016): 301–29.

5 For example, see, 'Offshore Processing Centres in Nauru and Papua New Guinea: Contract Management of Garrison Support and Welfare Services', Australian National Audit Office, 17 January 2017, available online: https://www.anao.gov.au/work/performance-audit/offshore-processing-centres-nauru-and-papua-new-guinea-contract-management (accessed 1 November 2021).

6 M. Alimardanian, 'Dark Development: Human Ipact and Politics of Ambiguity in "Papua New Guinea Solutio"', *Current Anthropology* (forthcoming, 2022).

7 For example, see 'A Pathway Forward, Inquiry into the Destruction of 46,00-Year-Old Cave at the Juukan Gorge in the Pilbara Region of Western Australia', Joint Committees, Parliamentary Business, Parliament of Australia, available online: https://www.aph.gov.au/Parliamentary_Business/Committees/Joint/Northern_Australia/CavesatJuukanGorge/Report/section?id=committees%2freportjnt%2f024757%2f77690 (accessed 1 November 2021).

Australian Corruption and the Pacific: Dollars, Displacement and Deaths

1 H. Davidson (2019), '"Six Years and I Didn't Achieve Anything": Inside Manus, a Tropical Purgatory', *The Guardian Australia*, 21 June. Available online: https://www.theguardian.com/australia-news/2019/jul/21/six-years-and-i-didnt-achieveanything-inside-manus-a-tropical-purgatory (accessed 26 October 2021).

2 H. Davidson (2019), '"Life on Manus: How Australia Transformed a Tropical Island into a Prison – Video', *The Guardian Australia*, 30 June. Available online: https://www.theguardian.com/australia-news/video/2019/jul/30/life-on-manus-

howaustralia-transformed-a-tropical-island-into-a-prison-video (accessed 26 October 2021).

3 H. Davidson, and C. Knaus (2019), 'Paladin Staff on Manus Walk off Job over Pay and Working Conditions', *The Guardian Australia*, 26 February. Available online: https://www.theguardian.com/australia-news/2019/feb/26/paladin-staff-on-manus-walkoff-job-over-pay-and-working-conditions (accessed 26 October 2021).

4 C. Knaus, and H. Davidson (2019), 'Australia's Offshore Contracts: How Mllions were Spent for Dubious Outcomes', *The Guardian Australia*, 23 February. Available online: https://www.theguardian.com/australia-news/2019/feb/23/australias-offshorecontracts-how-millions-were-spent-for-dubious-outcomes (accessed 26 October 2021).

5 B. Doherty, (2015), 'Exclusive: Woman Allegedly Raped in Manus Detention Centre Accuses Transfield of Cover-Up', *The Guardian Australia*, 23 February. Available online: https://www.theguardian.com/australia-news/2015/aug/27/exclusivewoman-allegedly-raped-in-manus-detention-centre-accuses-transfield-of-cover-up (accessed 26 October 2021).

6 B. Boochani (2018), '"Sam Could have Been Saved": Where Does the Money for Healthcare Go on Manus?', *The Guardian*, translated by Omid Tofighian, 28 November. Available online: https://www.theguardian.com/commentisfree/2018/nov/28/sam-could-have-been-saved-where-does-the-money-for-healthcare-go-onmanus (accessed 26 October 2021).

7 B. Boochani, and O. Tofighian (2020), 'A Human Being Feels They are on a Precipice: COVID-19's Threshold Moment', *Andrew and Renata Kaldor Centre for International Law, UNSW Law, COVID-19 Watch*, 16 June. Available online: https://www.kaldorcentre.unsw.edu.au/publication/%E2%80%98-human-being-feels-theyare-precipice%E2%80%
99-covid-19%E2%80%99s-threshold-moment (accessed 26 October 2021).

Part Eight

This Election is an Opportunity to Vote for Humanity and Freedom

1 Published with permission of Guardian News & Media, translated by Omid Tofighian, 15 May 2019.

'The Boats are Coming' is One of the Greatest Lies Told to the Australian People

1 Published with permission of Guardian News & Media, translated by Omid Tofighian, 1 July 2019.

2 Editors' note: Peter Dutton stated in 2018 that some women asylum seekers were 'trying it on' when they made allegations of rape and sexual abuse and were transferred to Australia for treatment in a bid to be granted asylum, see Davidson, H. 'Peter Dutton says women using rape and abortion claims as ploy to get to Australia', *The Guardian*, 20 June 2019, https://www.theguardian.com/australia-news/2019/jun/20/peter-dutton-says-women-using-and-abortion-claims-as-ploy-to-get-to-australia (accessed 30/06/2022).

The Truth About Self-harm in Offshore Detention

1 *The Saturday Paper*, translated by Omid Tofighian, 7 September 2019.

Purification by Love

1 *Atmos*, vol. 2: Latitude, translated by Omid Tofighian, 18 October 2019, available online: https://atmos.earth/volumes/latitude/ (accessed 30 April 2022).

Emotion, Responsibility and Hope for Different Futures

1 See Tazreiter on the concept of the 'border of disappearance' C. Tazreiter (2020b), 'Moved by the Oceans: The Haunting Presence of the Disappeared', in M. Gržinić, J. Pristovšek, S. Uitz and C. Jauernik (eds), *Genealogy of Amnesia*, KHM Catalogue, 186–9, Vienna: Weltmuseum Wien. Available online: https://www.weltmuseumwien.at/en/exhibitions/stories-of-traumatic-pasts/ (accessed 4 February 2022); C. Tazreiter (2020a), 'Emotions, Borders and the Role of Visual Culture in Refugee Arrivals', in S. Turnbull, M. Bhatia and G. Lousley (eds), *Borders, Racisms, and State Violence*, Special Issue, *Critical Criminology*, 2 (28). Available online: https://rdcu.be/b4H4N (accessed 4 February 2022); Tazreiter C. (2017), 'The Unlucky in the 'Lucky Country': Asylum Seekers, Irregular Migrants and Refugees and Australia's Politics of Disappearance', in L. Hill and C. van Ham (guest eds), Special Issue, *Australian Journal of Human Rights*, 23 (2): 242–60.

2 More recently, I have also worked in collaborations with Boochani, with other refugees, and with Omid Tofighian, aimed at articulating new visions of more just futures (B. Boochani, C. Tazreiter and O. Tofighian (2021), 'The Multiple Faces of the People Smuggler', in Ruth Balint and Julie Kalman (eds), *SMUGGLED: An Illegal History of Journeys to Australia*, 176–90, Sydney: New South Press; C. Tazreiter, and O. Tofighian, with B. Boochani (2022), 'Spectres of Subjugation/Inter-subjugation/Resubjugation of People Seeking Asylum: The Kyriarchal System in Australia's Necropoleis', in P. Billings (ed.), *Regulating Refugee Protection through Social Welfare Law, Policy and Praxis*, 68–90, London: Routledge; C. Tazreiter (2021), 'Race, Migration and Visual Culture: The Activist Artist Challenging the

Ever-Present Colonial Imagination', in B. Miyamoto and M. Ruiz (eds), *Art & Migration*, Rethinking Art History Series, 113–32, Manchester: Manchester University Press.)

3 B. Boochani (this collection), 'The Truth about Self-Harm in Offshore Detention'.

4 B. Boochani (this collection), '"The Boats are Coming" is One of the Greatest Lies Told to the Australian People'.

Prison Notebooks and the Oceanic–Kurdish Connection: Boochani's Political Reflectivity

1 S. Soukup (2015), 'Gramsci Comes to Indiana', *Persons & Polis*. Available online: https://cultureoflife.org/2015/04/06/gramsci-comes-to-indiana/ (accessed, 19 October 2021): 1.

2 A. Gramsci (1971), *Selections from the Prisons Notebooks of Antonio Gramsci*, New York: International Publishers.

3 B. Boochani (2016a), 'A Letter from Manus Island', 9 December 2017. Available online: https://www.thesaturdaypaper.com.au/news/politics/2017/12/09/letter-manusisland/15127380005617 (accessed 28 October 2021).

4 A. Öcalan (2017), *The Political Thought of Abdullah Öcalan*, London: Pluto Press.

5 D. Buller (2013), 'Slain Kurdish Activist Cansiz Leaves Stamp on Militant PKK', Reuters, 11 January. Available online: https://www.reuters.com/article/uk-france-kurdscansiz-idUKBRE90A0Z920130111?edition-redirect=uk (29 October 2021).

6 S. Talebi (2016), 'Critical Trauma Studies: Understanding Violence, Conflict and Memory in Everyday Life', 101–10, New York: New York University Press.

7 IranWire (2020), 'Sepideh's Diary: A Shocking Glimpse into Women Prisons in Iran. Available online: https://iranwire.com/en/features/7382 (accessed 28 October 2021).

8 B. Boochani (2016), 'This is Manus Island. My prison. My torture. My humiliation', 19 February. Available online: https://www.theguardian.com/commentisfree/2016/feb/19/this-is-manus-island-my-prison-my-torture-my-humiliation (accessed 28 October 2021).

9 B. Boochani (2017), 'I Write from Manus Island as a Duty to History', 6 December 2021. https://www.theguardian.com/commentisfree/2017/dec/06/i-write-from-manusisland-as-a-duty-to-history (accessed 28 October 2021).

10 B. Boochani (2016), 'The Gay, Transgender and Bisexual Men on Manus are Forced into Silence', 16 May. Available online: https://www.theguardian.com/commentisfree/2018/may/16/the-gay-transgender-and-bisexual-men-on-manusare-forced-into-silence (accessed 28 October 2021).

11 B. Boochani (2016), 'For Refugees Kidnapped and Exiled to the Manus Prison, Hope is Our Secret Weapon', 3 October. Available online: https://www.theguardian.com/australia-news/2016/oct/03/for-refugees-kidnapped-and-exiled-to-the-manusprison-hope-is-our-secret-weapon (accessed 28 October 2021).

12 B. Boochani (2016), 'This is Manus Island. My prison. My torture. My humiliation', 19 February. Available online: https://www.theguardian.com/commentisfree/2016/feb/19/this-is-manus-island-my-prison-my-torture-my-humiliation (accessed 28 October 2021).
13 B. Boochani (2016), 'Manus Island's Appalling Health Care Record', 16 April. Available online: https://www.thesaturdaypaper.com.au/news/politics/2016/04/16/manusislands-appalling-health-care-record/14607288003132 (accessed 28 October 2021).
14 B. Boochani (2017), 'I Write from Manus Island as a Duty to History', 6 December 2021. https://www.theguardian.com/commentisfree/2017/dec/06/i-write-from-manusisland-as-a-duty-to-history (accessed 28 October 2021).
15 E. Hau'ofa (1994), 'Our Sea of Islands', *Contemporary Pacific*, 6 (1): 148–61. Available online: http://www.jstor.org/stable/23701593 (accessed 13 September 2021).

Part Nine

As I Learn to Live in Freedom, Australia is Still Tormenting Refugees

1 *The Age* and *Sydney Morning Herald*, translated by Omid Tofighian, 17 May 2020.

'A Human Being Feels They Are on a Precipice': Covid-19's Threshold Moment

1 *Andrew and Renata Kaldor Centre for International Law,* University of New South Wales Law, Covid-19 Watch, 16 June 2020.

Boochani's 'Political Poetics': Subverting and Reimagining the Fiction of Politics

1 J. Ranciere (2018), 'The Politics of Fiction', *Qui Parle*, 27 (2): 287.
2 B. Boochani (2017), 'A Letter from Manus Island', *The Saturday Paper*, 9–15 December. Available online: https://www.thesaturdaypaper.com.au/news/politics/2017/12/09/letter-manus-island/15127380005617 (accessed 13 October 2021).
3 L. O'Shea (2019), 'How We Fight the Border Industrial Complex', *Overland*, 3 September. Available online: https://overland.org.au/2019/09/how-we-fight-theborder-industrial-complex/ (accessed 13 October 2021).
4 B. Boochani (2019), 'The Boats are Coming is One of the Greatest Lies Told to the Australian People', *The Guardian*, 2 July. Available online: https://www.theguardian.com/commentisfree/2019/jul/02/the-boats-are-coming-is-one-of-the-greatest-liestold-to-the-australian-people (accessed 13 October 2021).
5 J. Ranciere (2018), 'The Politics of Fiction', *Qui Parle*, 27 (2): 269.

6 Ranciere defines the structure of rationality as: 'a mode of presentation of things that cuts out a frame and places elements within it so as to compose a situation and make it perceptible and intelligible'. It is, moreover, Ranciere argues, 'a form of linkage of events' – that is, the 'causal connections' joining those events – that confers to the linkage 'the modality of the real, the possible or the necessary' (J. Ranciere (2018), 'The Politics of Fiction', *Qui Parle*, 27 (2): 269). Ranciere's argument in his paper is a complex one that I do not explore here. Nonetheless, some of that paper's ideas have influenced my thinking about contemporary politics, literature and the possible.

7 J. Ranciere (2018), 'The Politics of Fiction', *Qui Parle*, 27 (2): 269.

8 J. Ranciere (2018), 'The Politics of Fiction', *Qui Parle*, 27 (2): 269–70.

9 Boochani's discussion of the 'surreal' of politics (Tofighian in Boochani 2018: xxix, 367–9) is comparable to Ranciere's discussion of 'real politics'.

10 J. Ranciere (2018), 'The Politics of Fiction', *Qui Parle*, 27 (2): 270.

11 B. Boochani (2017), 'I Write from Manus as a Duty to History', *The Guardian*, 6 December. Available online: https://www.theguardian.com/commentisfree/2017/dec/06/i-write-from-manus-island-as-a-duty-to-history (accessed 13 October 2021).

12 A. Surma (2018), 'In a Different Voice: "A Letter from Manus Island" as Poetic Manifesto', *Continuum*, 32 (4): 524n.25.

13 B. Boochani (2018), 'Manus Prison Poetics/Our Voice: Revisiting "A Letter from Manus Island", A Reply to Anne Surma', *Continuum*, 32 (4): 527–31.

14 J. Dean (2009), *Democracy and Other Neoliberal Fantasies: Communicative Capitalism and Left Politics*, Durham, NC, and London: Duke University Press: 71.

15 J. Dean (2009), *Democracy and Other Neoliberal Fantasies: Communicative Capitalism and Left Politics*, Durham, NC, and London: Duke University Press: 72.

16 B. Boochani, and O. Tofighian (2020), 'A Human Being Feels They are on a Precipice: COVID-19's Threshold Moment', *Kaldor Centre For International Refugee Law*, 16 June. Available online: https://www.kaldorcentre.unsw.edu.au/publication/'-human-beingfeels-they-are-precipice'-covid-19's-threshold-moment (accessed 13 October 2021).

17 A. Vogl, C. Fleay, C. Loughnan, P. Murray and S. Dehm (2020), 'COVID-19 and the Relentless Harms of Australia's Punitive Immigration Detention Regime', *Crime, Media, Culture: An International Journal*, 17 (1): 43–51, for a discussion of the ways in which Covid's impacts are disproportionately experienced by refugees, people seeking asylum, and other non-citizens, as well as the ways in which the Australian government's treatment of these groups during the pandemic has reinforced already discriminatory practices.

18 B. Boochani, and O. Tofighian (2020), 'A Human Being Feels They are on a Precipice: COVID-19's Threshold Moment', *Kaldor Centre For International Refugee Law*, 16 June. Available online: https://www.kaldorcentre.unsw.edu.au/

publication/‘-human-beingfeels-they-are-precipice’-covid-19’s-threshold-moment (accessed 13 October 2021).

19 B. Boochani, and O. Tofighian (2020), ‘A Human Being Feels They are on a Precipice: COVID-19’s Threshold Moment’, *Kaldor Centre For International Refugee Law*, 16 June. Available online: https://www.kaldorcentre.unsw.edu.au/publication/‘-human-beingfeels-they-are-precipice’-covid-19’s-threshold-moment (accessed 13 October 2021).

20 B. Boochani, and O. Tofighian (2020), ‘A Human Being Feels They are on a Precipice: COVID-19’s Threshold Moment’, *Kaldor Centre For International Refugee Law*, 16 June. Available online: https://www.kaldorcentre.unsw.edu.au/publication/‘-human-beingfeels-they-are-precipice’-covid-19’s-threshold-moment (accessed 13 October 2021).

21 B. Boochani (2019), ‘The Paladin Scandal is Only a Drop in the Ocean of Corruption on Manus and Nauru’, *The Guardian*, 27 February. Available online: https://www.theguardian.com/commentisfree/2019/feb/27/the-paladin-scandal-is-only-adrop-in-the-ocean-of-corruption-on-manus-and-nauru (accessed 13 October 2021).

22 See also R. Andersson (2019), *No Go World: How Fear is Redrawing Our Maps and Infecting Our Politics*, Oakland, CA: University of California Press, and T. Miller (2019), *Empire of Borders: The Expansion of the US Border around the World*, London and New York: Verso.

23 B. Boochani, and O. Tofighian (2020), ‘A Human Being Feels They are on a Precipice: COVID-19’s Threshold Moment’, *Kaldor Centre For International Refugee Law*, 16 June. Available online: https://www.kaldorcentre.unsw.edu.au/publication/‘-human-beingfeels-they-are-precipice’-covid-19’s-threshold-moment (accessed 13 October 2021).

24 B. Boochani, and O. Tofighian (2020), ‘A Human Being Feels They are on a Precipice: COVID-19’s Threshold Moment’, *Kaldor Centre For International Refugee Law*, 16 June. Available online: https://www.kaldorcentre.unsw.edu.au/publication/‘-human-beingfeels-they-are-precipice’-covid-19’s-threshold-moment (accessed 13 October 2021).

Journalism as Dialogue: Creating Collective Activism Through the Prison Writings of Behrouz Boochani

1 B. Boochani (2016) ‘This is Manus Island. My Prison. My Torture. My Humiliation’, *The Guardian*, 18 February. Available online: https://www.theguardian.com/commentisfree/2016/feb/19/this-is-manus-island-my-prison-my-torture-myhumiliation (accessed 15 April 2022).

2 F. H. McKay, S. L. Thomas and S. Kneebone (2012), ‘“It Would be Okay if They Came through the Proper Channels”: Community Perceptions and Attitudes toward Asylum Seekers in Australia’, *Journal of Refugee Studies*, 25 (1): 113–33;

A. L. Haw (2021), '"Hapless Victims' or Making Trouble": Audience Responses to Stereotypical Representations of Asylum Seekers in Australian News Discourse', *Journalism Practice*, 1–19, DOI: 10.1080/17512786.2021.1930574.

3 E. Davey (2019), 'Life in Stasis: Behrouz Boochani's Manus Prison Literature', *Los Angeles Review of Books*, 28 May. Available online: https://lareviewofbooks.org/article/life-in-stasis-behrouz-boochanis-manus-prison-literature/ (accessed 15 April 2022).

4 M. Rae, R. Holman and A. Nethery (2018), 'Self-represented Witnessing: The Use of Social Media by Asylum Seekers in Australia's Offshore Immigration Detention Centres', *Media Culture & Society*, 40 (4): 484, DOI: 10.1177/0163443717746229.

5 M. Rae, R. Holman and A. Nethery (2018), 'Self-represented Witnessing: The Use of Social Media by Asylum Seekers in Australia's Offshore Immigration Detention Centres', *Media Culture & Society*, 40 (4): 488, DOI: 10.1177/0163443717746229.

6 P. Deandrea (2018), 'Journeys in Translation: Refugee Poems', *From the European South*, 3: 28. Available online: http://europeansouth.postcolonialitalia.it (accessed 15 April 2022).

7 Boochani's memoir, *No Friend but the Mountains*, is praised for its genre-crossing style and creative language, L. Stonebridge (2021), 'Survival Time / Human Time: Hannah Arendt and Behrouz Boochani', In *Writing and Righting: Literature in the Age of Human Right*, 93–110, Oxford: University of Oxford Press; E. Davey (2019), 'Life in Stasis: Behrouz Boochani's Manus Prison Literature', *Los Angeles Review of Books*, 28 May. Available online: https://lareviewofbooks.org/article/life-in-stasis-behrouz-boochanis-manus-prison-literature/ (accessed 15 April 2022); even his entries on his Facebook page are considered poetic, M. Rae, R. Holman and A. Nethery (2018), 'Self-represented Witnessing: The Use of Social Media by Asylum Seekers in Australia's Offshore Immigration Detention Centres', *Media Culture & Society*, 40 (4): 486. DOI: 10.1177/0163443717746229: 486.

8 B. Boochani (2018), 'Mohamed's Life Story is a Tragedy. But It's Typical for Fathers Held on Manus', *The Guardian*, 27 March. Available online: https://www.theguardian.com/commentisfree/2018/mar/27/mohameds-life-story-is-a-tragedy-but-its-typicalfor-fathers-held-on-manus (accessed 15 April 2022).

9 B. Boochani (2018), 'Australia Needs a Moral Revolution', *The Guardian*, 30 August. Available online: https://www.theguardian.com/commentisfree/2018/aug/31/australia-needs-a-moral-revolution (accessed 15 April 2022).

10 G. Whitlock (2020), '*No Friend but the Mountains*: How Should I Read This?', *Biography*, 43 (4): 714, DOI: 10.1353/bio.2020.0102.

11 B. Boochani (2018), 'Refugees' Lives Have become Weapons in a Rugged Political Contest', *The Guardian*, 19 June. Available online: https://www.theguardian.com/commentisfree/2018/jun/20/our-lives-are-have-become-weapons-in-a-ruggedpolitical-contest (accessed 15 April 2022).

12 B. Boochani (2017), 'I Write from Manus Island as a Duty to History', *The Guardian*, 5 December. Available online: https://www.theguardian.com/commentisfree/2017/dec/06/i-write-from-manus-island-as-a-duty-to-history (accessed 15 April 2022).

13 M. Mansoubi (2020), 'Translating Manus and Nauru: Refugee Writing', *artseverywhere*, 7 September. Available online: https://www.artseverywhere.ca/manus-nauru/(accessed 15 April 2022).

14 L. Stonebridge (2020), 'Manus Island is the Soul of the System: Lyndsey Stonebridge Talks to Omid Tofighian', *The Age of Superdiversity*, n.p. Available online: https://superdiversity.net/2020/06/18/manus-island-is-the-soul-of-the-system-lyndseystonebridge-talks-to-omid-tofighian/amp/ (accessed 15 April 2022).

15 L. Stonebridge (2021), 'Survival Time / Human Time: Hannah Arendt and Behrouz Boochani', In *Writing and Righting: Literature in the Age of Human Right*, 107, Oxford: University of Oxford Press.

16 L. Elkin (2017), 'Foreword', In *Translation as Transhumance*, by M. Gansel. Translated by Ros Schwartz, vii. New York: Feminist Press.

17 G. Whitlock (2020), '*No Friend but the Mountains*: How Should I Read This?', *Biography*, 43 (4): 705–23, DOI: 10.1353/bio.2020.0102; A. Poletti (2020), 'This Place Really Needs a Lot of Intellectual Work: Behrouz Boochani's Innovation in Life Writing as a Transnational Intellectual Practice', *Biography*, 43 (4): 755–62, DOI: doi:10.1353/bio.2020.0077; B. Boochani, and O. Tofighian (2018), 'The Last Days in Manus Prison', *Meanjin*, Summer, Melbourne: Melbourne University Press. Available online: https://meanjin.com.au/essays/the-last-days-in-manus-prison/ (accessed 15 April 2022); O. Tofighian (2018a), 'Translator's Tale: A Window to the Mountains', B. Boochani, *No Friend but the Mountains: Writing from Manus Prison*, translated by Omid Tofighian, xi–xxxiv, Sydney: Picador; O. Tofighian (2018b), 'Truth to Power: My Time Translating Behrouz Boochani's Masterpiece', The Conversation, 16 August. Available online: https://theconversation.com/truth-to-power-my-time-translating-behrouz-boochanis-masterpiece-101589 (accessed 15 April 2022).

18 Boochani claims that 'Australia Needs a Moral Revolution', B. Boochani (2018), 'Australia Needs a Moral Revolution', *The Guardian*, 30 August. Available online: https://www.theguardian.com/commentisfree/2018/aug/31/australia-needs-a-moral-revolution (accessed 15 April 2022). When exploring the urgent nature of such statements, and the radical potential they contain, consider the co-authored piece, '"A Human Being Feels They are on a Precipice": COVID-19's Threshold Moment'. Boochani and Tofighian draw significant parallels between the disastrous state of the detention camps and our current experience of the coronavirus pandemic. Going further they call for global decolonial action: 'We must fight for a

society in which racism, violence and marginalisation are no longer profitable, where refugees and asylum seekers are treated with dignity, and where there are no more Black deaths in custody', B. Boochani, and O. Tofighian (2020), '"A Human Being Feels They Are on a Precipice": COVID-19's Threshold Moment', *Kaldor Centre for International Refugee Law, UNSW Sydney*, 16 June. Available online: https://www.kaldorcentre.unsw.edu.au/publication/'-human-being-feels-they-are-precipice'-covid-19's-threshold-moment (accessed 15 April 2022).

Part Ten

For the Refugees Australia Imprisons Music is Liberation, Life and Defiance

1 Published with permission of Guardian News & Media, translated by Omid Tofighian, 7 September 2020.

'White Australia' Policy Lives on in Immigration Detention

1 *New York Times*, translated by Omid Tofighian, 20 September 2020.

On Documentation, Language and Social Media

1 B. Doherty, H. Davidson and P. Karp (2016), 'Papua New Guinea Court Rules Detention of Asylum Seekers on Manus Island Illegal', *The Guardian*, 26 April. Available online: https://www.theguardian.com/australia-news/2016/apr/26/papua-new-guineacourt-rules-detention-asylum-seekers-manus-unconstitutional (accessed 5 October 2021).
2 L. Briskman (2013), 'Technology, Control, and Surveillance in Australia's Immigration Detention Centres', *Refuge*, 29 (1): 9–19.
3 A. Grasso (forthcoming), *Twitter and Refugeehood: Practices of Decolonial Resistance in Contemporary Australia*, Palgrave Macmillan.
4 O. Tofighian (2020), 'Introducing Manus Prison Theory: Knowing Border Violence', *Globalizations*, 1–19.
5 B. Boochani (2017), 'A Kyriarchal System: New Colonial Experiments/New Decolonial Resistance', *9th Annual Maroon Conference Magazine*, translated by Omid Tofighian, Charles Town, Jamaica: Charles Town Maroon Council, 20–1: https://ctmcweb2020.maroons-jamaica.com/magazine-2017/ (accessed 25 March 2022).
6 Also see B. Boochani (2017), 'Diary of Disaster: The Last Days Inside Manus Island Detention Centre', *The Guardian*, translated by Omid Tofighian, 30 October. Available

online: https://www.theguardian.com/commentisfree/2017/oct/30/diary-of-disaster-the-last-days-inside-manus-island-detention-centre (accessed 5 October 2021).

7 B. Boochani (2017), 'All We Want is Freedom – Not Another Prison Camp', *The Guardian*, translated by Omid Tofighian, 13 November. Available online: https://www.theguardian.com/commentisfree/2017/nov/13/all-we-want-is-freedom-notanother-prison-camp (accessed 2 September 2021).

8 C. Aare (2018) 'A Narratological Investigation of Eyewitness Reporting: How a Journalistic Mission Affects Narrative Structures of the Text', *Associacao Brasileira de Pesquisadores em Jornalismo*, 14 (3): 680.

9 B. Boochani (2017), 'A Kyriarchal System: New Colonial Experiments/New Decolonial Resistance', *9th Annual Maroon Conference Magazine*, translated by Omid Tofighian, Charles Town, Jamaica: Charles Town Maroon Council, 20–1: https://ctmcweb2020.maroons-jamaica.com/magazine-2017/ (accessed 25 March 2022).

10 B. Boochani (2016), 'Mehdi Savari: Actor, Prisoner, and Improbable Star of Manus Island', *New Matilda*, translated by Omid Tofighian, 23 June. Available online: https://newmatilda.com/2016/06/23/mehdi-savari-actor-prisoner-and-improbable-star-ofmanus-island/ (accessed 2 September 2021). ; B. Boochani (2017), 'A Kyriarchal System: New Colonial Experiments/New Decolonial Resistance', *9th Annual Maroon Conference Magazine*, translated by Omid Tofighian, Charles Town, Jamaica: Charles Town Maroon Council, 20–1: https://ctmcweb2020.maroons-jamaica.com/magazine-2017/ (accessed 25 March 2022); B. Boochani (2017), '"The Man Who Loves Ducks": The Refugee Saving Animals on Manu', *The Guardian*, translated by Omid Tofighian, 13 September. Available online: https://www.theguardian.com/australia-news/2017/sep/14/the-man-wholovesducks-the-refugee-saving-animals-on-manus (accessed 2 September 2021); B. Boochani (2017), 'The Tortuous Demise of Hamed Shamshiripour, Who Didn't Deserve to Die on Manus Island', *The Huffington Post*, translated by Omid Tofighian, 14 August. Available online: http://www.huffingtonpost.com.au/behrouz-boochani/the-tortuous-demise-of-hamed-shamshiripour-who-didnt-deserve-t_a_23076393/ (accessed 2 September 2021); B. Boochani (2019), 'This Election is an Opportunity to Vote for Humanity and Freedom', *The Guardian*, translated by Omid Tofighian, 15 May. Available online: https://www.theguardian.com/commentisfree/2019/may/15/this-electionis-anopportunity-to-vote-for-humanity-and-freedom (accessed 2 September 2021).

11 B. Boochani (2016), 'For Refugees Kidnapped and Exiled to the Manus Prison, Hope is Our Secret Weapon', *The Guardian*, translated by Moones Mansoubi, 3 October. Available online: https://www.theguardian.com/australia-news/2016/oct/03/for-refugees-kidnapped-and-exiled-to-the-manus-prison-hope-is-our-secretweapon (accessed 2 September 2021).

12 M. Rae, R. Holman and A. Nethery (2018), 'Self-Represented Witnessing: The Use of Social Media by Asylum Seekers in Australia's Offshore Immigration Detention Centres', *Media, Culture & Society*, 40 (4): 482.

13 A. C. Russel and N. D. Diaz (2011), 'Photography in Social Work Research: Using Visual Image to Humanize Findings', *Qualitative Social Work*, 12 (4): 433–53.

14 B. Boochani (2017), 'A Letter from Manus Island', *The Saturday Paper*, 9–15 December. Available online: https://www.thesaturdaypaper.com.au/news/politics/2017/12/09/letter-manus-island/15127380005617 (accessed 2 September 2021).

15 B. Boochani (2020), 'As I Learn to Live in Freedom, Australia is Still Tormenting Refugees', *The Age and Sydney Morning Herald*, translated by Omid Tofighian, 17 May. Available online: https://www.smh.com.au/national/as-i-learn-to-live-in-freedomaustralia-is-still-tormenting-refugees-20200513-p54smg.html (accessed 2 September 2021).

Carceral Coloniality as a History of the Present

1 J. Roitman (2013), *Anti-Crisis*, Durham, NC: Duke University Press.

2 M. de Certeau(1992), *The Writing of History*, New York: Columbia University Press.

3 B. Boochani (2020), '"White Australia Policy' Lives on in Immigrant Detention', *The New York Times*, 20 September. Available online: https://www.nytimes.com/2020/09/20/opinion/australia-white-supremacy-refugees.html (accessed 19 February 2022).

4 B. Boochani (2020), '"White Australia Policy' Lives on in Immigrant Detention', *The New York Times*, 20 September. Available online: https://www.nytimes.com/2020/09/20/opinion/australia-white-supremacy-refugees.html (accessed 19 February 2022).

5 A. Mountz (2011), 'The Enforcement Archipelago: Detention, Haunting, and Asylum on Islands', *Political Geography*, 30 (3): 118–28.

6 G. Hage (2000), *White Nation: Fantasies of White Supremacy in a Multicultural Society*, Sydney: Pluto Press.

7 O. Tofighian, 'Translator's Tale: A Window to the Mountains', B. Boochani, *No Friend but the Mountains: Writing from Manus Prison*, translated by O. Tofighian, xxvii, Picador, 2018.

8 O. Tofighian, 'No Friend but the Mountains: Translator's Reflections', B. Boochani, *No Friend but the Mountains: Writing from Manus Prison*, translated by O. Tofighian (Sydney: Picador, 2018), 370.

9 O. Tofighian, 'No Friend but the Mountains: Translator's Reflections', B. Boochani, *No Friend but the Mountains: Writing from Manus Prison*, translated by O. Tofighian (Sydney: Picador, 2018), 370.

Plates

1 Measures: 40 m. long and 4–5 m. wide. Approximately 130 people were living in this tunnel from late 2013 to early 2014. It had about 56 sets of bunk beds, with less than 20 cm between each bed. The Second World War-era hangar with a corrugated metal roof, contained only one or two fans.

2 Text copied from Boochan's Facebook page: 'After taking two Nepali refugees by force to deport them, immigration have started to hand out negative status papers to asylum seekers. Too many officers are with them, knocking on doors to wake people up and tell them "go back to your country". The whole prison is in shock at this moment and people with negative status are so scared. It's totally barbaric. Why didn't you try to deport them four years ago? Why did you take four years to process them and subject them to four years of suffering? PNG police attacked Mike prison 4am to deport two Nepali asylum seekers. They took one of them while he was crying and the other one escaped and now is lost. There were about 10 police officers. We don't know where they are now. The asylum seekers from Nepal were under a lot of pressure for a long time. Five of them signed under pressure and went back to their countries last week. Immigration has said to the people with negative status sign this paper and get $20000, or we will deport you by force.' Translated by Moones Mansoubi.

3 Text copied from Boochani's Facebook page: 'I took this photo from a beautiful tree that was cut yesterday. In other words, they killed it. The Australian gov and the big companies in Manus prison have cut thousands of trees during last three years. They have cut many beautiful trees because of building the prisons here and huge accommodations for their employees. I don't know whether they got permission from the PNG environmental organisation or not. Also, I don't know if there are any NGOs in PNG to protect jungles and trees? But the point is clear and that is this system has destroyed Manus nature to build a prison. There was a big forest surrounding the prison but it was destroyed by Australian government for the purpose of deterrence. A jungle was destroyed to stop people coming to Australia by boat. Everything in Manus prison is plastic such as cutlery, plates, cups and thongs. Unintentionally, everyone produces kilos of plastic rubbish every day. I have a question for the authorities: what do they do with thousands of tons of plastic and where do they bury them? Manus nature is amazingly beautiful and I think it has become a victim -like us- under this cruel policy. Translated by Moones Mansoubi.'

References

Aare, C. (2018) 'A Narratological Investigation of Eyewitness Reporting: How a Journalistic Mission Affects Narrative Structures of the Text', *Associação Brasileira de Pesquisadores em Jornalismo*, 14(3): 676–99.

Abood, P. and Mansoubi, M. (2019) 'On Being', Paper presented at the University of New South Wales Conference on New Australian Modernities: Antigone Kefala and Australian Migrant Aesthetics, Association for the Study of Australian Literature (ASAL), Sydney.

Agozino, B. (2020) 'Fuck the Law: Decolonizing Nomophilitis with the Discourse of Love', *Globalizations*, 17(7): 1091–1103.

Alimardanian, M. (forthcoming, 2022) 'Dark Development: Human Impact and Politics of Ambiguity in "Papua New Guinea Solution"', *Current Anthropology*.

Allam, L. (2020) 'Aboriginal People in Prison and Out-of-Home Care Suffering under "Punitive" Covid-19 Restrictions', *The Guardian*. Available online: https://www.theguardian.com/australia-news/2020/may/27/aboriginal-people-in-prison-and-out-of-home-care-suffering-under-punitive-covid-19-restrictions

Amnesty International (2016) 'Island of Despair: Australia's "Processing" of Refugees on Nauru'. Available online: https://www.amnesty.org.au/wp-content/uploads/2016/10/ISLAND-OF-DESPAIR-FINAL.pdf

Amnesty International (2019) 'Award-Winning Journalist Behrouz Boochani Freed from Manus Island'. Available online: https://www.amnesty.org.uk/press-releases/award-winning-journalist-behrouz-boochani-freed-manus-island

Andersson, R. (2019) *No Go World: How Fear is Redrawing Our Maps and Infecting Our Politics*, Oakland, CA: University of California Press.

Australian National Audit Office (2017) 'Offshore Processing Centres in Nauru and Papua New Guinea: Contract Management of Garrison Support and Welfare Services'. Available online: https://www.anao.gov.au/work/performance-audit/offshore-processing-centres-nauruand-papua-new-guinea-contract-management

Awal, Md. R., Cao, R., Mitrovic, S. and Ka-Wei Lee, R. (2020) 'On Analyzing Antisocial Behaviors amid COVID-19 Pandemic' (arXiv:2007.10712). Available online: https://doi.org/10.48550/arXiv.2007.10712

Bekas, S. ([1970] 1990) 'Dîwanî Şêrko Bêkes, Qesidey Koç', in *Collection of Poems*, vol. I, Stockholm: Sara Publishers.

Belçim Galip, Ö. (2020) 'From Mountains to Oceans: The Prison Narratives of Behrouz Boochani', *Biography*, 43(4): 724–35. DOI: 10.1353/BIO.2020.0103.

Bennett, S. and Tofighian, O. (2020) 'Translation as Freedom, Experimentation and Sharing: Omid Tofighian on Translating *No Friend but the Mountains*', *Biography* (University of Hawai'i Press), 43(4): 748-54.

Bhatia, M. and Canning, V. (eds) (2021) *Stealing Time: Migration, Temporalities and State Violence*, Cham: Palgrave Macmillan.

Boochani, B. (2015) 'Becoming MEG45', translated by Moones Mansoubi, *Mascara Literary Magazine*. Available online: http://mascarareview.com/behrouz-boochani/

Boochani, B. (2016) 'Australia, Exceptional in Its Brutality', translated by Moones Mansoubi, *Overland*. Available online: https://overland.org.au/2016/04/australia-exceptional-in-its-brutality/

Boochani, B. (2016) 'Faysal Ishak Ahmed's Life was Full of Pain. Australia Had a Duty to Protect Him', translated by Omid Tofighian, *The Guardian*. Available online: https://www.theguardian.com/commentisfree/2016/dec/30/faysal-ishak-ahmeds-life-was-full-of-pain-australia-had-a-duty-to-protect-him?CMP=share_btn_fb

Boochani, B. (2016) 'For Refugees Kidnapped and Exiled to the Manus Prison, Hope is Our Secret Weapon', translated by Moones Mansoubi, *The Guardian*. Available online: https://www.theguardian.com/australianews/2016/oct/03/forrefugeeskidnapped andexiled-to-the-manus-prison-hope-is-our-secret-weapon

Boochani, B. (2016) 'Island of the Damned', translated by Moones Mansoubi, *The Saturday Paper*. Available online: https://www.thesaturdaypaper.com.au/opinion/topic/2016/02/27/life-manus-island-the-damned/14564916002937

Boochani, B. (2016) 'Malcolm Turnbull, Why Didn't You Answer My Question on Q&A', translated by Omid Tofighian, *The Guardian*. Available online: https://www.theguardian.com/commentisfree/2016/jun/21/malcolm-turnbull-why-didnt-you-answer-my-question-on-qa-about-manus-island

Boochani, B. (2016) 'Manus Island's Appalling Health Care Record', translated by Moones Mansoubi, *The Saturday Paper*. Available online: https://www.thesaturdaypaper.com.au/news/politics/2016/04/16/manus-islands-appalling-health-care-record/14607288003132#hrd

Boochani, B. (2016) 'Mehdi Savari: Actor, Prisoner, and Improbable Star of Manus Island', translated by Omid Tofighian, *New Matilda*. Available online: https://newmatilda.com/2016/06/23/mehdi-savari-actor-prisoner-and-improbable-star-of-manus-island/

Boochani, B. (2016) 'The Day My Friend Hamid Khazaei Died', translated by Moones Mansoubi, *The Guardian*. Available online: https://www.theguardian.com/australia-news/2016/nov/28/the-day-my-friend-hamid-kehazaei-died

Boochani, B. (2016) 'This is Manus Island. My Prison. My Torture. My Humiliation', translated by Moones Mansoubi, *The Guardian*. Available online: https://www.theguardian.com/commentisfree/2016/feb/19/this-is-manus-island-my-prison-my-torture-my-humiliation

Boochani, B. (2016) 'What It's Like in Solitary Confinement on Manus Island', translated by Moones Mansoubi, *The Huffington Post*. Available online: https://www.huffingtonpost.com.au/behrouzboochani/whatitslikeinsolitaryconfinement on-manus-island_a_21456114/

Boochani, B. (2017) 'A Kyriarchal System: New Colonial Experiments/New Decolonial Resistance', *9th Annual Maroon Conference Magazine*, translated by Omid Tofighian, Charles Town, Jamaica: Charles Town Maroon Council, 20–1. Available online: https://ctmcweb2020.maroons-jamaica.com/magazine-2017/

Boochani, B. (2017) 'A Letter from Manus Island', translated by Omid Tofighian, *The Saturday Paper*. Available online: https://www.thesaturdaypaper.com.au/a-letter-from-manus-island

Boochani, B. (2017) 'All We Want is Freedom – Not Another Prison Camp', translated by Omid Tofighian, *The Guardian*. Available online: https://www.theguardian.com/commentisfree/2017/nov/13/all-we-want-is-freedom-not-another-prison-camp

Boochani, B. (2017), 'A Merciless Fear Provoked by Last Night's Events Has Gripped the Manus Island Camp,' translated by Omid Tofighian, *The Guardian*, Available online: https://www.theguardian.com/commentisfree/2017/nov/01/a-merciless-fear-provoked-by-the-events-last-night-has-gripped-the-camp

Boochani, B. (2017) 'Days before the Forced Closure of Manus, We Have No Safe Place to Go', translated by Omid Tofighian, *The Guardian*. Available online: https://www.theguardian.com/commentisfree/2017/oct/27/days-before-the-forced-closure-of-manus-we-have-no-safe-place-to-go

Boochani, B. (2017) 'Diary of Disaster: The Last Days Inside Manus Island Detention Centre', translated by Omid Tofighian, *The Guardian*. Available online: https://www.theguardian.com/commentisfree/2017/oct/30/diary-of-disaster-the-last-days-inside-manus-island-detention-centre

Boochani, B. (2017) 'For Six Months I Was Jesus', in M. Green and A. Dao (eds), *They Cannot Take the Sky: Stories from Detention*, 3–25, Sydney: Allen & Unwin.

Boochani, B. (2017) 'I Write from Manus Island as a Duty to History', translated by Omid Tofighian, *The Guardian*. Available online: https://www.theguardian.com/commentisfree/2017/dec/06/i-write-from-manus-island-as-a-duty-to-history

Boochani, B. (2017) 'Manus is a Landscape of Surreal Horror', translated by Omid Tofighian, *The Guardian*. Available online: https://www.theguardian.com/commentisfree/2017/nov/02/manus-is-a-landscape-of-surreal-horror

Boochani, B. (2017) '"The Man Who Loves Ducks": The Refugee Saving Animals on Manus', translated by Omid Tofighian, *The Guardian*. Available online: https://www.theguardian.com/australia-news/2017/sep/14/the-man-who-loves-ducks-the-refugee-saving-animals-on-manus

Boochani, B. (2017) 'The Tortuous Demise of Hamed Shamshiripour, Who Didn't Deserve to Die on Manus Island', translated by Omid Tofighian, *The Huffington Post*. Available online: http://www.huffingtonpost.com.au/behrouz-boochani/the-tortuous-demise-of-hamed-shamshiripour-who-didnt-deserve-t_a_23076393/

Boochani, B. (2017) 'There Was Our silence and Their Violence as Manus camp Was Evacuated', translated by Moones Mansoubi, *The Guardian*. Available online: https://www.theguardian.com/commentisfree/2017/dec/01/there-was-our-silence-and-their-violence-as-manus-camp-was-evacuated

Boochani, B. (2017) '"This is Hell out Here": How Behrouz Boochani's Diaries Expose Australia's Refugee Shame', translated by Moones Mansoubi and Omid Tofighian, *The Guardian*. Available online: https://www.theguardian.com/world/2017/dec/04/this-is-hell-behrouz-boochani-diaries-expose-australia-refugee-shame

Boochani, B. (2018) 'Australia Needs a Moral Revolution', translated by Omid Tofighian, *The Guardian*. Available online: https://www.theguardian.com/commentisfree/2018/aug/31/australia-needs-a-moral-revolution

Boochani, B. (2018) 'Four Years after Reza Barati's Death, We Still Have No Justice', translated by Omid Tofighian, *The Guardian*. Available online: https://www.theguardian.com/commentisfree/2018/feb/17/four-years-after-reza-baratis-death-we-still-have-no-justice

Boochani, B. (2018) 'Mohamed's Life Story is a Tragedy. But It's Typical for Fathers Held on Manus', translated by Omid Tofighian, *The Guardian*. Available online: https://www.theguardian.com/commentisfree/2018/mar/27/mohameds-life-story-is-a-tragedy-but-its-typical-for-fathers-held-on-manus

Boochani, B. (2018) *No Friend but the Mountains: Writing from Manus Prison*, translated by Omid Tofighian, Sydney: Picador Australia.

Boochani, B. (2018) 'Refugees' Lives Have become Weapons in a Rugged Political Contest', translated by Moones Mansoubi, *The Guardian*. Available online: https://www.theguardian.com/ commentisfree/2018/jun/20/our-lives-are-have-become-weapons-in-a-rugged-political-contest

Boochani, B. (2018) 'Salim Fled Genocide to Find Safety. He Lost His Life in the Most Tragic Way', translated by Omid Tofighian, *The Guardian*. Available online: https://www.theguardian.com/commentisfree/2018/may/25/salim-fled-genocide-to-find-safety-he-lost-his-life-in-the-most-tragic-way

Boochani, B. (2018) '"Sam Could have Been Saved": Where Does the Money for Healthcare Go on Manus?', translated by Omid Tofighian, *The Guardian*. Available online: https://www.theguardian.com/commentisfree/2018/nov/28/sam-could-have-been-saved-where-does-the-money-for-healthcare-go-on-manus

Boochani, B. (2018) 'The Gay, Transgender and Bisexual Men on Manus are Forced into Silence', translated by Moones Mansoubi, *The Guardian*. Available online: https://www.theguardian.com/commentisfree/2018/may/16/the-gay-transgender-and-bisexual-men-on-manus-are-forced-into-silence

Boochani, B. and Kamali Sarvestani, A. (directors) (2018) *Chauka, Please Tell Us the Time*, Eindhoven: Sarvin Productions.

Boochani, B. and Tofighian, O. (2018) 'The Last Days in Manus Prison', *Meanjin*, Summer, Melbourne: Melbourne University Press. Available online: https://meanjin.com.au/essays/the-last-days-in-manus-prison/

Boochani, B. (2019) 'How Many More People Must Die on Manus before Australia Ends Indefinite Detention', translated by Omid Tofighian, *The Guardian*. Available online: https://www.theguardian.com/commentisfree/2019/jun/03/how-many-more-people-must-die-on-manus-before-australia-ends-indefinite-detention

Boochani, B. (2019) 'This Election is an Opportunity to Vote for Humanity and Freedom', translated by Omid Tofighian, *The Guardian*. Available online: https://www.theguardian.com/commentisfree/2019/may/15/this-election-is-an-opportunity-to-vote-for-humanity-and-freedom

Boochani, B. (2019) 'Writing is an Act of Resistance', TEDxSydney 2019, video. Available online: https://tedxsydney.com/talk/writing-is-an-act-of-resistance-behrouz-boochani/

Boochani, B. and Tazreiter, C (2019) 'Notes on Exile: Behrouz Boochani in Conversation with Claudia Tazreiter', *Australian Journal of Human Rights*, 25(3). DOI: https://doi.org/10.1080/1323238X.2019.1685768.

Boochani, B. and Tofighian, O. (2019) 'In Conversation: Manus Prison Theory: Borders, Incarceration and Collective Agency', Griffith Review, *Crimes and Punishments*, 65: 275–88

Boochani, B. (2020) 'As I Learn to Live in Freedom, Australia is Still Tormenting Refugees', translated by Omid Tofighian, *The Age* and *Sydney Morning Herald*. Available online: https://www.smh.com.au/national/as-i-learn-to-live-in-freedom-australia-is-stilltormenting-refugees-20200513-p54smg.html

Boochani, B. (2020) 'For the Refugees Australia Imprisons, Music is Liberation, Life and Defiance', translated by Omid Tofighian, *The Guardian*. Available online: https://www.theguardian.com/commentisfree/2020/sep/07/for-the-refugees-australia-imprisons-music-is-liberation-life-and-defiance?mc_cid=b065785f36&mc_eid=8b9d450e65

Boochani, B. (2020) '"White Australia" Policy Lives on in Immigrant Detention', translated by Omid Tofighian, *New York Times*. Available online: https://www.nytimes.com/2020/09/20/opinion/australia-white-supremacy-refugees.html

Boochani, B. and Tofighian, O. (2020) 'A Human Being Feels They are on a Precipice: COVID-19's Threshold Moment', Andrew and Renata Kaldor Centre for International Law, UNSW Law, COVID-19 Watch. Available online: https://www.kaldorcentre.unsw.edu.au/publication/%E2%80%98humanbeingfeelstheyareprecipice%E2%80%99-covid-19%E2%80%99s-threshold-moment

Boochani, B. and Tofighian, O. (2020) 'No Friend but the Mountains and Manus Prison Theory: In Conversation', *Borderlands Journal*, 19(1): 8–26.

Boochani, B., Tazreiter, C. and Tofighian, O. (2021) 'The Multiple Faces of the People Smuggler', in R. Balint and J. Kalman (eds), *Smuggled: An Illegal History of Journeys to Australia*, 176–90, Sydney: NewSouth Publishing.

Bradbury-Jones, C., and Isham, L. (2020) 'The Pandemic Paradox: The Consequences of COVID-19 on Domestic Violence', *Journal of Clinical Nursing*, 29(13–14): 2047–9. DOI: https://doi.org/10.1111/jocn.15296.

Briskman, L. (2013) 'Technology, Control, and Surveillance in Australia's Immigration Detention Centres', *Refuge*, 29(1): 9–19.

Buller, D. (2013) 'Slain Kurdish Activist Cansiz Leaves Stamp on Militant PKK', *Reuters*. Available online: https://www.reuters.com/article/uk-france-kurds-cansiz-idUKBRE90A0Z920130111?edition-redirect=uk

Business & Human Rights Resource Centre (2015) 'No Business in Abuse Website'. Available online: https://www.business-humanrights.org/en/latest-news/no-business-in-abuse-website/

Caruth, C. (2007) 'Unclaimed Experience: Trauma, Narrative and History', Baltimore, MD: Johns Hopkins University Press.

Castree, N. (2009) 'The Spatio-Temporality of Capitalism', *Time & Society*, 18(1): 26–61.

Chandler, J. (2014) 'Welcome to Manus, the Island that has Been Changed Forever by Australian Asylum-Seeker Policy', *The Guardian*. Available online: https://www.theguardian.com/australia-news/2014/dec/16/-sp-welcome-to-manus-island-changed-forever-australian-asylum-seeker-policy

Chandler, J. (2015) 'Manus in Balance', *The Monthly*. Available online: https://www.themonthly.com.au/issue/2015/february/1422709200/jo-chandler/manus-balance#mtr

Davey, E. (2019) 'Life in Stasis: Behrouz Boochani's Manus Prison Literature', *Los Angeles Review of Books*. Available online: https://lareviewofbooks.org/article/life-in-stasis-behrouz-boochanis-manus-prison-literature/

Davidson, H. (2016) 'Manus Island Residents Air Grievances about Hosting Australian Detention Centre', *The Guardian*. Available online: https://www.theguardian.com/australia-news/2016/jan/22/manus-island-residents-air-grievances-about-hosting-australian-detention-centre

Davidson, H. (2019) '"Life on Manus: How Australia Transformed a Tropical Island into a Prison" –Video', *The Guardian*. Available online: https://www.theguardian.com/australianews/video/2019/jul/30/lifeonmanushowaustraliatransfomed-a-tropical-island-into-a-prison-video

Davidson, H. (2019) 'Peter Dutton says women using rape and abortion claims as ploy to get to Australia', *The Guardian*, https://www.theguardian.com/australianews/
2019/jun/20/peter-dutton-says-women-using-and-abortion-claims-as-ployto-get-to-australia

Davidson, H. (2019) '"Six Years and I Didn't Achieve Anything": Inside Manus, a Tropical Purgatory', *The Guardian*. Available online: https://www.theguardian.com/australia-news/2019/jul/21/six-years-and-i-didnt-achieve-anything-inside-manus-a-tropical-purgatory

Davidson, H. (2019) 'Sprent Dabwido: Former Nauru President and Leader of Nauru 19 Dies, Aged 46', *The Guardian*. Available online: https://www.theguardian.com/world/2019/may/08/sprent-dabwido-former-nauru-president-and-leader-of-nauru-19-dies-aged-46

Davidson, H. and Knaus, C. (2019) 'Paladin Staff on Manus Walk off Job over Pay and Working Conditions', *The Guardian*. Available online: https://www.theguardian.com/australia-news/2019/feb/26/paladin-staff-on-manuswalkoffjobover-pay-and-working-conditions

Davies, A. and Doherty, B. (2018) 'Corruption, Incompetence and a Musical: Nauru's Cursed History', *The Guardian*. Available online: https://www.theguardian.com/world/2018/sep/04/corruption-incompetence-and-a-musical-naurus-riches-to-rags-tale

de Certeau, M. (1984) *The Practice of Everyday Life*, 122–5, Berkeley, CA: University of California Press.

de Certeau, M. (1992) *The Writing of History*, New York: Columbia University Press.

Dean, J. (2009) *Democracy and Other Neoliberal Fantasies: Communicative Capitalism and Left Politics*, Durham, NC, and London: Duke University Press.

Deandrea, P. (2018) 'Journeys in Translation: Refugee Poems', *European South*, 3: 27–42. Available online: http://europeansouth.postcolonialitalia.it

Deathscapes: Mapping Race and Violence in Settler States. Available online: https://www.deathscapes.org/

Doherty, B. (2015) 'Exclusive: Woman Allegedly Raped in Manus Detention Centre Accuses Transfield of Cover-Up', *The Guardian Australia*. Available online: https://www.theguardian.com/australianews/2015/aug/27/exclusivewomanallegedlyraped-in-manus-detention-centre-accuses-transfield-of-cover-up

Doherty, B., Davidson, H. and Karp, P. (2016) 'Papua New Guinea Court Rules Detention of Asylum Seekers on Manus Island Illegal', *The Guardian*. Available online: https://www.theguardian.com/australia-news/2016/apr/26/papua-new-guinea-court-rules-detention-asylum-seekers-manus-unconstitutional

Doherty, B. (2017) 'Decay, Defiance and Despair: Inside the Manus Island Refugee Camp', *The Guardian*. Available online: https://www.theguardian.com/australia-news/2017/nov/16/decay-despair-defiance-inside-the-manus-island-refugeecamp

Doherty, B. (2019) 'Behrouz Boochani, Voice of Manus Island Refugees, is Free in New Zealand', *The Guardian*. Available online: https://www.theguardian.com/australia-news/2019/nov/14/behrouz-boochani-free-voice-manusislandrefugeesnewzealanda ustralia

Elkin, L. (2017) 'Foreword', in M. Gansel, *Translation as Transhumance*, translated by Ros Schwartz, vi–ix, New York: Feminist Press.

Felman, S. (1991) 'Camus' *The Plague*, or a Monument to Witnessing', in S. Felman and D. Laub, *Testimony: Crises of Witnessing in Literature, Psychoanalysis and History*, 93, New York: Routledge.

Felman, S. and Laub, D. (1991) *Testimony: Crises of Witnessing in Literature, Psychoanalysis and History*, New York: Routledge.

Fricker, M. (2007) *Epistemic Injustice: Power and the Ethics of Knowing*, Oxford: Oxford University Press.

Galbraith, J. (2019) 'A Reflection on Chauka, Please Tell Us the Time', *Alphaville: Journal of Film and Screen Media*, 18: 193–8.

Gramsci, A. (1971) *Selections from the Prisons Notebooks of Antonio Gramsci*, New York: International Publishers.

Grasso, A. (2022) 'Twitter and Refugeehood: Practices of Decolonial Resistance in Contemporary Australia', PhD thesis, University of Naples 'L'Orientale'.

Grasso, A. (forthcoming) *Twitter and Refugeehood: Practices of Decolonial Resistance in Contemporary Australia*, Chm: Palgrave Macmillan.

Hage, G. (2000) *White Nation: Fantasies of White Supremacy in a Multicultural Society*, Sydney: Pluto Press.

Haw, A. L. (2021) '"Hapless Victims or Making Trouble": Audience Responses to Stereotypical Representations of Asylum Seekers in Australian News Discourse', *Journalism Practice*, 1–19. DOI: 10.1080/17512786.2021.1930574.

Hau'ofa, E. (1994) 'Our Sea of Islands', *Contemporary Pacific*, 6(1): 148–61. Available online: http://www.jstor.org/stable/23701593

Homa, A. (2020) *Daughters of Smoke and Fire*, New York: The Overlook Press.

Homa, A. (2020) 'Resistance is Life: On Writing and Resiliency', *Women Writers, Women[’s] Books*. Available online: http://booksbywomen.org/resistance-is-life-on-writing-and-resiliency/

Human Rights Law Centre (2020) 'Police Officers Involved in Tanya Day's Death Avoid Prosecution'. Available online: https://www.hrlc.org. au/news/2020/8/26/police-officers-involved-in-tanya-days-death-avoid-prosecution

Human Rights Resource Centre (2015) 'No Business in Abuse Website'. Available online: https//www.business-humanrights.org/en/latest-news/no-businessinabusewebsite/

Gholian, S. (2020) 'Sepideh's Diary: A Shocking Glimpse into Women Prisons in Iran', translated by Zahra Moravvej, *Iran Wire*. Available online: https://iranwire.com/en/features/7382

Giannacopoulos, M. (2020) 'Debtscape: Australia's Constitutional Nomopoly', *Borderlands*, 18(2): 116–36. Available online: https://www.exeley.com/borderlands/doi/10.21307/borderlands-2019-013

Innerarity, D. (2012) *The Future and Its Enemies*, Stanford, CA: Stanford University Press.

Kamali Sarvestani, A. (director) (2021) *Tall Fences, Taller Trees*, Eindhoven: Sarvin Productions.

Kanapahti, S. (2019) 'After Six Years We Leave Manus Island to Go to "Nowhere": An Asylum Seeker's Story', *Sydney Morning Herald*. Available online: www.smh.com.au/national/after-six-years-we-leave-manus-island-to-go-to-nowhere-an-asylum-seeker-s-story-20190905-p52o9t.html

Kanapahti, S. (2019) 'As a Refugee Detained Indefinitely by Australia, I wish You a Happy New Year', *The Guardian*. Available online: https://www.theguardian.com/commentisfree/2020/jan/01/as-a-refugee-detained-indefinitely-by-australia-i-wish-you-a-happy-new-year

Kanapahti, S. (2019) 'From Manus Island to Port Moresby', *The Saturday Paper*. Available online: https://www.thesaturdaypaper.com.au/opinion/topic/2019/09/14/manus-island-port-moresby/15683832008783#hrd

Kanapahti, S. (2019) Twitter post @Shamindan1. Available online: https://twitter.com/Shamindan1/status/1147640595201978368.

Kanapahti, S. (2019) Twitter post @Shamindan1, 18 December. Available online: https://twitter.com/ Shamindan1/status/1207106981892214784

Kēhaulani Kauanui, J. (2016) '"A Structure, Not an Event": Settler Colonialism and Enduring Indigeneity', *Lateral*, 5(1). DOI: https://doi. org/10.25158/L5.1.7. Available online: https://csalateral.org/issue/5-1/forum-alt-humanitiessettlercolonialismendur ingindigeneity-kauanui/

Kidd, I. J., Medina, J. and Pohlhaus, G., Jr (eds) (2017) *The Routledge Handbook of Epistemic Injustice*, London and New York: Routledge.

King, M. L., Jr, (1963) 'Letter from Birmingham Jail', *The Atlantic*. Available online: https://www.theatlantic.com/magazine/archive/2018/02/letter-from-a-birmingham-jail/552461/

Knaus, C. and Davidson, H. (2019) 'Australia's Offshore Contracts: How Millions were Spent for Dubious Outcomes', *The Guardian Australia*. Available online: https://www.theguardian.com/australia-news/2019/feb/23/australias-offshore-contracts-how-millions-were-spent-for-dubious-outcomes

Lamb, D., Gnanapragasam, S., Greenberg, N., Bhundia, R., Carr, E., Hotopf, M., Razavi, R., Raine, R., Cross, S., Dewar, A., Docherty, M., Dorrington, S., Hatch, S., Wilson-Jones, C., Leightley, D., Madan, I., Marlow, S., McMullen, I., Rafferty, A.-M., Parsons, M., Polling, C., Serfioti, D., Gaunt, H., Aitken, P.,. Morris-Bone, J., Simela, C., French, V., Harris, R., Stevelink, S. A. M., Wessely, S. (2021) 'Psychosocial Impact of the COVID-19 Pandemic on 4378 UK Healthcare Workers and Ancillary Staff: Initial Baseline Data from a Cohort Study Collected During the First Wave of the Pandemic', *Occupational and Environmental Medicine*, 78: 801–8. DOI: 10.1136/oemed-2020-107276.

Laub, D. (1991) 'Bearing Witness or the Vicissitudes of Listening', in S. Felman and D. Laub, *Testimony: Crises of Witnessing in Literature, Psychoanalysis and History*, 60, New York: Routledge.

Laurie, J. (2014) 'Full Airplane Interview from August 21, 1983, with Ninoy Aquino'. Available online: https://youtube/eBD4vJS0dPk?t=360

Levi, P. (1996) *Survival in Auschwitz: The Nazi Assault on Humanity*, translated by Stuart Woolf, 123, New York: Touchstone.

Levinas, E. (1990) 'The Name of a Dog, or Natural Rights', in *Difficult Freedom: Essays on Judaism*, 151–3, Baltimore, MD: Johns Hopkins University Press.

Mansoubi, M. (2020) 'Translating Manus and Nauru: Refugee Writing', *artseverywhere*. Available online: https://www.artseverywhere.ca/manus-nauru/

McKay, F. H., Thomas, S. L. and Kneebone, S. (2012) '"It Would be Okay if They Came through the Proper Channels": Community Perceptions and Attitudes toward Asylum Seekers in Australia', *Journal of Refugee Studies*, 25(1): 113–33.

McKinnon, C. (2020) 'Enduring Indigeneity and Solidarity in Response to Australia's Carceral Colonialism', *Biography*, 43(4): 691–704.

Measham, F. (2019) 'Love in a Time of Apocalypse', *Meanjin*, 78(3): 1–5. Available online: https://meanjin.com.au/essays/love-in-a-time-of-apocalypse/

Miller, T. (2019) *Empire of Borders: The Expansion of the US Border around the World*, London and New York: Verso.

Mohammad, I. (2017) 'Four Years on Manus Island', *The Saturday Paper*. Available online: https://www.thesaturdaypaper.com.au/2017/07/18/fouryearsmanusisland/15003000004932

Mountz, A. (2011) 'The Enforcement Archipelago: Detention, Haunting, and Asylum on Islands', *Political Geography*, 30(3): 118–28.

Mountz, A. (2020) *The Death of Asylum: Hidden Geographies of the Enforcement Archipelago*, Minneapolis, MN: University of Minnesota Press.

Nethery, A. (2009) '"A Modern-Day Concentration Camp": Using History to Make Sense of Australian Immigration Detention Centres', in K. Neumann and G. Tavan (eds), *Does History Matter? Making and Debating Citizenship, Immigration and Refugee Policy in Australia and New Zealand*, 65–80, Canberra: ANU Press.

O'Brien, B. (2016) 'Extraterritorial Detention Contracting in Australia and the UN Guiding Principles on Business and Human Rights', *Business and Human Rights Journal*, 1(2): 333–40.

Öcalan, A. (2017) *The Political Thought of Abdullah Öcalan*, London: Pluto Press.

O'Shea, L. (2019) 'How We Fight the Border Industrial Complex', *Overland*. Available online: https://overland.org.au/2019/09/how-we-fight-the-border-industrial-complex/

Paik, A. N. (2021) '"Create a Different Language": Behrouz Boochani & Omid Tofighian', Public Books. Available online: https://www.publicbooks.org/createadifferent languagebehrouz-boochani-omid-tofighian/

Parliament of Australia (2021) 'A Pathway Forward: Inquiry into the Destruction of 46,000-Year-Old Cave at the Juukan Gorge in the Pilbara Region of Western Australia', Joint Committees, Parliamentary Business. Available online: https://www.aph.gov.au/Parliamentary_Business/Committees/Joint/Northern_38502.indb26714/06/202212:55268NotesAustralia/CavesatJuukanGorge/Report/section?id=committees%2freportjnt%2f024757%2f77690

Pausch, D. (2010) 'Medien des Erinnerns [Modes of Remembering]', in *Gedächtnis und Erinnerung. Ein interdisziplinäres Handbuch* [*Memory and Recollection: An Interdisciplinary Handbook*], ed. by C. Gudehus, A. Eichenber and H. Welzer, 127–35, Stuttgart: Metzler.

Perera, S. (2002) 'What is a Camp . . .?' *Borderlands Journal*, 1(1): para. 19. Available online: http://www.borderlands.net.au/vol1no1_2002/perera_camp.html

Poletti, A. (2020) 'This Place Really Needs a Lot of Intellectual Work: Behrouz Boochani's Innovation in Life Writing as a Transnational Intellectual Practice', *Biography*, 43(4): 755–62. DOI: doi:10.1353/bio.2020.0077.

Rae, M., Holman, R. and Nethery, A. (2018) 'Self-represented Witnessing: The Use of Social Media by Asylum Seekers in Australia's Offshore Immigration Detention Centres', *Media Culture & Society*, 40(4): 479–95. DOI: 10.1177/0163443717746229.

Rancière, J. (2004) *The Politics of Aesthetics: The Distribution of the Sensible*, translated by G. Rockhill, London: Continuum.

Rancière, J. (2018) 'The Politics of Fiction', *Qui Parle*, 27(2): 269–89.

Reid, J. A., Chenneville, T., Gardy, S. M. and Baglivio, M. T. (2021) 'An Exploratory Study of COVID-19's Impact on Psychological Distress and Antisocial Behavior among Justice-Involved Youth', *Crime & Delinquency*, 1–21. DOI: https://doi.org/10.1177/00111287211054729.

Roitman, J. (2013) *Anti-Crisis*, Durham, NC: Duke University Press.

Rooney, M. N. (2014) 'Reflections on How the Manus Island Detention Centre Promotes Gender-Based Violence', *Dev Policy Blog*. Available online: https://devpolicy.org/reflections-on-how-the-manus-island-detention-centre-promotes-gender-based-violence-20140509/?print=print

Rooney, M. N. (2018) 'Manus Island: How a Small Community Agreed to Host an Australian Detention Centre in Return for Economic Benefits', *The Independent*. Available online: https://www.independent.co.uk/news/long_reads/manus-island-australia-detention-centre-immigration-papua-new-guinea-chauka-bird-a8198991.html

Rooney, M. N. (2018) 'The Chauka Bird and Morality on Our Manus Island Home', *The Conversation*. Available online: https://theconversation.com/friday-essay-the-chauka-bird-and-morality-on-our-manus-island-home-90107

Rooney, M. N. (2021) 'As Basket and Papu: Making Manus Social Fabric', *Oceania*, 91(1): 86–105. DOI: https://doi.org/10.1002/ocea.5289.

Rothberg, M. (2009) *Multidirectional Memory: Remembering the Holocaust in the Age of Decolonization*, Stanford, CA: Stanford University Press.

Russell, A. C. and Diaz, N. D. (2011) 'Photography in Social Work Research: Using Visual Image to Humanize Findings', *Qualitative Social Work*, 12(4): 433–53.

Schüssler Fiorenza, E. (1992) *But She Said: Feminist Practices of Biblical Interpretation*, Boston, MA: Beacon Press.

Schüssler Fiorenza, E. (2001) 'Glossary', in *Wisdom Ways: Introducing Feminist Biblical Interpretation*, 207–16, New York: Orbis Books.

Schüssler Fiorenza, E. (2020) 'Biblical Interpretation and Kyriachal Globalization', in Susanne Scholz (ed.), *The Oxford Handbook of Feminist Approaches to the Hebrew Bible*, 3–20, Oxford: Oxford University Press.

Soukup, S. (2015) 'Gramsci Comes to Indiana', *Persons & Polis*. Available online: https://cultureoflife.org/2015/04/06/gramsci-comes-to-indiana/

Stonebridge, L. (2020) 'Manus Island is the Soul of the System: Lyndsey Stonebridge Talks to Omid Tofighian', *The Age of Superdiversity*. Available online: https://superdiversity.net/2020/06/18/manus-island-is-the-soul-of-the-system-lyndseystonebridge-talks-to-omid-tofighian/amp/

Stonebridge, L. (2021) 'Survival Time / Human Time: Hannah Arendt and Behrouz Boochani', in *Writing and Righting: Literature in the Age of Human Right*, 93–110, Oxford: Oxford University Press.

Surma, A. (2018) 'In a Different Voice: "A Letter from Manus Island" as Poetic Manifesto', *Continuum*, 32(4): 518–26.

Talebi, S. (2016) *Critical Trauma Studies: Understanding Violence, Conflict and Memory in Everyday Life*, 101–10, New York: New York University Press.

Tazreiter, C. (2017) 'The Unlucky in the "Lucky Country": Asylum Seekers, Irregular Migrants and Refugees and Australia's Politics of Disappearance', in L. Hill and C. van Ham (guest eds), Special Issue, *Australian Journal of Human Rights*, 23(2): 242–60.

Tazreiter, C. (2020) 'Emotions, Borders and the Role of Visual Culture in Refugee Arrivals', in S. Turnbull, M. Bhatia and G. Lousley (eds), Borders, Racisms, and State Violence, Special Issue, *Critical Criminology*, 2(28). Available online: https://rdcu.be/b4H4N

Tazreiter, C. (2020) 'Moved by the Oceans: The Haunting Presence of the Disappeared', in M. Gržinić, J. Pristovšek, S. Uitz and C. Jauernik (eds), *Genealogy of Amnesia, KHM Catalogue*, 186–9, Vienna: Weltmuseum Wien. Available online: https://www.weltmuseumwien.at/en/exhibitions/stories-of-traumatic-pasts/

Tazreiter, C. (2021) 'Race, Migration and Visual Culture: The Activist Artist Challenging the Ever-Present Colonial Imagination', in B. Miyamoto and M. Ruiz (eds), *Art & Migration, Rethinking Art History Series*, 113–32, Manchester: Manchester University Press.

Tazreiter, C. and Tofighian, O. with Boochani, B. (2022) 'Spectres of Subjugation/Inter-subjugation/Resubjugation of People Seeking Asylum: The Kyriarchal System in Australia's Necropoleis', in P. Billings (ed.), *Regulating Refugee Protection through Social Welfare Law, Policy and Praxis*, 68–90, London: Routledge.

Tofighian, O. (2018) 'Behrouz Boochani and the Manus Prison Narratives: Merging Translation with Philosophical Reading', *Continuum: Journal of Media and Cultural Studies*, 32(3): 532–40.

Tofighian, O. (2018) 'No Friend but the Mountains: Translator's Reflections', in B. Boochani, *No Friend but the Mountains: Writing from Manus Prison*, translated by Omid Tofighian, 359-374 ,Sydney: Picador.

Tofighian, O. (2018) 'Translator's Tale: A Window to the Mountains', in B. Boochani, *No Friend but the Mountains: Writing from Manus Prison*, translated by Omid Tofighian, xi–xxxiv, Sydney: Picador.

Tofighian, O. (2018) 'Truth to Power: My Time Translating Behrouz Boochani's Masterpiece', *The Conversation*. Available online: https://theconversation. com/truth-to-power-my-time-translating-behrouz-boochanis-masterpiece-101589

Tofighian, O. (2020) 'Introducing Manus Prison Theory: Knowing Border Violence', *Globalizations*, 17(7): 1138–56.

Tofighian, O. with Boochani, B. (2020) 'Narrative, Resistance and Manus Prison Theory', *Review of Middle East Studies, Special Focus: Pluralism in Emergencies*, 54(2): 174–95

Tofighian, O. (2021) 'Horrific Surrealism: New Storytelling for Australia's Carceral-Border Archipelago', in H. Gilbert, D. Pigram and R. Swain (eds), *Marrugeku: Telling that Story – 25 Years of Trans-Indigenous and Intercultural Performance*, 306–19, Aberystwyth: Performance Research Books.

Tofighian, O. and Boochani, B. (2021) 'The Weaponisation of Time: Indefinite Detention as Torture', in M. Bhatia and V. Canning (eds), *Stealing Time: Migration, Temporalities and State Violence*, 65–82, Cham: Palgrave Macmillan.

Tofighian, O. (forthcoming, 2023) 'Manus Island and Manus Prison Theory', in R. Braidotti, E. Jones and G. Klumbytė (eds), *More Posthuman Glossary*, 77–80, London: Bloomsbury.

Vogl, A., Fleay, C., Loughnan, C., Murray, P. and Dehm, S. (2020) 'COVID-19 and the Relentless Harms of Australia's Punitive Immigration Detention Regime', *Crime, Media, Culture: An International Journal*, 17(1): 43–51.

Wahlquist, C. and Doherty, B. (2016) 'Manus Detainee Climbs Tree in Rejection of PNG Refugee Status', *The Guardian*. Available online: https://www.theguardian.com/australia-news/2016/apr/24/manus-asylum-seeker-deemed-refugee-climbs-tree-to-protest-settlement-in-png

Walden, M. (2019) 'Asylum Seekers in Detention 200 Times more Likely to Commit Self-Harm than Australians, Research Finds', *ABC News*. Available online: https://www.abc.net.au/news/2019-10-14/asylum-seekers-in-detention-200-more-likely-to-commit-self-harm/11600148

Wallis, J. and Dalsgaard, S. (2016) 'Money, Manipulation and Misunderstanding', *Journal of Pacific History*, 51(3): 301–29.

White, H. (2016) 'Historical Truth, Estrangement, and Disbelief', in C. Fogu, W. Kansteiner and T. Presner (eds), *Probing the Ethics of Holocaust Culture*, 71, Cambridge, MA: Harvard University Press.

Whitlock, G. (2020) 'No Friend but the Mountains: How Should I Read This?', *Biography*, 43(4): 705–23. DOI: 10.1353/bio.2020.0102.

Whittaker, A. (2018) '"Dragged Like a Dead Kangaroo": Why Language Matters for Deaths in Custody', *The Guardian*. Available online: https://www.theguardian.com/commentisfree/2018/sep/07/draggedlikeadeadkangaroowhy-language-matters-for-deaths-in-custody

Wolfe, P. (2006) 'Settler Colonialism and the Elimination of the Native', *Journal of Genocide Research*, 8(4): 388.

Woodly, D. (2021) *Reckoning: Black Lives Matter and the Democratic Necessity of Social Movements*, New York: Oxford University Press.

Young, J. E. (1997) 'Toward a Received History of the Holocaust', *History and Theory*, 36(4): 34.

Contributors

Mahnaz Alimardanian is Applied Anthropologist and Adjunct Research Fellow at the Faculty of Humanities and Social Sciences, La Trobe University, Melbourne, Australia. She provides community-based research services at PiiR Consulting. Her research and publications are situated at the intersection of fields of social, legal and philosophical anthropology.

Lida Amiri is Lecturer in Comparative Literature at Utrecht University, Netherlands. In 2020, she completed her dissertation at the University of Liverpool, UK. Currently, she is working on her first monograph on Afghanistan's diaspora communities, translingualism and contemporary literature.

Behrouz Boochani is a Kurdish Iranian writer and film-maker. He graduated from Tarbiat Moallem University (Kharazmi) and Tarbiat Modares University, both in Tehran, Iran. He has an MA in Political Geography and Geopolitics. From 2013 to 2019, he was a political prisoner incarcerated by the Australian Government on Manus Island, Papua New Guinea. He is co-director (with Arash Kamali Sarvestani) of the 2017 feature-length film *Chauka, Please Tell Us the Time*, and author of *No Friend but the Mountains: Writing from Manus Prison*. At the 2019 Victorian Premier's Literary Awards, his book won the Victorian Prize for Literature in addition to the Non-Fiction category.

Victoria Canning is Senior Lecturer in Criminology at the University of Bristol, UK. She is currently Co-coordinator of the European Group for the Study of Deviance and Social Control, Associate Director in Border Criminologies at Oxford University and Trustee of Statewatch. She researches violence, harm and torture, and has worked for more than a decade on migrant rights and women's rights. She is co-creator of the Right to Remain Asylum Navigation Board (with Lisa Matthews), and her first monograph *Gendered Harm and Structural Violence in the British Asylum System* won the 2018 British Society of Criminology Book Prize.

Helen Davidson is an award-winning journalist and correspondent for *The Guardian*. She covered Australia's refugee and asylum-seeker policy from

2014 to 2020, reporting from Sydney, Darwin, Port Moresby and Manus Island. She was on *The Guardian*'s Walkley nominated Nauru Files team.

Ben Doherty is International Affairs correspondent for *The Guardian* newspaper in Australia, and has spent a decade reporting across the Asia-Pacific, including postings in South-East Asia and South Asia. His work focuses on human rights and humanitarian issues, forced migration and asylum. He has won Australia's highest journalism honour, the Walkley Award, three times, as well as three United Nations Association Media Peace Prizes. He holds Master's degrees in International Law and International Relations from the University of Oxford and from University of New South Wales, studied at the Queensland conservatorium of music, and is a fellow at the Reuters Institute for the Study of Journalism at Oxford. A former professional footballer with the Brisbane and Melbourne Australian football clubs, he is the author of a novel, *Nagaland*, a love story for modern India.

Roza Germian was born in the second year of the eight year-long Iran–Iraq War, in 1981, in the multi-ethnic (disputed) city of Kirkuk under the Baathist rule in Iraq, in which the majority of its population were of Kurdish background. The invasion of Kuwait in 1990 by Iraq ignited the first Gulf War, and in 1994 her family fled to Turkey. After spending close to two years there as refugees they were granted asylum by Australia, and landed in Brisbane, Queensland, in 1996 when she was 15 years of age. Roza has a BA in Communications majoring in Journalism. She has a double Master's degree in International Relations and International Communications from Macquarie University. She has been working as a journalist, broadcaster and editor for almost ten years.

Mehran Ghadiri is a political scientist and international relations analyst who left his economic development role in Nauru after several years of witnessing the realities of Australia's offshore border regime. He has many years of first-hand experience of working in a broad range of roles directly in support of refugees resettled and living in Australia. As well as his unique insights into the inner workings of Australia's refugee system and detention industry, he brings a nuanced understanding of the global forces that create and manipulate refugee flows for financial and political gain. He is currently writing a detailed analysis of the political, economic and societal effects of Australia's policies in Nauru.

Arianna Grasso received her PhD in the Department of Literary, Linguistic and Comparative Studies, University of Naples 'L'Orientale', Italy. Her research interests include Australian populism, refugee discourse and digital media studies. She is currently working on the analysis of digital discursive practices as enacted by refugees in the context of Australian border policy. In June 2021, she was awarded the Outstanding Doctoral Researcher prize, sponsored by Palgrave Macmillan, with her paper 'Twitter and Refugeehood: Practices of Resistance in Contemporary Australia'.

Erik Jensen is the founding editor of *The Saturday Paper* and editor-in-chief of Schwartz Media. He is the author of *Acute Misfortune: The Life and Death of Adam Cullen* (2014), *On Kate Jennings* (2017) and the poetry collection *I Said the Sea was Folded* (2021), all published by Black Inc.

Sajad Kabgani is an independent researcher. He received his PhD in educational philosophy from the University of New South Wales, Australia, focusing on Lacanian psychoanalysis and literature. He was translation consultant for Behrouz Boochani's book *No Friend but the Mountains*. He has published scholarly articles on a range of themes and topics and his current research engages with extinction studies, posthumanism, ethics and capitalist temporality, all examined through the lens of continental philosophers such as Emmanuel Lévinas, Jacques Rancière, Jacques Lacan and Gilles Deleuze

Shaminda Kanapathi is a human rights activist, writer and translator, was detained by the Australian Government from 2013 to 2020 in Papua New Guinea (PNG, in Manus Island and Port Moresby). During his detention in PNG, he was a media spokesman for the Australian and international media and was highly active in writing, giving speeches and addressing questions from around the world.

Moones Mansoubi is a community, arts and cultural development worker based in Sydney, Australia. Her work is dedicated mainly to supporting and collaborating with migrants and people seeking asylum in Australia. She has managed numerous community and cultural projects and was the first translator of Behrouz Boochani's work when he began writing from Manus Island. She was translation consultant for Boochani's book *No Friend but the Mountains*. Her translation of the article 'An Island off Manus' (*The Saturday Paper*, 6 May 2017) was included in Boochani's winning nomination for an Amnesty International Australia Media Award in 2017. She has a Master's in International Relations and is passionate about social justice and social cohesion. She is currently coordinator of the Community Refugee Welcome Centre in Inner West Sydney and a producer for SBS Persian.

Anne McNevin is Associate Professor of Politics at The New School, New York, USA. Her research focuses on the transformation of borders, sovereignty, citizenship and migration.

Fatima Measham is a writer and speaker living west of the Werribee River in Wadawurrung Country, Australia. She was a consulting editor, columnist and podcast producer for *Eureka Street*, covering issues of social justice, identity and politics. Her recent work focuses on nature, wildlife and conservation. She was on the judging panel that considered *No Friend but the Mountains* for the Victorian Premier's Literary Awards.

Steven Ratuva is an award-winning political sociologist, Distinguished Professor and Director of the Macmillan Brown Centre for Pacific Studies at the University of Canterbury, New Zealand. His expertise and interests are interdisciplinary and span various disciplines such as sociology, anthropology, politics, development studies, peace studies, history and cultural studies. He has worked in a number of universities around the world, including in the USA as Senior Fulbright Fellow at University of California, Los Angeles, Duke University, North Carolina, and Georgetown University, Washington, DC, and as advisor-consultant for a number of international organizations.

Jordana Silverstein is Senior Research Fellow in the Peter McMullin Centre on Statelessness in the Melbourne Law School at the University of Melbourne, Australia. A cultural historian, she is the author of *Anxious Histories: Narrating the Holocaust in Jewish Communities at the Beginning of the Twenty-First Century* and co-editor of *Refugee Journeys: Histories of Resettlement, Representation and Resistance.* She was convenor of the Non-Fiction judging panel, and on the panel for the Victorian Prize for Literature, which awarded *No Friend but the Mountains* in the 2019 Victorian Premier's Literary Awards.

Anne Surma's research explores the use of public language and its effects in the shaping of cultural norms. She has published articles and book chapters examining how the literary arts may variously unsettle the language of 'common sense' and the dehumanizing logic governing mainstream political discourses concerning people seeking asylum.

Claudia Tazreiter is Professor in Ethnic and Migration Studies, Institute for Research on Migration, Ethnicity and Society (REMESO), University Linköping, Sweden. Her research is in the fields of political sociology, social theory, visual cultures, race, ethnicity and migration. The focus of this research is on the social and affective impacts of forced and irregular migration, on human rights culture, the role of civil society in social change, and visual cultures of dissent.

Omid Tofighian is an award-winning lecturer, researcher and community advocate, combining philosophy with interests in citizen media, popular culture, displacement and discrimination. He is affiliated with the School of the Arts and Media, University of New South Wales, Australia; and the School of Law, Birkbeck College, University of London, UK. His publications include *Myth and Philosophy in Platonic Dialogues*, the translation of Behrouz Boochani's multi-award-winning book *No Friend but the Mountains* and as co-editor of special issues for journals *Literature and Aesthetics* (2011), *Alphaville: Journal of Film and Screen Media* (2019) and *Southerly* (2021).

Helena Zeweri is Assistant Professor of Global Studies at the University of Virginia, Charlottesville, VA, USA. Helena's research sits at the intersection of global migration, immigrant-led political activism, and settler colonialism, and has focused on Australia, the United States and the global Afghan diaspora. She is currently writing a book on the logics of care and criminality within migrant-targeted social welfare in Australia. Her next project is an ethnographic and historical study of Afghan diasporic political activism since the Global War on Terror.

Elahe Zivardar, aka Ellie Shakiba, is an Iranian artist, architect, journalist and documentary film-maker who was imprisoned by the Australian Government in Nauru during 2013–19. She was accepted as a refugee by the USA in 2019 and currently lives and works in Washington, DC. During her detention in Nauru, she was highly active in using photos and video to document the horrific treatment and conditions endured by people seeking asylum and imprisoned offshore. She continues to actively advocate for the freedom of the remaining detainees, and against the adoption of similar refugee detention policies by other countries, through her art, documentary film-making, animation, journalism, publications and as an advisor to multiple refugee rights campaigns in Australia, the UK and EU.

Index